Ultimate Data Engineering with Databricks

Develop Scalable Data Pipelines Using Data Engineering's Core Tenets Such as Delta Tables, Ingestion, Transformation, Security, and Scalability

Mayank Malhotra

www.orangeava.com

Copyright © 2024, Orange Education Pvt Ltd, AVA™

All rights reserved. No part of this book may be reproduced, stored in a retrieval system, or transmitted in any form or by any means, without the prior written permission of the publisher, except in the case of brief quotations embedded in critical articles or reviews.

Every effort has been made in the preparation of this book to ensure the accuracy of the information presented. However, the information contained in this book is sold without warranty, either express or implied. Neither the author nor **Orange Education Pvt Ltd** or its dealers and distributors, will be held liable for any damages caused or alleged to have been caused directly or indirectly by this book.

Orange Education Pvt Ltd has endeavored to provide trademark information about all of the companies and products mentioned in this book by the appropriate use of capital. However, **Orange Education Pvt Ltd** cannot guarantee the accuracy of this information. The use of general descriptive names, registered names, trademarks, service marks, etc. in this publication does not imply, even in the absence of a specific statement, that such names are exempt from the relevant protective laws and regulations and therefore free for general use.

First published: February 2024

Published by: Orange Education Pvt Ltd, AVA™

Address: 9, Daryaganj, Delhi, 110002

ISBN: 978-81-96994-78-5

www.orangeava.com

Dedicated To

My beloved Parents:

Shri Jagdish Malhotra
Rita Malhotra

and

My wife Jayshree

About the Author

Mayank Malhotra's journey in the tech world began as a big data engineer, quickly evolving into a versatile data engineering expert. His extensive experience spans various cloud platforms such as AWS, Azure, and Databricks, as well as On-Prem Infrastructure, showcasing his adaptability and depth of knowledge. A BTech graduate, Mayank's academic foundation laid the groundwork for his successful career.

In the realm of data engineering, Mayank has tackled a diverse range of projects, from data migration and modeling to data transformation and quality validation. His ability to navigate complex data landscapes has not only honed his skills but also made him a sought-after expert in the field. One of his key beliefs, "Be the senior you needed as a junior," reflects his passion for mentoring. He thrives on guiding others, sharing insights, and discussing new design approaches in data engineering, making him a valuable mentor and leader.

With an impressive accumulation of 5x Databricks certifications, Mayank's credentials speak to his commitment and expertise. His aptitude for creating sophisticated data solutions is evidenced by his remarkable achievements, including being honored three times in his organization for delivering defect-free code–a testament to his exceptional skill and attention to detail. His enthusiasm for exploring new technologies and solving challenging problems keeps him at the forefront of the industry, continuously pushing the boundaries of what's possible in data engineering.

Outside of his professional life, Mayank is driven by a curiosity to explore and learn. This quest for knowledge and new experiences not only fuels his professional growth but also shapes his personal interests.

Looking ahead, Mayank aspires to become one of the most accomplished data engineers, adept at solving a wide spectrum of data-related challenges. He believes in rising to the level of problems one solves, a philosophy that propels him to constantly seek out and conquer new and more complex challenges.

Mayank's journey in data engineering is not just about technical mastery but also about the impact and inspiration he brings to the field. His story is a testament to the power of continuous learning, adaptability, and the pursuit of excellence. As he continues to navigate and shape the world of data, Mayank Malhotra stands as a beacon of expertise and inspiration for many aspiring data engineers.

About the Technical Reviewer

Nawaz Abbas started his career with Accenture 12 years ago. His journey in the field of Information Technology has given him a chance to explore multiple domains such as Banking, Security, and Consumer sectors, with exposure to various technologies in the field of Big Data and Analytics.

He likes to be involved in building and designing data pipelines using various Big Data Technologies like PySpark, Databricks, Scala, Java, Kafka, Hive, Airflow, and more. More recently, he has taken on the roles of a Technical Lead and/or Big Data Engineer. He has worked on various AWS components, including AWS Lambda, SNS, Athena, S3, EC2, Load Balancer, Elastic Beanstalk, ASG, and more.

As an avid reader, Nawaz likes to remain close to newer technologies and stay connected to the latest industry trends. In his free time, you might find him spending time with his family, traveling, watching soccer, playing cricket, or participating in CSR events.

Acknowledgements

As I reflect on the journey of writing this book, my heart is filled with gratitude for the incredible support and inspiration I have received from numerous individuals.

First and foremost, my deepest appreciation goes to my parents and wife, whose unwavering encouragement and belief in my abilities were the bedrock of this endeavor. I extend my sincere thanks to the various courses and companies that have been instrumental in my learning journey. The invaluable experiences and insights gained during my time with them have significantly shaped my understanding and approach to data engineering.

A special note of gratitude is reserved for Mr. Nawaz Abbas, whose meticulous technical scrutiny and invaluable feedback were pivotal in refining the content of this book. His expertise and guidance have been a guiding light, ensuring the technical accuracy and relevance of the material presented.

I am also deeply grateful to my childhood friend, Abhishek Rawat, who not only motivated me to write this book but also guided me in every aspect whenever I faced challenges.

This book is not just a compilation of knowledge but a testament to the collaborative spirit and collective wisdom of all those who have been part of this journey. To everyone who has played a role, no matter how big or small, I offer my heartfelt thanks. Your contributions have been the threads in the tapestry of this achievement.

Preface

In an age where data is the new currency, mastering the art of data engineering has become more crucial than ever. This book, *Ultimate Data Engineering with Databricks*, is a culmination of my experiences and learnings, designed to guide you through the intricacies of data engineering in the modern cloud environment.

The journey begins with **Chapter 1**, *Fundamentals of Data Engineering with Databricks*, providing a solid foundation for those new to the field or looking to strengthen their core understanding. Following this, **Chapter 2**, *Mastering Delta Tables in Databricks*, dives into the specifics of handling data at scale, a skill pivotal in today's data-intensive world.

As you progress through the chapters, from **Chapter 3**, *Data Ingestion and Extraction*, to **Chapter 4**, *Data Transformation and ETL Processes*, the focus shifts to the practical aspects of managing and manipulating data. The subsequent chapters, **Chapter 5**, *Data Quality and Validation* and **Chapter 6**, *Data Modeling and Storage*, emphasize the importance of maintaining data integrity and efficiently organizing data for optimal use.

Chapter 7, *Data Orchestration and Workflow Management*, introduces you to the critical task of managing various data processes cohesively, ensuring a smooth flow of data across systems. In **Chapter 8**, *Performance Tuning and Optimization*, you will learn to refine these processes for efficiency and effectiveness, a key to handling big data challenges.

With data becoming an increasingly valuable asset, **Chapter 9**, *Data Security and Governance* addresses the vital need to protect and manage it responsibly. Finally, **Chapter 10**, *Scalability and Deployment Considerations* prepares you to scale your solutions and ensure they are robust and adaptable in the ever-evolving technological landscape.

This book is more than just a guide; it's a companion in your data engineering journey. Whether you are a beginner or an experienced professional, the chapters are designed to provide valuable insights and practical knowledge. The aim is not just to educate but to inspire you to innovate and excel in the realm of data engineering.

As you turn these pages, may you find the information both enlightening and empowering, equipping you with the skills to tackle the dynamic challenges of data engineering head-on.

Downloading the code bundles and colored images

Please follow the links or scan the QR codes to download the *Code Bundles and Images* of the book:

https://github.com/ava-orange-education/Ultimate-Data-Engineering-with-Databricks

The code bundles and images of the book are also hosted on
https://rebrand.ly/ea3eeb

In case there's an update to the code, it will be updated on the existing GitHub repository.

Errata

We take immense pride in our work at **Orange Education Pvt Ltd,** and follow best practices to ensure the accuracy of our content to provide an indulging reading experience to our subscribers. Our readers are our mirrors, and we use their inputs to reflect and improve upon human errors, if any, that may have occurred during the publishing processes involved. To let us maintain the quality and help us reach out to any readers who might be having difficulties due to any unforeseen errors, please write to us at :

errata@orangeava.com

Your support, suggestions, and feedback are highly appreciated.

DID YOU KNOW

Did you know that Orange Education Pvt Ltd offers eBook versions of every book published, with PDF and ePub files available? You can upgrade to the eBook version at **www.orangeava.com** and as a print book customer, you are entitled to a discount on the eBook copy. Get in touch with us at: **info@orangeava.com** for more details.

At **www.orangeava.com**, you can also read a collection of free technical articles, sign up for a range of free newsletters, and receive exclusive discounts and offers on AVA™ Books and eBooks.

PIRACY

If you come across any illegal copies of our works in any form on the internet, we would be grateful if you would provide us with the location address or website name. Please contact us at **info@orangeava.com** with a link to the material.

ARE YOU INTERESTED IN AUTHORING WITH US?

If there is a topic that you have expertise in, and you are interested in either writing or contributing to a book, please write to us at **business@orangeava.com**. We are on a journey to help developers and tech professionals to gain insights on the present technological advancements and innovations happening across the globe and build a community that believes Knowledge is best acquired by sharing and learning with others. Please reach out to us to learn what our audience demands and how you can be part of this educational reform. We also welcome ideas from tech experts and help them build learning and development content for their domains.

REVIEWS

Please leave a review. Once you have read and used this book, why not leave a review on the site that you purchased it from? Potential readers can then see and use your unbiased opinion to make purchase decisions. We at Orange Education would love to know what you think about our products, and our authors can learn from your feedback. Thank you!

For more information about Orange Education, please visit **www.orangeava.com**.

Table of Contents

1. Fundamentals of Data Engineering 1
    Introduction 1
    Structure 3
    Role of Data Engineering in Modern Organizations 3
        Data Engineering's Role in Enabling Data Analytics and
        Machine Learning.. 4
        Data Engineering Supports Data-Driven Decision-Making 5
    Understanding Data Engineering Concepts and Principles 7
        Core Concepts and Principles in Data Engineering 8
        Overview of Data Pipelines, Data Integration, and
        Data Transformation 9
    Overview of Databricks 10
        Databricks as a Unified Analytics Platform 10
        Key Features and Benefits of Using Databricks for Data
        Engineering 11
        Overview of Databricks Architecture and Components 12
        Components of Databricks Architecture 14
        Understanding the Databricks Workspace and
        Its Functionalities 15
        Introducing Databricks Notebooks and Its Role in
        Data Engineering 16
    Setting Up Databricks Environment and Workspace 18
        Best Practices for Managing Databricks Notebooks..................... 21
    Conclusion 23
    Key Terms 23

2. Mastering Delta Tables in Databricks 25
    Introduction 25
    Structure 26

  Understanding the Benefits of Delta Tables in Databricks 26
   Enhanced Data Reliability and Consistency with Delta Tables.... 27
   Efficient Data Processing and Query Optimization 28
   Improved Data Versioning and Time Travel Capabilities in
   Delta Tables 30
    Data Versioning 30
    Time Travel 31
    Use Case Example 31
  Overview of Delta Lake Architecture and Concepts 32
   Introduction to Delta Lake 32
   Delta Lake Architecture 34
   Understanding Delta Lake's File Organization and
   Transaction Log 36
    File Organization in Delta Lake 36
    Transaction Log in Delta Lake 37
  Implementing Schema Evolution and Table Updates with Delta 39
   Handling Schema Changes and Evolution Using Delta 40
    Introduction to Schema Evolution 40
   Understanding Schema Evolution Challenges 41
   Leveraging Delta Lake for Schema Evolution 42
   Techniques for Handling Schema Changes 43
   Best Practices for Schema Evolution 45
 Conclusion 46
 Key Terms 46

3. Data Ingestion and Extraction 49
 Introduction 49
 Structure 50
 Ingesting Data into Databricks 50
  Understanding the Importance of Data Ingestion 51
  Choosing the Appropriate Data Ingestion Method 52
  Identifying Key Considerations for Data Ingestion 53

Implementing Data Ingestion Best Practices 55
　Implementing Efficient Data Extraction Techniques 57
　　　Overview of Data Extraction Methods from Various Sources...... 57
　　　Extracting Data from Databases Using Connectors and JDBC ...59
　　　　　Working with JDBC Connector..59
　　　　　Best Practices for Efficient Extraction 61
　　　Techniques for Extracting Data from Cloud Storage Platforms...62
　　　　　AWS S3 Connector Sample Code..63
　Implementing Efficient Data Extraction Techniques 64
　　　Working with Structured Data Formats..64
　　　Handling Unstructured and Semi-Structured data........................66
　　　Techniques for Extracting Data from APIs and Web Scraping......69
　Conclusion 71
　Key Terms 72

4. **Data Transformation and ETL Processes** 75
　Introduction 75
　Structure 76
　Building Scalable Data Transformation Pipelines................................. 76
　　　Understanding the Importance of Data Transformation in Data Engineering... 77
　　　Designing Scalable and Efficient Data Transformation Pipelines... 78
　　　Techniques for Data Transformation in Databricks...................... 80
　Applying ETL Methodologies 81
　　　Overview of the ETL Process and Its Key Components...................82
　　　Extracting Data from Various Sources for Transformation...........84
　　　　　Example: Extracting Data from a Relational Database 85
　　　Applying Transformations and Business Logic to Prepare Data for Analysis 86
　　　　　Example: Data Transformation with Apache Spark 87

  Loading Transformed Data into Target Systems or
Data Warehouses 88
    Case Study: Loading Transformed Data into a
Data Warehouse 90
  Optimizing Data Processing and Performance in Databricks 90
    Strategies for Optimizing Data Processing in Databricks 91
    Leveraging Databricks Runtime Configurations for
Performance Improvements 92
    Performance Tuning for Data Transformation
Operations in Databricks 94
  Conclusion 95
  Key Terms 96

5. **Data Quality and Validation** 97
  Introduction 97
  Structure 98
  Ensuring Data Quality and Integrity in Databricks 98
    Importance of Data Quality 99
    Designing Data Quality Checks and Validation Processes 99
    Techniques for Identifying and Handling Data Quality Issues 101
    Implementing Data Profiling and Monitoring in Databricks 102
  Implementing Data Validation Techniques and Rules 105
    Overview of Data Validation Methodologies 106
    Applying Data Validation Rules and Constraints 107
    Techniques for Validating Data Completeness, Consistency,
and Accuracy 108
    Implementing Automated Data Validation Processes in
Databricks 110
    Case Study 111
  Handling Data Anomalies and Outliers 114
    Strategies for Managing and Correcting Data Anomalies and
Outliers 116

Business Use Case: Sales Forecasting with Outliers 117

Conclusion 118

Multiple Choice Questions 119

Answers 120

6. Data Modeling and Storage **121**

Introduction 121

Structure 122

Designing Effective Data Models 122

Importance of Data Modeling 123

Types of Data Modeling 125

Principles of Effective Data Modeling for
Analytical Workloads 127

Schema-on-Read and Schema-on-Write models 128

Schema-on-Read 128

Schema-on-Write 129

Hybrid Approaches 129

Best Practices for Designing Data Models 129

Utilizing Structured and Unstructured Data Storage Options 131

Overview of Structured and Unstructured
Data Storage Options 132

Structured Data Storage 132

Unstructured Data Storage 132

Hybrid Approaches 133

Utilizing Data Lakes and Data Warehouses 133

Data Lakes 133

Data Warehouses 134

Hybrid Approach 134

Choosing the Appropriate Storage Format 134

Data Partitioning and Optimization Strategies 137

Understanding Data Partitioning 138

Different Techniques for Partitioning Data 139

   Benefits of Tailored Data Partitioning 140

   Considerations for Data Partitioning 141

  Strategies for Data compaction and Optimization in Databricks 141

 Conclusion 143

 Key Terms 144

7. Data Orchestration and Workflow Management 145

 Introduction 145

 Structure 146

 Implementing Workflow Automation with Databricks 147

  Overview of Workflow Automation 147

  Introduction to Databricks Jobs and Notebooks for Workflow Automation 148

  Designing and Implementing Automated Data Pipelines in Databricks 149

 Managing Dependencies and Scheduling Data Pipelines 151

  Understanding Dependencies Between Data Pipelines and Tasks 152

  Techniques for Managing Dependencies in Databricks Workflows 153

  Scheduling and Orchestrating Data Pipelines Using Databricks Jobs 154

  Best Practices for Handling Complex Workflows and Task Dependencies 156

 Monitoring and Error Handling in Workflow Execution 157

  Strategies for Monitoring Workflow Execution 158

  Implementing Logging and Alerting Mechanisms for Error Detection 159

  Techniques for Handling Workflow Failures and Retries 161

  Utilizing Databricks Monitoring and Debugging Tools for Workflow Optimization 163

 Conclusion 164

  Key Terms 165

8. Performance Tuning and Optimization 167
  Introduction 167
  Structure 168
  Techniques for Optimizing Databricks Performance 168
    Overview of Key Performance Optimization Techniques in
    Databricks 169
    Utilizing Caching and Data Skipping for
    Faster Query Execution 170
      Practical Use Case: E-commerce Sales Analysis 172
    Techniques for Optimizing Data Shuffling and
    Data Serialization 173
  Resource Management and Cluster Optimization 175
    Understanding Resource Management in Databricks Clusters ..176
    Best Practices for Cluster Configuration and Sizing 177
    Techniques for Optimizing Cluster Utilization and
    Cost Efficiency 178
    Strategies for Managing Cluster Auto-Scaling and
    Workload Isolation 180
  Identifying and Resolving Performance Bottlenecks 181
    Techniques for Performance Profiling and
    Bottleneck Identification 182
    Analyzing Query Execution Plans and Identifying
    Performance Hotspots 183
    Strategies for Optimizing Complex Transformations and Joins..... 185
  Conclusion 186
  Key Terms 187

9. Scalability and Deployment Considerations 189
  Introduction 189
  Structure 190
  Scaling Data Engineering Solutions in Databricks 190

Importance of Scalability in Data Engineering Solutions............190
Techniques for Scaling Data Pipelines and
Processing Workflows...191
Horizontal and Vertical Scaling Options in Databricks...............193
Horizontal Scaling (Scale-Out)...193
Vertical Scaling (Scale-Up)..193
Strategic Scaling in Databricks...194
Cloud Deployment Options and Considerations..................................194
Overview of Cloud Deployment Options for Databricks...............195
Evaluating Different Cloud Providers and Services......................197
Exploring Databricks with AWS..198
Handling Data Growth and Future-Proofing Strategies...............200
Strategies for Managing and Accommodating
Data Growth in Databricks..201
Techniques for Future-Proofing Data Engineering Solutions...202
Evaluating Emerging Technologies and Trends in
Data Engineering..204
Conclusion..205
Key Terms...205

10. **Data Security and Governance**..**207**
   Introduction..207
   Structure...208
   Unity Catalog..208
   Understanding the Unity Catalog in Databricks..........................208
   Overview of Metadata Management and Data Discovery in
   Unity Catalog..209
   Leveraging Unity Catalog for Efficient Data Governance
   and Metadata Management..211
   Ensuring Data Privacy and Compliance in Databricks........................212
   Importance of Data Privacy and Compliance..............................213
   Implementing Privacy Measures and Techniques in Databricks....215

  Ensuring Compliance with Data Protection Regulations 216
  Techniques for Anonymization, Pseudonymization, and
  Data Masking 218

 Implementing Access Controls and Data Encryption 220
  Overview of Access Controls and Authorization in Databricks 220
  Designing and Implementing Access Policies for
  Data Protection 222
  Techniques for Encrypting Data at Rest and in Transit in
  Databricks 223
  Implementing Key Management and Secure
  Credential Storage Practices 225

 Data Governance Best Practices 227
  Importance of Data Governance 227
  Techniques for Data Lineage, Metadata Management, and
  Data Cataloging 229
  Best Practices for Data Documentation, Stewardship, and
  Data Lifecycle Management 231

 Conclusion 232
 Key Terms 233

Last Words 235
 Recap of the Journey 235
 Continuous Learning and Upgradation 235
 Encouragement for Practical Application 236
 Final Motivational Note 236
 Index 237

xx

CHAPTER 1
Fundamentals of Data Engineering

"In God we trust. All others must bring data."

– W. Edwards Deming

Introduction

In today's data-driven world, organizations are faced with the challenge of efficiently managing and extracting value from vast amounts of data. This has led to the emergence of data engineering as a critical discipline that focuses on the collection, transformation, and management of data to enable data-driven decision-making and support various data-intensive processes. In this chapter, we will explore the fundamentals of data engineering with a specific emphasis on using Databricks, a popular and powerful data engineering platform.

We will begin by understanding the role of data engineering in modern organizations and its significance in driving business success. With the exponential growth of data, organizations need robust data engineering practices to handle diverse data sources, perform complex transformations, and ensure data quality and integrity. Data engineering plays a pivotal role in bridging the gap between raw data and actionable insights, enabling organizations to unlock the true potential of their data assets.

Next, we will provide an overview of Databricks, a leading data engineering platform that empowers organizations to manage and process their data effectively at scale. Databricks offers a unified analytics platform that combines the power of Apache Spark with a collaborative workspace, making it a popular choice among data engineers and data scientists. We will explore the key features and advantages of Databricks that make it a compelling solution for data engineering.

To lay a strong foundation, we will delve into the core concepts and principles of data engineering. Understanding these fundamental concepts is crucial for building efficient and scalable data engineering solutions. We will cover topics such as data integration, data transformation, data pipelines, data quality, and data governance. By gaining a solid understanding of these concepts, you will be well-equipped to design and implement robust data engineering processes using Databricks.

Following that, we will dive into the specific features and capabilities of Databricks. We will explore how Databricks simplifies and accelerates data engineering tasks by providing an intuitive workspace for developing and executing data engineering workflows. Topics such as notebooks, clusters, libraries, and jobs will be covered in detail, highlighting their role in creating, executing, and managing data engineering pipelines. By the end of this section, you will have a comprehensive understanding of the Databricks environment and be ready to leverage its full potential for your data engineering projects.

To get you up and running with Databricks, we will walk through the process of setting up the Databricks environment and workspace. This will include creating a Databricks account and accessing the Databricks workspace. We will also discuss how to personalize the workspace by customizing preferences and settings to suit your needs. This practical guidance will ensure that you have a seamless experience while working with Databricks.

This chapter will provide you with a solid foundation in the fundamentals of data engineering with a focus on utilizing Databricks as the data engineering platform. By the end of this chapter, you will have a clear understanding of the role of data engineering in organizations, the significance of Databricks, the core concepts and principles of data engineering, and the process of setting up the Databricks environment and workspace. Armed with this knowledge, you will be well-prepared to explore the advanced topics covered in the subsequent chapters and become proficient in data engineering with Databricks.

Structure

In this chapter, the following topics will be covered:
- Role of Data Engineering in Modern Organizations
- Understanding Data Engineering Concepts and Principles
- Overview of Databricks and Its Significance in Data Engineering
- Introduction to Databricks and Its Core Features
- Setting up Databricks Environment and Workspace

Role of Data Engineering in Modern Organizations

In the vast landscape of modern organizations, data has become a precious commodity – a fuel that drives business success and innovation. However, raw data, like unrefined oil, holds limited value until it is transformed into something meaningful. This is where data engineering takes center stage.

Imagine data engineering as skilled artisans who refine and shape raw data into valuable insights. They possess the technical prowess to collect, organize, cleanse, and transform vast amounts of data from diverse sources into a structured and usable form. Just as skilled craftsmen sculpt raw materials into exquisite works of art, data engineers craft data into actionable information.

Data engineering brings order to chaos, creating a solid foundation for subsequent data analytics and machine learning initiatives. It lays the groundwork for advanced analytics, enabling organizations to gain insights, discover patterns, and make predictions. Without the expertise of data engineers, data analytics and machine learning models would stumble, unable to deliver accurate and meaningful results.

In a world where data is the currency of success, organizations that invest in robust data engineering practices gain a competitive advantage. They can swiftly adapt to changing market conditions, identify emerging trends, and make data-driven decisions with confidence. Data engineering has become an essential discipline that ensures organizations harness the power of their data assets and embark on a journey towards data-driven excellence.

Data Engineering's Role in Enabling Data Analytics and Machine Learning

Data analytics and machine learning have revolutionized the way organizations operate and make decisions. However, these transformative technologies rely on high-quality, well-prepared data to deliver accurate and actionable insights. This is where data engineering steps in, acting as the catalyst that enables the seamless integration of data analytics and machine learning into business processes. Let's explore how data engineering plays a crucial role in this dynamic landscape:

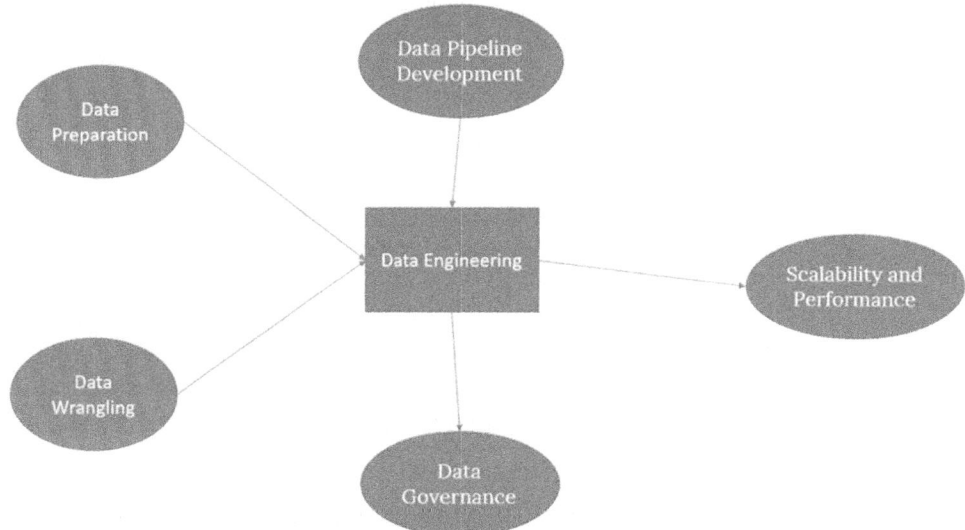

Figure 1.1: Roles of Data Engineering in Data Analytics and ML

- **Data Wrangling:** Like a skilled conductor leading an orchestra, data engineering orchestrates the harmonious transformation of raw data into a structured format suitable for analysis. It involves data cleansing, data integration, and data transformation processes. By wrangling the data into shape, data engineering ensures that data analytics and machine learning algorithms can operate efficiently and produce reliable results.

- **Data Preparation:** Data engineering takes on the role of a meticulous curator, preparing the data for analysis and modeling. This involves aggregating, summarizing, and filtering the data to create a refined dataset. Data engineers optimize the data for specific use cases, creating a solid foundation for data scientists and analysts to extract meaningful insights.

- **Data Pipeline Development:** Just as a well-designed plumbing system ensures a smooth flow of water, data engineering constructs data pipelines that enable the seamless flow of data from source to destination. These pipelines act as conduits, ingesting data from various sources, performing transformations, and delivering it to the analytics or machine learning systems. Data engineers design and implement robust, scalable, and fault-tolerant pipelines, ensuring the availability of timely and accurate data for analysis.
- **Scalability and Performance:** Data engineering architects have the infrastructure necessary for handling large volumes of data and processing it at scale. This involves designing distributed computing systems and leveraging technologies like Apache Spark, Hadoop, or cloud-based platforms. By optimizing performance and scalability, data engineering enables organizations to process massive datasets efficiently, unlocking the potential for advanced analytics and machine learning at scale.
- **Data Governance:** In the age of increasing data regulations and privacy concerns, data engineering ensures that data is handled in a compliant and secure manner. Data engineers establish data governance practices, implementing access controls, data encryption, and anonymization techniques to protect sensitive information. By safeguarding data assets, data engineering promotes trust and compliance within the organization.

By embracing these crucial responsibilities, data engineering enables organizations to leverage the full potential of data analytics and machine learning. It paves the way for data-driven decision-making, empowers business users with actionable insights, and drives innovation and competitive advantage in the modern era.

Data Engineering Supports Data-Driven Decision-Making

In today's fast-paced business landscape, organizations must make informed decisions quickly and effectively. Data engineering plays a vital role in supporting data-driven decision-making by providing reliable, high-quality data and facilitating its accessibility. Let's explore how data engineering enables organizations to harness the power of data for decision-making:

- **Data Integration:** Data engineering acts as the bridge between disparate data sources, enabling the integration of data from various systems, databases, and applications. By harmonizing and consolidating data from different sources, data engineering creates a unified view of the organization's information landscape. This integrated data forms the foundation for decision-making, allowing stakeholders to gain a holistic understanding of the business.

- **Data Transformation and Aggregation:** Data engineering transforms raw data into meaningful and actionable insights. Through data transformation processes such as cleansing, normalization, and aggregation, data engineers create structured datasets that are tailored to specific decision-making requirements. These transformed and aggregated datasets provide a consolidated and simplified view of complex data, making it easier for decision-makers to derive insights.

- **Data Quality Assurance:** Data engineering ensures the quality and reliability of data used for decision-making. Data engineers implement data validation techniques, perform data profiling, and establish data quality standards to identify and rectify inconsistencies, errors, and anomalies in the data. By ensuring data accuracy, completeness, and consistency, data engineering instills confidence in decision-makers, enabling them to rely on data with certainty.

- **Data Accessibility and Visualization:** Data engineering plays a crucial role in making data easily accessible and understandable for decision-makers. Data engineers design and develop data platforms, data warehouses, and data lakes that provide a centralized repository of clean and curated data. They also create intuitive data visualization tools and dashboards that allow stakeholders to explore and interpret data visually, facilitating better decision-making.

- **Scalability and Performance:** As data volumes grow exponentially, data engineering ensures that decision-making processes can scale seamlessly. Data engineers design and implement scalable data architectures and systems that can handle the increasing demands of data processing and analysis. By optimizing performance and ensuring efficient data retrieval and processing, data engineering enables timely decision-making even with large and complex datasets.

- **Data Governance and Compliance**: In an era of stringent data regulations, data engineering plays a critical role in ensuring data governance and compliance. Data engineers establish data governance frameworks, implement data security measures, and enforce data privacy regulations. By adhering to data governance practices, organizations maintain data integrity, protect sensitive information, and mitigate risks associated with data-driven decision-making. It gives them more confidence in their data.

By performing these essential functions, data engineering empowers organizations to make data-driven decisions with confidence. It enables stakeholders to access, analyze, and interpret data effectively, leading to better insights, improved operational efficiency, and competitive advantage.

As we delve deeper into the chapters of this book, we will explore the fundamental concepts, best practices, and proven strategies of data engineering with Databricks. We will equip you with the knowledge and skills to harness the power of Databricks for efficient data engineering, enabling you to drive data-driven decision-making in your organization.

Understanding Data Engineering Concepts and Principles

Data engineering plays a crucial role in modern organizations by enabling the collection, transformation, and processing of large volumes of data to support data-driven decision-making. It involves the design, development, and maintenance of systems and workflows that facilitate the smooth flow of data across various stages, from ingestion to storage and analysis.

At its core, data engineering focuses on the practical aspects of managing data. It encompasses the processes and techniques involved in extracting data from diverse sources, transforming it into a usable format, and loading it into storage systems for further analysis. Data engineering also involves ensuring data quality, integrity, and security throughout the data lifecycle.

Data engineering operates at the intersection of data science and software engineering. While data scientists focus on extracting insights from data, data engineers are responsible for building the infrastructure and pipelines that enable data scientists to work with data effectively. Data engineers work closely with data scientists, data analysts, and other stakeholders to understand their data requirements and translate them into scalable and efficient data engineering solutions.

The scope of data engineering extends beyond traditional relational databases to include big data technologies, cloud-based data platforms, and real-time streaming data. Data engineers need to have a solid understanding of data modeling, data integration, data transformation, and data governance principles to ensure the successful implementation of data engineering workflows.

In summary, data engineering encompasses the practices, tools, and methodologies used to handle data at scale, ensuring its availability, reliability, and usability for analysis and decision-making. It involves designing and implementing data pipelines, integrating disparate data sources, and transforming raw data into a structured and meaningful format.

By understanding the role and scope of data engineering, you'll gain valuable insights into the foundational concepts and principles that drive effective data engineering practices. This understanding sets the stage for exploring the core concepts and principles in data engineering, which we will cover next.

Core Concepts and Principles in Data Engineering

To effectively work with data, it's essential to grasp the core concepts and principles that underpin data engineering. These concepts form the building blocks of data engineering workflows and provide a solid foundation for designing scalable and efficient data solutions. Let's explore some of these key concepts and principles:

- **Data Modeling:** Data modeling involves designing the structure and relationships of data to support efficient data storage and retrieval. It includes defining entities, attributes, and relationships within a data model, which can be represented using various techniques such as entity-relationship diagrams or schema definitions.
- **Data Integration:** Data integration refers to the process of combining data from multiple sources into a unified view. It involves handling data from various formats, structures, and systems, and ensuring consistency, accuracy, and quality during the integration process. Techniques such as data consolidation, data transformation, and data cleansing are used to harmonize and standardize data across different sources.
- **Data Transformation:** Data transformation involves converting data from one format or structure to another. It includes tasks such as data cleaning, data enrichment, data aggregation, and data normalization. Data transformation is crucial for preparing data for analysis, ensuring that it is in a usable and meaningful format.
- **Data Pipelines:** Data pipelines are a series of processes that move data from its source to its destination, typically involving data ingestion, data transformation, and data loading. Pipelines can be designed to handle batch processing or real-time streaming, depending on the data

requirements. Effective data pipelines automate and orchestrate the flow of data, ensuring data is processed and delivered efficiently.

- **Data Governance:** Data governance refers to the overall management and control of data assets within an organization. It involves defining policies, procedures, and standards for data management, ensuring data quality, privacy, security, and compliance. Data governance establishes guidelines for data usage, access controls, and data lifecycle management.

Understanding these core concepts and principles will enable you to navigate the complexities of data engineering. As we delve deeper into the topic, we will explore practical techniques and best practices for implementing these concepts in data engineering workflows.

Overview of Data Pipelines, Data Integration, and Data Transformation

In data engineering, data pipelines, data integration, and data transformation are fundamental components that enable the smooth flow and processing of data. Let's explore each of these areas in more detail:

- **Data Pipelines:** Data pipelines are a series of interconnected steps that move data from its source to its destination. They facilitate the extraction, transformation, and loading (ETL) process. Data pipelines can be designed to handle batch processing, where data is processed in scheduled intervals, or real-time streaming, where data is processed as it arrives. These pipelines ensure the efficient and reliable movement of data, allowing organizations to derive valuable insights from their data.

- **Data Integration:** Data integration involves combining data from multiple sources into a unified view. Organizations often have data spread across various systems, databases, and applications. Data integration allows for the seamless consolidation and synchronization of data from these disparate sources. It ensures that data is accurate, consistent, and readily available for analysis and decision-making. Data integration techniques include data consolidation, data replication, data virtualization, and data federation.

- **Data Transformation:** Data transformation is the process of converting data from one format or structure to another. It encompasses various operations such as data cleaning, data enrichment, data aggregation, and data normalization. Data transformation is essential to ensure that data is in a usable and consistent format for analysis. It involves applying business rules, data validation, and data manipulation techniques to transform raw data into meaningful insights. Data transformation can be performed using programming languages, SQL queries, or dedicated data transformation tools.

By understanding the concepts of data pipelines, data integration, and data transformation, you'll be equipped to design and implement efficient data engineering workflows. These workflows enable the extraction, transformation, and loading of data, ultimately driving insights and value for organizations.

In the upcoming chapters, we will delve deeper into practical techniques, tools, and best practices for building robust and scalable data pipelines, integrating disparate data sources, and performing effective data transformations.

Overview of Databricks

Databricks is a powerful and versatile platform that serves as a unified analytics solution for modern organizations. It combines the power of data engineering, data science, and business intelligence in one comprehensive platform. With Databricks, organizations can seamlessly integrate their data engineering and data science workflows, enabling collaboration and accelerating insights.

Databricks as a Unified Analytics Platform

The platform provides a collaborative environment where data engineers and data scientists can work together, leveraging the same tools, frameworks, and data to drive innovation and make informed decisions. Databricks simplifies the data engineering process by offering a centralized hub for managing code, notebooks, and data, thereby facilitating productivity and streamlining development cycles. By unifying the various components of analytics, Databricks empowers organizations to unlock the full potential of their data and drive meaningful business outcomes.

- **Integration Simplified:** Databricks brings together data engineering, data science, and business intelligence capabilities in one platform, enabling seamless integration and collaboration across teams.
- **Centralized Workspace:** Databricks Workspace serves as a centralized hub for managing code, notebooks, and data, fostering productivity and streamlining development cycles.
- **Notebooks for Interactive Analysis:** With Databricks Notebooks, users can write and execute code, visualize data, and document their analyses, promoting interactivity and exploratory data analysis.

- **Breaking Down Silos:** Databricks enables multiple users to work on the same notebook simultaneously, fostering collaboration and breaking down silos between teams.
- **Version Control and Reproducibility:** Databricks integrates with version control systems like Git, ensuring code and data reproducibility and providing an audit trail of changes.
- **Flexibility and Portability:** Databricks supports multiple programming languages and integrates with popular data tools, providing flexibility and enabling seamless integration with existing data ecosystems.

Key Features and Benefits of Using Databricks for Data Engineering

Here are some key features and benefits of using Databricks for data engineering:

- **Scalable Data Processing with Apache Spark**
    - Databricks leverages Apache Spark, a fast and distributed data processing engine, enabling data engineers to handle large-scale data processing and analytics tasks efficiently.
    - The distributed nature of Spark allows for parallel processing, making it well-suited for handling massive datasets and performing complex transformations.
- **Seamless Integration with Popular Data Sources and Formats**
    - Databricks provides seamless integration with various data sources and formats, including databases, data lakes, cloud storage, and streaming platforms.
    - It supports connectors to popular databases like SQL Server, Oracle, and MySQL, as well as big data technologies like Hadoop, Apache Kafka, and Apache Cassandra.
- **Collaborative and Interactive Data Exploration and Analysis**
    - Databricks offers a collaborative environment where data engineers can interactively explore and analyze data through notebooks.
    - Notebooks provide an interactive interface to write and execute code, visualize data, and document insights, promoting collaboration and iterative analysis.

- **Scheduling Capabilities for Data Engineering Pipelines**
    - Databricks provides scheduling capabilities that allow data engineers to schedule and automate the execution of their data engineering pipelines.
    - Data engineers can define workflows, dependencies, and time-based triggers to ensure the pipelines run at specific intervals or in response to certain events.
- **Cost Optimization and Resource Management:**
    - Databricks provides features for cost optimization and resource management, allowing data engineers to optimize cluster configurations and allocate resources efficiently.
    - It offers autoscaling capabilities, which dynamically adjust the cluster size based on workload demands, ensuring optimal resource utilization and cost efficiency.

Overview of Databricks Architecture and Components

Databricks is built on a cloud-native architecture that combines the power of Apache Spark with a unified analytics platform. The architecture is designed to provide scalable, reliable, and high-performance data processing and analytics capabilities. It leverages cloud computing resources to enable organizations to efficiently handle large volumes of data and extract valuable insights.

At the core of Databricks architecture is Apache Spark, an open-source distributed computing framework known for its speed and scalability. Databricks extends Spark's capabilities by providing a managed platform that simplifies the deployment, configuration, and management of Spark clusters. This allows organizations to focus on their data and analytics tasks rather than the underlying infrastructure.

Databricks utilizes a distributed processing model, where data is partitioned and processed in parallel across a cluster of nodes. This distributed nature enables organizations to scale their data processing capabilities as needed, accommodating growing data volumes and computational requirements. It also ensures fault tolerance and high availability by replicating data and computations across multiple nodes in the cluster.

One of the key architectural components of Databricks is the Databricks Workspace. It serves as a collaborative environment where data engineers, data scientists, and analysts can work together on their projects. The Workspace provides a centralized interface for managing notebooks, which are interactive documents that combine code, visualizations, and narrative text. Notebooks enable users to write and execute code, perform data exploration and analysis, and document their work in a reproducible manner.

The following figure depicts the Databricks architecture:

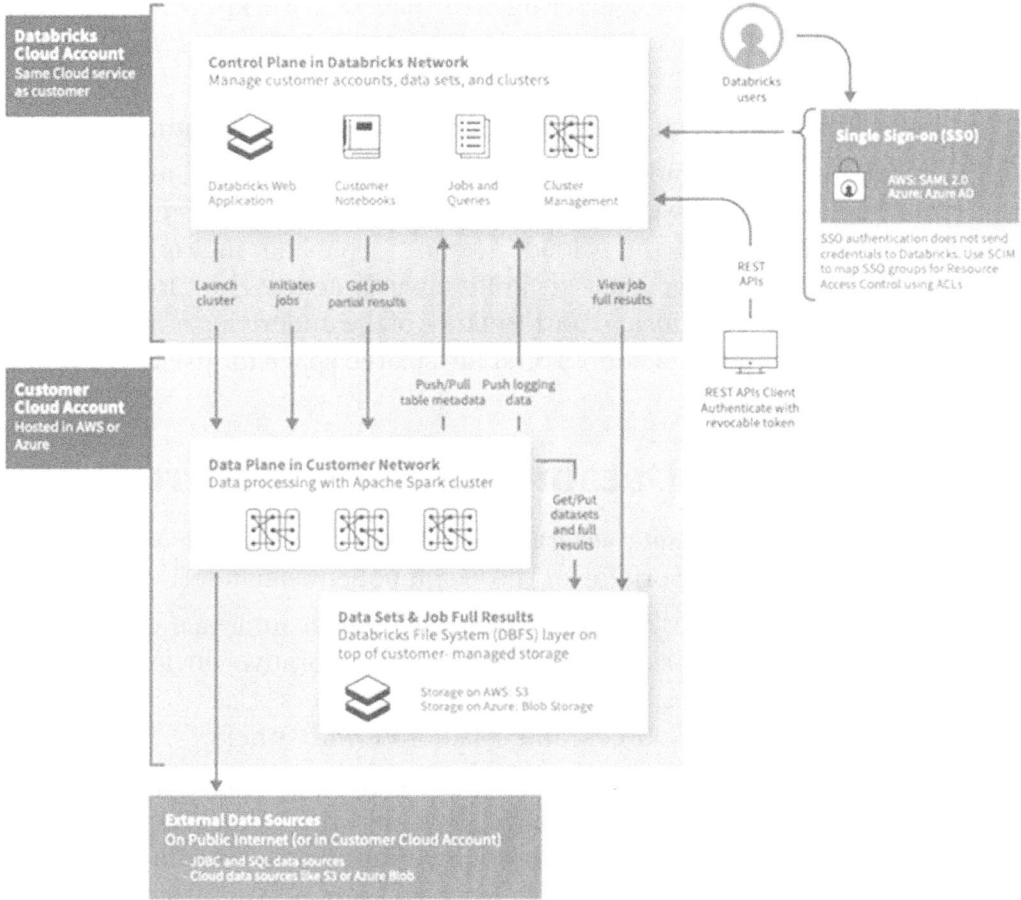

Figure 1.2: Basic Architecture of Databricks
(Credit: https://docs.databricks.com/getting-started/overview.html)

- **Databricks Cloud Account**

  The Databricks Cloud Account represents the managed infrastructure and services provided by Databricks. It includes the underlying infrastructure components required for running Databricks, such as the computing resources, networking, storage, and security mechanisms.

Databricks manages and maintains this infrastructure to ensure high availability, scalability, and performance for all customer accounts.

- **Customer Account**

    A Customer Account in Databricks architecture represents a user or organization-specific account within the Databricks Cloud Account. Each Customer Account has its own isolated environment for managing and executing data engineering and analytics workflows. It includes resources such as workspaces, notebooks, clusters, data storage, and collaboration features.

- **Interactions between Cloud Account and Customer Account**

    The Databricks Cloud Account provides the underlying infrastructure and services that power the Customer Accounts. The Customer Accounts are created within the Cloud Account, enabling multiple users or organizations to have their separate environments. The Cloud Account ensures the availability and performance of the underlying infrastructure, while the Customer Accounts offer an isolated space for users to interact with Databricks.

Components of Databricks Architecture

Within a Customer Account, several components interact to enable data engineering and analytics workflows. These components include:

- **Workspace**: The Workspace is a web-based user interface where users interact with Databricks. It provides a collaborative environment for managing notebooks, libraries, jobs, and clusters. Users can organize their work, share resources, and collaborate with others.

- **Notebooks**: Notebooks are interactive documents that allow users to write and execute code, visualize data, and document their analyses. Notebooks are at the core of data engineering and analytics in Databricks, supporting various programming languages and providing a platform for iterative development.

- **Clusters**: Clusters are virtual machines that provide the computing resources for executing data processing and analysis tasks. Users can create and manage clusters, specifying the desired compute capabilities, Spark versions, and libraries. Clusters enable scalable and parallel processing of data.

- **Data Storage**: Databricks integrates with various data storage systems, such as cloud storage solutions like Amazon S3, Azure Data Lake Storage, or Google Cloud Storage. These storage systems allow users to access and process data directly within Databricks, leveraging its computing capabilities.

Understanding the Databricks Workspace and Its Functionalities

The Databricks Workspace is a web-based user interface that serves as a central hub for interacting with Databricks. It provides a collaborative environment where users can manage their data engineering and analytics workflows, collaborate with team members, and access various resources. The Workspace offers several key functionalities that enhance productivity and facilitate efficient data engineering processes.

Key Functionalities of Databricks Workspace:

- **Notebooks:** The Workspace allows users to create, edit, and manage notebooks. Notebooks are interactive documents that combine code, visualizations, and narrative text. They provide an environment for data exploration, experimentation, and analysis. Within the Workspace, users can create new notebooks, organize them into folders, and easily share them with colleagues.

- **Libraries:** Databricks Workspace allows users to manage libraries, which are packages or modules containing reusable code and dependencies. Users can install, update, and uninstall libraries to extend the functionality of their notebooks. The Workspace provides a seamless way to manage libraries, making it easy to collaborate and ensure consistent environments for data engineering tasks.

- **Jobs:** The Workspace enables users to schedule and manage jobs. Jobs allow the automation of data engineering workflows by specifying tasks, execution schedules, and dependencies. Users can define jobs to run notebooks or submit code for execution at specified intervals or triggered by events. The Workspace provides a job management interface to monitor job runs, view logs, and set up notifications.

- **Clusters:** The Workspace provides the ability to create and manage clusters. Clusters are the computational resources used to execute data processing and analysis tasks. Users can configure clusters with the desired specifications, such as the number of nodes, instance types, and available libraries. The Workspace allows users to create clusters on-demand, manage their lifecycle, and monitor their performance.

- **Collaboration and Sharing:** The Workspace supports collaboration features, allowing team members to work together on notebooks and projects. Users can share notebooks, folders, and dashboards with specific individuals or entire teams. Collaborators can simultaneously edit notebooks, leave comments, and track changes, facilitating effective teamwork and knowledge sharing.
- **Version Control and Integration:** Databricks Workspace integrates with version control systems like Git, enabling users to manage and track changes to notebooks and code. It provides seamless integration with popular development tools, such as Jupyter, VS Code, and PyCharm, allowing users to leverage their preferred development environments while working with Databricks.

The Databricks Workspace provides a unified interface for managing notebooks, libraries, jobs, and clusters, enabling users to streamline their data engineering workflows. Its collaborative features, integration capabilities, and user-friendly interface enhance productivity, facilitate teamwork, and simplify the process of working with data in Databricks.

Introducing Databricks Notebooks and Its Role in Data Engineering

Databricks notebooks play a crucial role in enabling efficient data engineering workflows. Let's dive into the introduction of Databricks notebooks and their significance.

Databricks notebooks are interactive computing environments that allow data engineers to write, execute, and collaborate on code, queries, and visualizations. Notebooks provide a flexible and powerful interface for data engineering tasks, enabling users to perform data ingestion, transformation, analysis, and visualization within a single environment.

Role of Databricks Notebooks in Data Engineering:
- **Code Development and Execution:** Databricks notebooks support multiple programming languages, such as Python, Scala, R, and SQL. Data engineers can write code to implement various data engineering tasks, including data cleaning, data transformation, and data integration. Notebooks provide a live coding experience, allowing users to execute code cells and see the results immediately. This iterative development process accelerates the data engineering workflow.

- **Data Exploration and Visualization:** Notebooks offer interactive data exploration capabilities. Data engineers can query and analyze datasets, perform aggregations, apply filters, and generate visualizations within the notebook environment. Visualizations help data engineers gain insights into the data and identify patterns, outliers, and trends. Databricks notebooks provide rich visualization libraries and interactive plotting tools to create informative charts and graphs.

- **Collaboration and Documentation:** Databricks notebooks support collaboration among data engineering teams. Multiple users can work on the same notebook simultaneously, making it easier to collaborate, share ideas, and exchange knowledge. Notebooks also allow users to document their code, add narrative text, and explain the logic behind data engineering processes. This documentation capability enhances code readability, facilitates knowledge sharing, and promotes reproducibility.

- **Integration with External Tools and Services:** Databricks notebooks seamlessly integrate with a wide range of external tools and services. Data engineers can leverage popular libraries, frameworks, and APIs within their notebooks, such as Apache Spark, TensorFlow, scikit-learn, and AWS services. This integration allows data engineers to harness the power of these tools and services while performing data engineering tasks, enabling advanced analytics, machine learning, and cloud integration.

- **Reusability and Reproducibility:** Databricks notebooks promote code reusability and reproducibility. Data engineers can create modular and reusable code snippets, functions, and libraries within notebooks. These reusable components can be shared across multiple notebooks and projects, saving time and effort. Moreover, notebooks capture the entire code execution history, making it easy to reproduce previous results and track changes.

Databricks notebooks provide a versatile and interactive environment for data engineers to develop, execute, and collaborate on data engineering tasks. Their integration with various programming languages, data exploration capabilities, collaboration features, and seamless integration with external tools make them essential for efficient data engineering workflows.

Setting Up Databricks Environment and Workspace

Setting up a Databricks account and workspace is an important step to start working with the platform. Let's explore the steps involved in setting up a Databricks account and workspace:

1. **Account Creation:** To begin, you need to create a Databricks account. Visit the Databricks website (https://community.cloud.databricks.com/) and sign up for an account by providing the required information, such as your name, email address, and organization details. You may also need to choose a pricing plan that aligns with your requirements, but here we will create a free account, which will be sufficient to cover the scope of this book. You can go with the same.

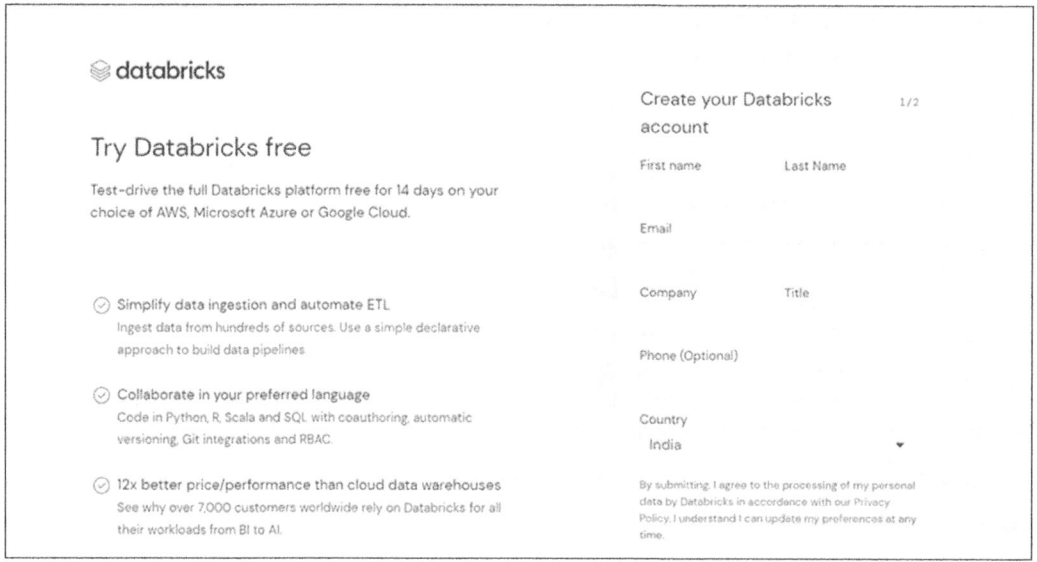

Figure 1.3: *Registration Page 1*

2. **Choosing the Cloud Provider:** Databricks offers integration with different cloud providers like Amazon Web Services (AWS), Microsoft Azure, and Google Cloud Platform (GCP). Select the cloud provider of your choice based on your organization's cloud infrastructure or preferences. If you don't have any of the accounts, you can click **Get Started with Community Edition.** As this is a free account, we will use this account in this book.

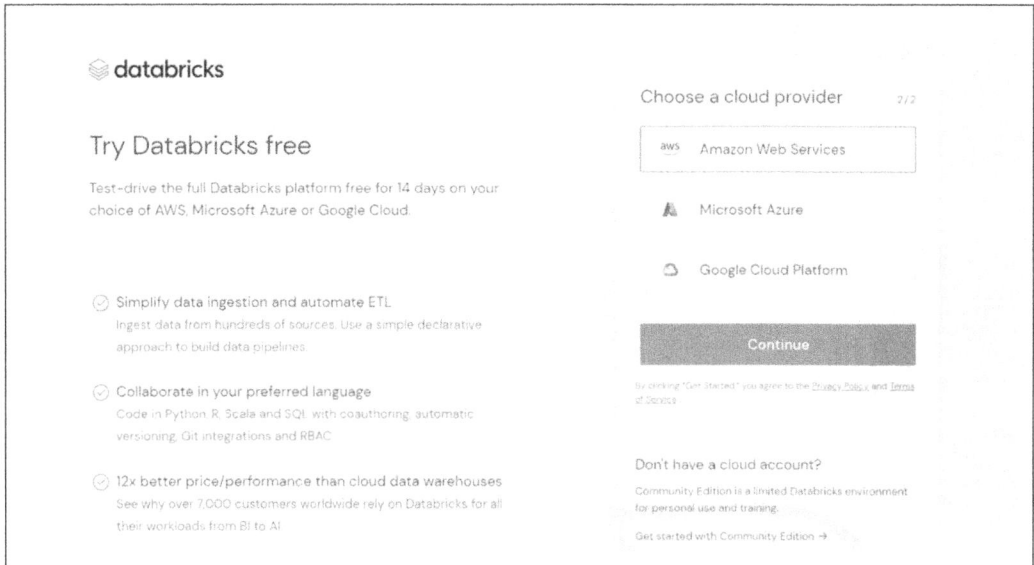

Figure 1.4: *Registration Page 2*

You will receive the following screenshot once you click Community Edition:

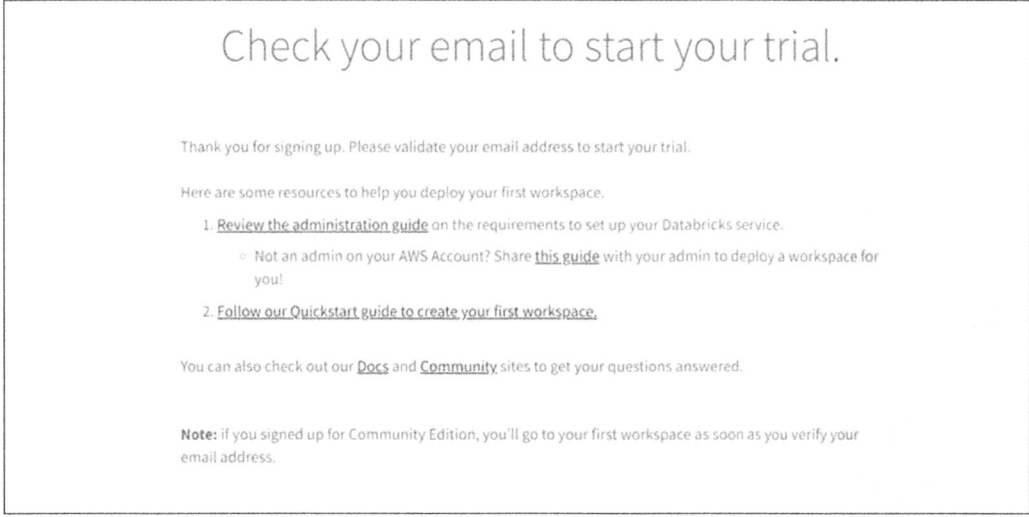

Figure 1.5: *Success page after completing the Registration Form*

After verifying the link received in your email ID and setting up the password, you will see the following window to ensure that your workspace has been set up:

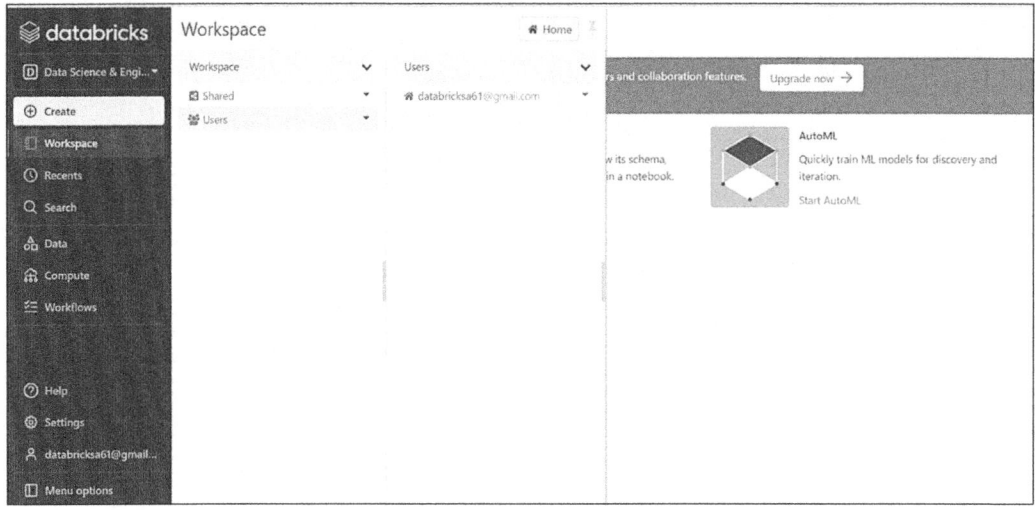

Figure 1.6: Home Page when you log in to the Databricks account

3. **Navigating the Workspace:** The Databricks Community Edition workspace provides a user-friendly interface for managing your notebooks and clusters. You can navigate through different sections like Home, Workspace, Clusters, and Jobs to access and organize your work.

4. **Creating Notebooks:** Notebooks are an integral part of Databricks and are used for developing and executing code. In the Databricks Community Edition, you can create new notebooks by navigating to the Workspace section and selecting `Create` or `Import` to create a new notebook or import an existing one.

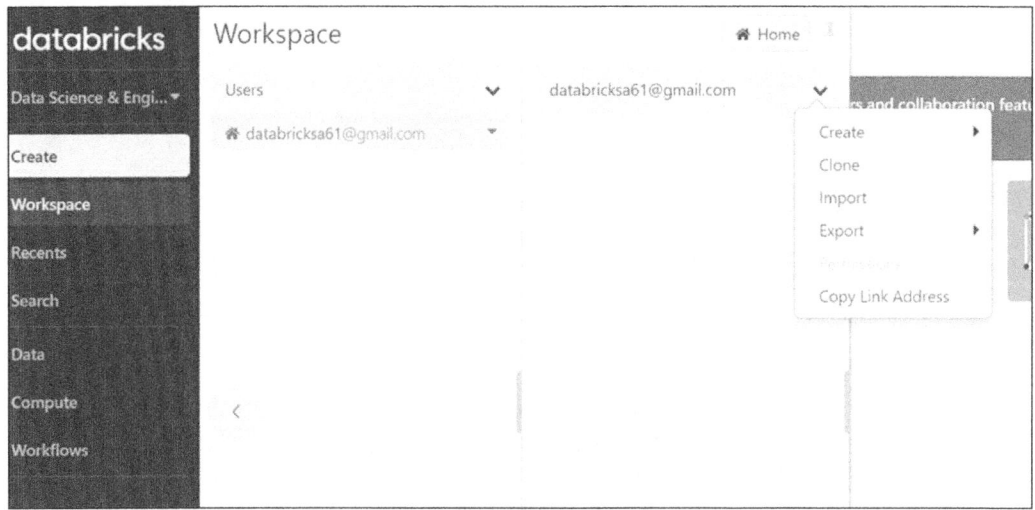

Figure 1.7: Workspace for your user

5. **Running Code in Notebooks:** Databricks notebooks support multiple programming languages, such as Python, Scala, and SQL. You can write code in the notebook cells and execute them to perform various data engineering tasks, including data ingestion, transformation, and analysis. We will explore this in upcoming chapters.

6. **Managing Clusters:** In Databricks, clusters provide the computational resources for executing your code. In the Community Edition, you can create and manage clusters to run your notebooks. You can select the cluster size and configuration based on your needs and budget. In this edition, we have the micro cluster, which is sufficient for learning, developing, and running all sample data pipelines.

7. **Connecting to Data Sources:** Databricks allows you to connect to various data sources, such as databases, data lakes, and cloud storage. In the Community Edition, you can establish connections to these data sources to access and process the data within your notebooks. We will explore these topics in future chapters.

By following these steps, you can successfully set up a Databricks account and workspace, allowing you to leverage the powerful capabilities of the platform for your data engineering tasks.

Best Practices for Managing Databricks Notebooks

Managing and organizing Databricks projects and notebooks is crucial for maintaining a structured and efficient data engineering environment. In this section, we will discuss some best practices to help you effectively manage and organize your projects and notebooks in Databricks.

- **Project Organization:** Create a logical structure for your projects by grouping related notebooks together. You can organize notebooks based on functional areas, data sources, or specific tasks. This helps in better navigation and understanding of your data engineering. Create folders within your Databricks workspace to organize your notebooks. Use folders to group related projects, modules, or datasets. A well-structured folder hierarchy makes it easier to navigate and locate specific notebooks and workflows.

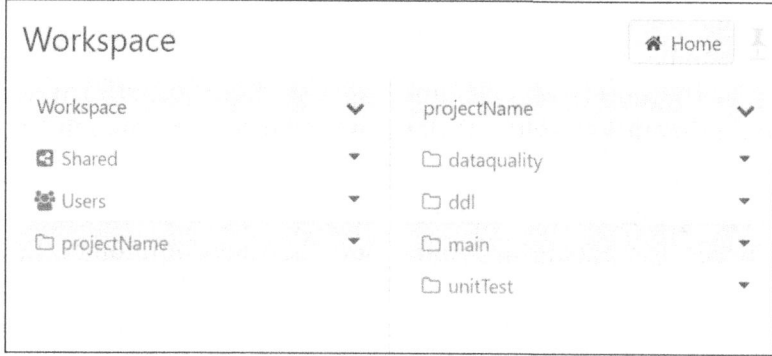

Figure 1.8: Folder Structure

- **Notebook Naming Conventions:** Adopt a consistent naming convention for your notebooks. Use descriptive and meaningful names that reflect the purpose or content of the notebook. This makes it easier to identify and search for specific notebooks within your workspace.

- **Notebook Documentation:** Document your notebooks to provide clear explanations of the code logic, data sources, transformations, and any other relevant information. Use Markdown cells or comments to add explanations, instructions, or references. Well-documented notebooks facilitate collaboration and enhance the maintainability of your projects. We will cover this topic in upcoming chapters.

- **Version Control:** Leverage version control systems like Git to manage the changes in your notebooks. Databricks integrates with popular version control platforms, allowing you to track modifications, collaborate with team members, and roll back to previous versions if needed. Version control ensures code traceability and helps in troubleshooting and auditing. If you don't have Git, you can get the last version of code change from Databricks' new in-built feature – `Revision history`. This feature can be found on the right-side of the notebook, as shown in *Figure 1.9*:

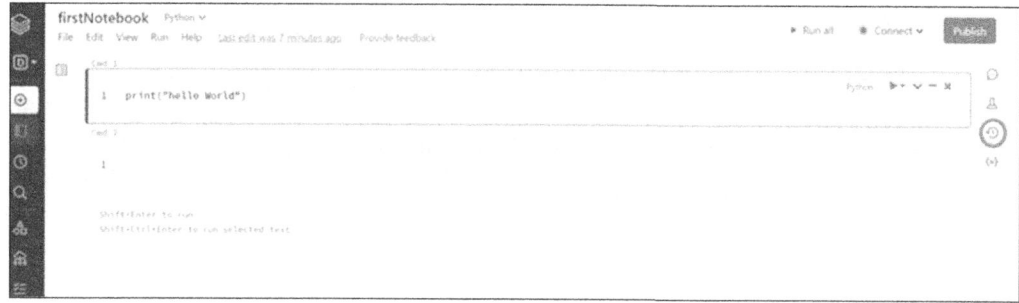

Figure 1.9: First Program

- **Notebook Dependencies**: Identify and manage dependencies between notebooks. If a notebook relies on the output of another notebook, ensure that the dependencies are properly documented and maintained. This helps in understanding the data flow and ensures that changes in one notebook do not break the functionality of others.

By following these best practices, you can maintain a well-organized and efficient environment for your Databricks projects and notebooks. These practices promote code reusability, collaboration, and scalability, enabling you to build robust and maintainable data engineering solutions.

Conclusion

In this chapter, we explored the fundamentals of data engineering with Databricks, a powerful platform for data processing and analytics. We began by understanding the role of data engineering in modern organizations and its significance in driving data-driven decision-making. We then delved into the introduction of Databricks and its core features, including its architecture, components, and the role of Databricks notebooks in data engineering workflows.

Furthermore, we discussed key concepts and principles in data engineering. We explored the benefits of using Databricks for data engineering. Additionally, we explored the process of setting up a Databricks environment and workspace, and best practices for managing and organizing Databricks projects and notebooks.

With this foundational knowledge, we are now well-equipped to dive deeper into the world of Databricks data engineering. In the upcoming chapters, we will explore topics such as Delta Tables for efficient data management, data transformation and ETL processes, data quality and integrity, designing effective data models, workflow automation, performance optimization, scaling data engineering solutions, data privacy and compliance, and data governance best practices. By mastering these topics, we will become proficient in leveraging Databricks for robust and efficient data engineering solutions.

Key Terms

- **Data Engineering**: The discipline that focuses on designing, developing, and maintaining systems and processes for the efficient and reliable management of data.

- **Databricks**: A unified analytics platform that combines data engineering, data science, and business analytics. It provides a collaborative environment for building data-driven solutions.
- **Data Pipeline**: A series of steps or processes that extract, transform, and load (ETL) data from various sources to a target destination, enabling data movement and transformation.
- **Data Integration**: The process of combining data from multiple sources into a unified view, ensuring data consistency, accuracy, and availability for analysis and decision-making.
- **Data Transformation**: The process of converting raw data into a desired format or structure by applying various operations such as filtering, aggregating, cleaning, and enriching the data.
- **Databricks Workspace**: A collaborative environment within Databricks where users can create, manage, and execute Databricks notebooks, organize projects, and collaborate with team members.
- **Databricks Notebooks**: Interactive, web-based documents that allow users to write, execute, and share code, visualizations, and explanatory text. Notebooks are widely used for data exploration, analysis, and data engineering workflows.
- **Cluster**: A group of virtual machines (VMs) in Databricks that collectively provide computing resources for executing data processing tasks. Clusters can be configured with different sizes and specifications based on workload requirements.
- **Delta Tables**: A data storage format in Databricks that provides ACID transactional capabilities, schema evolution, and time travel features for managing and processing large-scale data.
- **Workflow Automation**: The process of automating and orchestrating data engineering tasks and processes, such as data ingestion, transformation, and scheduling, to ensure efficiency and reliability.

CHAPTER 2
Mastering Delta Tables in Databricks

"In data, quality and structure go hand in hand. Master the tables, and you harness the power of your data."

Introduction

In today's data-driven world, organizations face the challenge of managing and processing vast amounts of data efficiently and reliably. This is where Delta Tables come into play. Delta Tables, a core feature of Databricks, provides a powerful and scalable solution for data management and processing, enabling data engineers to handle large-scale datasets easily.

This chapter delves deep into the world of Delta Tables, exploring their benefits, architecture, and the various techniques and strategies for optimizing their usage. By mastering Delta Tables, data engineers can unlock the full potential of their data, ensuring reliability, scalability, and performance in their data engineering workflows.

Throughout this chapter, we will explore the fundamental concepts and principles of Delta Tables, understand their architecture and components, and learn how they can enhance data management and processing in Databricks.

We will delve into important topics such as schema evolution, transactional capabilities, data versioning, and performance optimization techniques.

By the end of this chapter, you will have a comprehensive understanding of Delta Tables and be equipped with the knowledge and skills to leverage their capabilities effectively. So, let's dive into the world of Delta Tables and discover how they can revolutionize your data engineering journey in Databricks.

Structure

In this chapter, the following topics will be covered:
- Understanding the Benefits of Delta Tables in Databricks
- Overview of Delta Lake Architecture and Concepts
- Implementing Schema Evolution and Table Updates

Understanding the Benefits of Delta Tables in Databricks

Delta tables, introduced by Databricks, are an advanced data storage technology combining the best features of data lakes and data warehouses. They provide a reliable and scalable solution for managing and processing large volumes of data in a structured and efficient manner.

Traditionally, data lakes were known for storing vast amounts of raw and unprocessed data, while data warehouses excelled at structured and optimized data processing. However, this dichotomy often led to data reliability, consistency, and query performance challenges.

Delta tables bridge this gap by offering the best of both worlds. They are designed to provide ACID (Atomicity, Consistency, Isolation, Durability) transactional capabilities, which ensure data integrity and consistency during read and write operations. Like in a traditional database, you can update, delete, and merge data in Delta tables with full transactional support.

Moreover, Delta tables offer advanced data versioning and time travel capabilities. You can easily track changes to your data, revert to previous versions, and perform point-in-time queries to analyze data at specific historical moments. This data traceability and temporal analysis level is crucial for data governance, compliance, and audit purposes.

In addition, Delta tables leverage powerful optimizations such as indexing, data skipping, and caching to accelerate query performance. These optimizations enable faster data access, efficient data pruning, and selective scanning, significantly improving query response times.

Adopting Delta tables in your data engineering workflows gives you a reliable, scalable, and performant data storage and processing solution. With Delta tables ' trust and efficiency, you can confidently build robust data pipelines, implement data transformations, and empower data-driven decision-making.

In the next sections, we will explore Delta tables' various benefits and features in more detail, providing you with a comprehensive understanding of their significance in modern data engineering.

Enhanced Data Reliability and Consistency with Delta Tables

Delta tables provide several features that enhance data reliability and consistency compared to traditional data storage approaches. Some of the key aspects are as follows:

- **ACID Transactions:** Delta tables support ACID (Atomicity, Consistency, Isolation, Durability) transactions, ensuring that data operations are reliable and consistent. ACID transactions guarantee that a set of operations succeeds or fails, leaving the data in a consistent state.

  For example, consider a scenario where you need to update multiple records in a Delta table. With ACID transactions, if one of the records fails to update due to an error or interruption, all the other updates will be rolled back, and the table will remain unchanged. This ensures data consistency and prevents partial updates that could lead to data inconsistencies.

  In a non-ACID system, without transactional support, if an error occurs during the update process, some records may be updated while others are not, leaving the data inconsistent. ACID transactions ensure that such partial updates do not occur, maintaining the integrity of the data.

  ACID transactions also provide isolation, meaning that concurrent transactions running simultaneously do not interfere with each other. Each transaction is executed as if it is the only transaction running, preventing any conflicts or inconsistencies that could arise from concurrent operations.

The durability aspect of ACID transactions ensures that once a transaction is committed, the changes made to the data are permanent and will survive system failures or crashes. Even during a power outage or system failure, the changes made within a committed transaction will be preserved.

By supporting ACID transactions, Delta tables provide a reliable and consistent data processing environment, ensuring that your data remains valid and consistent throughout various operations, regardless of failures or concurrent activities. This feature must be included in Data Lake but provided in a data warehouse. Hence, it brought it into Delta Table.

- **Write Optimization:** Delta tables optimize write operations by leveraging a technique called write-ahead logs. This ensures that writes are durable and recoverable, even during failures or system crashes. Delta tables also employ a transaction log allowing easy rollbacks and recovery.
- **Data Versioning:** Delta tables enable easy data versioning, allowing you to track and access different versions of the data. This is particularly useful for auditing, reproducing past results, or performing historical analysis. You can easily query and access specific versions of the data using time travel functionality.
- **Schema Evolution:** Delta tables support schema evolution, which means you can modify the schema over time without requiring a full table rewrite. This flexibility allows for easier data evolution and accommodates changes in data requirements without disrupting existing workflows.
- **Data Consistency Checks:** Delta tables perform automatic data consistency checks during write operations, ensuring that data adheres to defined schema constraints. This helps maintain the integrity and consistency of the data stored in Delta tables.

By leveraging these features, Delta tables provide enhanced data reliability and consistency, enabling you to trust the integrity of your data and have confidence in its accuracy and consistency throughout the data engineering process.

Efficient Data Processing and Query Optimization

Delta tables offer efficient data processing and query optimization capabilities, resulting in faster and more performant data operations. The following features contribute to the efficient processing of data and optimization of queries:

- **Predicate Pushdown:** Delta tables optimize query execution by pushing down predicates to the storage layer. This means that data filtering happens at the storage level, reducing the amount of data transferred and improving query performance.
- **Data Skipping:** Delta tables utilize data skipping techniques to avoid reading irrelevant data during query execution. By leveraging statistics and metadata about the data, Delta can intelligently skip entire files or partitions that do not contain relevant data for the query, further reducing I/O overhead. For example, consider a Delta table that stores sales data across multiple regions and dates. Each file in the table might contain data for a specific region and date range. If a user queries for sales data from a particular region during a specific week, Delta Lake will first consult the metadata associated with each file, which includes information such as the minimum and maximum dates and regions covered in each file. By analyzing this metadata, Delta Lake can quickly determine which files do not contain data for the specified region and date range and exclude them from the scan.
- **Column Pruning:** Delta tables perform column pruning, meaning only the necessary columns are read from storage during query execution. This minimizes data transfer and storage I/O, improving query performance, especially when dealing with wide tables or tables with large-sized columns.
- **Indexing Mechanisms:** Delta tables employ indexing techniques to optimize data processing and query performance further. Two key indexing mechanisms in Delta are Z-Ordering and Bloom filters.
  - **Z-Ordering**: Z-Ordering is a technique that organizes data to improve data locality and enable efficient range-based filtering. With Z-Ordering, data is reorganized based on the values of one or more columns, ensuring that related data is stored close. This arrangement facilitates better data skipping and filtering during query execution. By storing related data together, Z-Ordering improves the efficiency of range-based queries, such as filtering data based on a specific date range or a particular customer ID.
  - **Bloom Filters**: Bloom filters are probabilistic data structures that provide an efficient way to quickly determine whether a value is present in a set. In Delta tables, Bloom filters determine if a specific value exists in a column or a partition without reading all the data. By precomputing and storing Bloom filters for each column or partition, Delta can quickly skip irrelevant data during query execution. This

helps to reduce I/O overhead and speeds up query processing, especially when dealing with large datasets.

By leveraging Z-Ordering and Bloom filters, Delta tables optimize data access patterns and reduce the amount of data that needs to be read from storage during query execution. This results in improved query performance and faster data processing, enabling efficient data analysis and exploration in data engineering workflows.

By leveraging these optimization techniques, Delta tables ensure that queries execute efficiently by minimizing data transfer, reducing I/O overhead, and providing timely results. Whether you're running complex analytics or ad-hoc queries, Delta's query optimization capabilities contribute to improved overall performance and faster time-to-insight.

Improved Data Versioning and Time Travel Capabilities in Delta Tables

Delta tables offer advanced data versioning and time travel features, allowing you to access and analyze data at specific points in time. Here's an explanation of the benefits and functionalities as follows:

Data Versioning

Delta tables keep track of every change made to the data, enabling easy access to different dataset versions. This versioning capability offers several advantages as follows:

- **Historical Analysis:** You can analyze data as it appeared at different points in time, facilitating historical analysis and trend identification. This is particularly useful for tracking changes, understanding data evolution, and conducting retrospective analysis.
- **Data Auditing:** Delta tables maintain a comprehensive transaction log that records all modifications made to the data. This log provides an audit trail, allowing you to trace and investigate the changes made, helping with compliance, data governance, and debugging scenarios.
- **Reproducibility:** With data versioning, you can reproduce analysis results by accessing the exact version of the data used in a specific analysis or experiment. This promotes reproducibility, ensuring consistent and reliable results.

Time Travel

Delta tables introduce the concept of time travel, which enables you to query the state of the data at a particular point in time. Here's how time travel works:

- **Querying Historical Data:** You can run SQL queries against Delta tables specifying a specific version or timestamp to retrieve the data as it existed at that particular moment. This allows you to reconstruct past states of the data and perform analysis on historical snapshots.
- **Point-in-Time Recovery:** In case of data corruption or accidental data changes, Delta tables' time travel feature allows you to restore the data to a previous state by rolling back to a specific version or timestamp. This ensures data integrity and provides a safety net for data recovery.
- **Data Comparison:** Time travel lets you compare data versions to identify changes, anomalies, or discrepancies. By querying different versions of the data, you can perform data diffing and identify alterations between datasets.

By providing data versioning and time travel capabilities, Delta tables offer enhanced data visibility, audibility, and the ability to explore data at different points in time. These features empower data engineers to perform detailed analyses, ensure data integrity, and make informed decisions based on historical data states.

Use Case Example

Scenario: Imagine you are a data engineer at a famous e-commerce company. Your company runs flash sales every week. Due to the rush during these sales, sometimes there are discrepancies in the sales records. At the end of the month, the finance team wants to reconcile the sales transactions. It needs to compare the sales data immediately after a specific flash sale with the current state to identify any discrepancies or adjustments made post-sale.

Problem Statement: To help the finance team, you decided to provide them with the sales data immediately after the flash sale that took place on the 15th of October. This SQL command fetches the `sales_data` as it appeared right after the sale on the 15th of October:

```sql
-- Retrieve sales data as it was on 15th October, post flash sale.
SELECT * FROM sales_data TIMESTAMP AS OF '2023-10-15 23:59:59'
```

Figure 2.1: SQL Query to retrieve sales data

To further assist, you provide a comparative analysis between the data from the 15th of October and the current state. This will show the new transactions or modifications after the flash sale:

```sql
-- Find transactions after the 15th of October
SELECT * FROM sales_data
EXCEPT
SELECT * FROM sales_data TIMESTAMP AS OF '2023-10-15 23:59:59'
```

Figure 2.2: SQL Query to find transactions

Overview of Delta Lake Architecture and Concepts

Managing and processing large volumes of data efficiently and reliably in modern data engineering is paramount. This is where Delta Lake comes into play. Delta Lake is an open-source storage layer that provides advanced data management capabilities on top of cloud storage, such as AWS S3, Azure Data Lake Storage, or Google Cloud Storage. It extends the functionality of Apache Spark, making it easier to handle big data workloads and ensuring data reliability, scalability, and performance.

In this chapter, we will delve into the architecture and core concepts of Delta Lake. We will explore how Delta Lake addresses key challenges in data engineering and provides a powerful framework for managing and processing data at scale. By understanding the underlying principles of Delta Lake, data engineers can leverage its features to build robust and efficient data pipelines, enabling them to unlock the full potential of their data assets.

Let's now dive into the first topic of this chapter, Introduction to Delta Lake, where we will explore the fundamental concepts and features that make Delta Lake a game-changer in data engineering.

Introduction to Delta Lake

Delta Lake was developed by Databricks, a company founded by the creators of Apache Spark, to address the challenges organizations face when working with big data at scale. Delta Lake was first introduced in 2017 as an open-source storage layer for data lakes, designed to provide reliability, performance, and advanced features on top of existing data lakes.

Before Delta Lake, traditional data lakes faced several limitations. One of the main challenges was the lack of transactional support, which made it difficult to ensure data integrity and consistency. Without transactional capabilities, data engineers had to implement complex, error-prone mechanisms to handle data updates and rollbacks. Additionally, data lakes often suffer from schema evolution issues, making it challenging to manage evolving data structures and enforce data quality standards.

To recognize these limitations, Databricks developed Delta Lake to enhance data lakes and address these challenges. Delta Lake combines the power of Apache Spark's distributed processing capabilities with additional features that provide ACID transactions, schema enforcement and evolution, time travel, and optimization techniques. It enables organizations to achieve reliable, scalable, and performant data management and analytics on their data lakes.

Since its introduction, Delta Lake has gained widespread adoption and has become a popular choice for managing and processing big data workloads. It has been embraced by various industries, including finance, healthcare, e-commerce, and telecommunications, where data engineers and data scientists rely on its capabilities to build robust and efficient data pipelines.

The ongoing development and contributions from the open-source community have further enriched Delta Lake, making it a mature and reliable technology for data engineering and analytics. With its rich history and continuous evolution, Delta Lake has emerged as a leading solution for organizations seeking to overcome the challenges associated with big data processing and management in modern data architectures.

Delta Lake is a powerful data storage and processing framework that addresses common challenges data engineers face when working with large-scale datasets. It combines the scalability and processing capabilities of Apache Spark with a transaction log and a set of optimizations for data storage and query performance.

Let's explore the key concepts and features of Delta Lake with this Tabular comparison with Data Warehouse and Data Lake:

	DATA LAKE	DATA WAREHOUSE	DELTA LAKE
Data Storage	Stores raw, unstructured, and structured data in its native format	Stores structured and processed data in a schema-based format	Stores structured and processed data in a schema-based format

	DATA LAKE	DATA WAREHOUSE	DELTA LAKE
Data Structure	Schema-on-read	Schema-on-write	Schema-on-read
Data Processing	Suitable for complex and diverse data processing tasks	Optimized for complex analytical queries	Combines the benefits of both Data Lakes and Data Warehouses
ACID Compliance	Typically lacks full ACID transaction support	Provides ACID transaction support	Provides ACID transaction support
Time Travel	Limited or no built-in support for time travel functionality	Limited or no built-in support for time travel functionality	Provides built-in support for time travel functionality
Scalability	Highly scalable and can handle large volumes of data	Scalability may vary based on the underlying technology	Highly scalable and can handle large volumes of data
Data Governance	Limited built-in data governance and metadata management capabilities	Provides robust data governance and metadata management capabilities	Provides robust data governance and metadata management capabilities
Performance	Flexible and may require additional processing for optimal performance	Optimized for fast analytical queries	Optimized for both read and write performance
Data Integration	Supports diverse data sources and formats	Supports structured data sources and formats	Supports diverse data sources and formats
Cost Efficiency	Generally cost-effective due to the use of cost-efficient storage options	Typically, more expensive due to the need for high-performance infrastructure	Offers a cost-effective solution with performance optimizations

Table 2.1: Comparison of key concepts and features of Delta Lake with Data Warehouse and Data Lake

Delta Lake Architecture

In this section, we will delve into the architecture and fundamental concepts of Delta Lake, an advanced data storage and processing solution. Delta Lake offers robust features enabling organizations to manage and analyze large-scale data workloads effectively. By understanding the key components and concepts of Delta Lake, data engineers and analysts can harness its capabilities to build reliable and scalable data pipelines and analytics solutions.

Figure 2.3 shows the roles of Data Engineering in Data Analytics and ML:

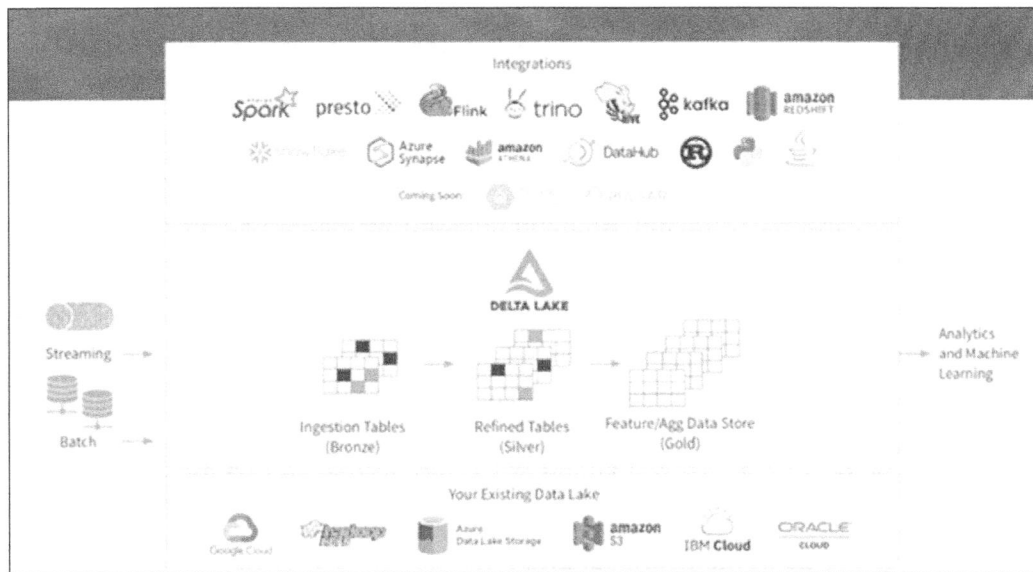

***Figure* 2.3**: *Delta Lake Architecture (Source Credits: https://delta.io/)*

The preceding figure offers a visual representation of the Delta Lake architecture and its integrations with other platforms and tools. Here's a breakdown based on the image:

- **Data Inputs**:
    - **Streaming**: This implies that Delta Lake can ingest real-time data, typically from sources that produce data in continuous, small packets.
    - **Batch**: Delta Lake also supports batch processing, which means it can handle large chunks of data that are ingested at periodic intervals.
- **Delta Lake Core**:
    - **Ingestion Tables (Bronze)**: This is the initial stage where raw data is ingested into Delta Lake. This raw data is often unrefined and may contain imperfections.
    - **Refined Tables (Silver)**: Once the data is cleaned, transformed, and enriched, it moves to this stage. The data is more structured and ready for further analysis.
    - **Feature/Aggregated Data Store (Gold)**: This is the final layer where data is further aggregated or enriched to derive meaningful insights. The data here is in a form that is most optimal for analytics and machine learning operations.

- **Integrations**:
  - The figure showcases a plethora of tools and platforms that integrate with Delta Lake, indicating its flexibility and compatibility.
    - **Processing Engines**: Apache Spark, Presto, Snowflake, Flink, Trino, Hive, and Kafka.
    - **Cloud Data Warehouses and Tools**: Azure Synapse, Amazon Athena, DataHub, Amazon Redshift, Google BigQuery, and Pulsar.
    - A note indicates that Google BigQuery integration is "Coming Soon."
- **Your Existing Data Lake**:
  - Delta Lake integrates seamlessly with existing data lakes. The storage solutions showcased here include Google Cloud (with the GCP logo), Hadoop HDFS, Azure Data Lake Storage, Amazon S3, IBM Cloud, and Oracle Cloud.
- **Analytics and Machine Learning**:
  - This arrow indicates that once the data goes through the Delta Lake processes, it's primed and ready for analytics and machine learning tasks. This is where actionable insights are derived from the data.

The overall architecture highlights Delta Lake's capability to process both streaming and batch data, refine it through multiple layers (bronze, silver, gold), and make it ready for analysis. The architecture also emphasizes Delta Lake's extensive integration capabilities, making it a versatile platform for various data engineering tasks.

Understanding Delta Lake's File Organization and Transaction Log

This section will delve into the intricate details of Delta Lake's file organization and transaction log mechanisms. These components are pivotal in ensuring data integrity, reliability, and efficient data processing within Delta Lake.

File Organization in Delta Lake

Delta Lake utilizes a unique file organization format that combines data and metadata into a single set of files. This format enables efficient data access and facilitates query optimization and data management capabilities. Let's explore the following key aspects of Delta Lake's file organization:

- **Delta Table**: Delta Lake organizes data into tables, represented as directories in a file system. Each table consists of multiple files collectively forming a Delta Lake dataset. Using tables provides schema enforcement and data consistency for all operations performed on the dataset. It ensures the data conforms to a predefined schema, preventing schema drift and maintaining data integrity.
- **File Versions**: Delta Lake supports versioning of data files, enabling easy tracking and retrieval of historical data snapshots. Each version represents a point-in-time state of the dataset. This versioning capability is achieved by storing multiple versions of the dataset files in the file system. It allows users to query the data as it appeared at specific points in the past, enabling powerful time travel queries. Additionally, versioning enables easy rollbacks to previous versions in case of data corruption or incorrect updates.
- **File Compaction**: Delta Lake employs file compaction to optimize storage and improve query performance. File compaction involves consolidating multiple small files into larger, more efficient files. This process reduces the metadata overhead of smaller files and improves data reading efficiency. It also helps in reducing storage costs by minimizing the number of files. Delta Lake automatically triggers file compaction based on defined criteria, such as file size or number of files, ensuring optimal performance and resource utilization.

The file organization in Delta Lake ensures efficient data access, query optimization, and simplified data management. By organizing data into tables, maintaining file versions, and performing file compaction, Delta Lake provides a reliable and scalable platform for managing large-scale data sets. These capabilities are essential for data engineering and analytics workflows, enabling organizations to derive valuable insights from their data robustly and efficiently.

Transaction Log in Delta Lake

The transaction log is a fundamental component of Delta Lake that ensures data reliability, consistency, and ACID (Atomicity, Consistency, Isolation, Durability) compliance. It records all changes made to the Delta Lake dataset, enabling features like ACID transactions, data versioning, and data recovery. Let's delve into the following key aspects of the transaction log in Delta Lake:

- **Write-Ahead Log (WAL)**: The transaction log in Delta Lake is implemented using a Write-Ahead Log (WAL) mechanism. The changes are first recorded in the transaction log when a write operation is performed on the Delta Lake dataset, such as inserting, updating, or deleting data. This log captures the metadata changes and the corresponding data modifications associated with each transaction.

The operational essence of WAL in Delta Lake lies in its process of recording every change in a transaction log before the change is applied to the data. This pre-emptive logging forms the backbone of data consistency, enabling the system to maintain an immutable history of data modifications. In the event of a system interruption or failure, this log is instrumental in data recovery, allowing Delta Lake to revert to the last consistent state, thereby minimizing data corruption risks.

While WAL offers these significant advantages in data integrity and recovery, it also introduces considerations around performance. Delta Lake addresses this by optimizing the logging process to minimize overhead during write operations. This is particularly crucial in a distributed system like Databricks, where managing logs efficiently across a cluster is essential for performance and scalability. Additionally, the integration of checkpointing mechanisms complements WAL by providing periodic snapshots of the data state, further streamlining the recovery process by reducing the amount of log data that needs to be replayed.

Overall, the WAL in Delta Lake is a sophisticated feature that enhances the platform's ability to handle large-scale, complex data operations, providing a stable and reliable environment for data processing and analytics.

- **ACID Transactions**: Delta Lake provides full ACID transactional capabilities, ensuring data consistency and integrity even in concurrent read and write operations. ACID transactions guarantee that all changes to the dataset are atomic, consistent, isolated, and durable. The transaction log plays a crucial role in achieving transactional consistency by maintaining a log of the changes made to the dataset. Delta Lake can use the transaction log to revert the dataset to a consistent state in case of failures or rollbacks.

- **Data Versioning**: The transaction log enables data versioning in Delta Lake. Each transaction in the log is assigned a unique transaction ID, and the log maintains a chronological order of these transactions. This versioning capability allows users to access and query the data simultaneously. By leveraging the transaction log, Delta Lake enables powerful time travel queries, enabling data exploration and analysis at any specific dataset.

- **Data Recovery and Consistency**: Delta Lake uses the transaction log to recover the dataset and ensure data consistency in case of system failures or crashes. The log captures all the changes made to the dataset, allowing Delta Lake to replay and restore them to their last consistent state. This capability ensures that data remains consistent, even during unexpected failures.

The transaction log in Delta Lake provides critical functionality for maintaining data reliability, consistency, and ACID compliance. It records all changes made to the dataset, supports ACID transactions, enables data versioning, and facilitates data recovery in case of failures. By leveraging the transaction log, Delta Lake offers robust data management and processing capabilities, making it a powerful tool for data engineering and analytics workflows.

Implementing Schema Evolution and Table Updates with Delta

Schema evolution and table updates are common challenges in data engineering, where data schemas often evolve to accommodate changing business requirements. Delta Lake provides robust capabilities for managing these schema changes and updates efficiently and streamlined. This subsection will explore how Delta Lake empowers data engineers and analysts to implement schema evolution and make table updates seamlessly.

In this hands-on focused section, we will dive into the practical aspects of implementing schema evolution and table updates using Delta Lake. We will cover techniques for handling schema changes, such as adding, modifying, and deleting columns in Delta tables. Additionally, we will discuss strategies for managing backward compatibility and performing data migrations.

Through a combination of theoretical concepts and practical exercises, you will gain a comprehensive understanding of the techniques and best practices involved in implementing schema evolution and table updates with Delta Lake. By the end of this section, you will be equipped with the knowledge and skills necessary to confidently manage and evolve your data schemas using Delta Lake's powerful capabilities.

So, let's embark on this journey of implementing schema evolution and table updates with Delta Lake and discover how it simplifies adapting your data structures to meet evolving business needs.

Handling Schema Changes and Evolution Using Delta

We will explore how to handle schema changes and evolution using Delta Lake. This involves adapting the dataset's structure to accommodate changes in business requirements while ensuring data integrity and compatibility. We will dive into the techniques and best practices for managing schema evolution in Delta Lake.

Introduction to Schema Evolution

Schema evolution refers to the process of modifying or evolving the structure of a data schema over time. In the context of Delta Lake, schema evolution involves changing the dataset's structure, such as adding new columns, modifying existing columns, or removing columns altogether while ensuring data integrity and compatibility with existing data.

To illustrate schema evolution, let's consider an example. Suppose you have a Delta table called **SalesData** that stores information about sales transactions, including columns such as **OrderID**, **ProductID**, **CustomerID**, **Quantity**, and **Price**. Over time, your business requirements change, and you need to introduce new fields to capture additional information, such as **Discount** and **OrderDate**.

With Delta Lake's schema evolution capabilities, you can easily add new columns to the existing table without affecting the existing data. The schema evolution process involves updating the metadata of the Delta table to include the new columns, allowing you to incorporate the changes into your data pipeline seamlessly.

For example, you can use the following command in Delta Lake to add the **Discount** and **OrderDate** columns to the **SalesData** table:

```
ALTER TABLE SalesData
ADD COLUMNS (Discount DOUBLE, OrderDate DATE);
```

Figure 2.4: Code to alter table schema by adding 2 new columns

This command modifies the **SalesData** table schema, extending it to include the new columns. The existing data remains intact, and any new data ingested into the table will include the newly added columns. This flexibility of schema evolution in Delta Lake enables you to adapt your data schema to evolving business requirements without disrupting existing data or data processing workflows.

Schema evolution also encompasses other operations like modifying existing columns (for example, changing the data type or length of a column) or removing columns from the schema. Delta Lake provides comprehensive support for these operations, allowing you to evolve and manage your data schema efficiently.

Understanding Schema Evolution Challenges

To effectively handle schema changes and evolution using Delta Lake, it is important to understand the challenges associated with evolving schemas in data systems. Let's explore some of the following challenges:

- **Data Consistency:** One of the main challenges in schema evolution is ensuring data consistency throughout the process. When modifying a schema, it is crucial to ensure that existing data remains valid and compatible with the new schema. Inconsistent or incompatible data can lead to quality issues and hinder downstream data processing and analysis.
- **Backward Compatibility:** Schema evolution should strive to maintain backward compatibility whenever possible. Backward compatibility ensures that existing data and applications that rely on the previous schema can function seamlessly without requiring extensive modifications. Managing backward compatibility is important to minimize disruption and facilitate a smooth transition to the new schema.
- **Data Migration:** Schema evolution often requires migrating existing data to conform to the updated schema. Data migration involves transforming and reorganizing the data to align with the new schema structure. This process requires careful planning and execution to ensure data integrity, completeness, and consistency throughout the migration.
- **Data Validation and Cleansing:** Schema evolution may necessitate data validation and cleansing to ensure the integrity and quality of the data. As the schema changes, existing data may need to be validated and cleansed to meet the updated schema requirements. This includes handling missing values, data type conversions, and other data quality issues.
- **Impact on Data Processing Workflows:** Schema changes can affect existing data processing workflows, including ETL (Extract, Transform, Load) pipelines, analytics processes, and downstream applications. It is essential to assess the impact of schema evolution on these workflows

and ensure that they continue to function correctly with the updated schema.

Leveraging Delta Lake for Schema Evolution

When it comes to handling schema changes and evolution using Delta Lake, you can employ various techniques and approaches. These techniques allow you to introduce new, modify existing, and remove columns from Delta tables while ensuring data integrity and compatibility. Let's explore some of the following techniques:

- **Schema Enforcement:** Delta Lake allows you to enforce schema constraints on your data, ensuring that only data adhering to the defined schema can be written into the Delta table. This helps maintain data consistency and prevents data with incompatible schemas from being introduced.

- **Schema Evolution Compatibility:** Delta Lake is designed to handle schema evolution in a compatible manner. It provides backward-compatible schema evolution, allowing you to add new columns to existing tables without breaking the compatibility with previously written data. This ensures smooth transitions between different versions of the schema.

- **Flexible Metadata Management:** Delta Lake maintains comprehensive metadata about the data schema, including column names, data types, and more. This metadata is stored in a transaction log, allowing Delta Lake to track and manage schema changes efficiently. The metadata helps ensure data consistency, compatibility, and integrity throughout the schema evolution process.

- **Unified Data Storage:** Delta Lake stores data in a unified format, combining the data and its metadata in a single, transactional format. This unified storage simplifies data management and schema changes, as all the relevant information is stored together. It provides atomicity, consistency, isolation, and durability (ACID) properties, ensuring data integrity and schema modifications.

- **Time Travel Capability:** Delta Lake's time travel capability allows you to access and query historical versions of your data, including previous schema versions. This feature is invaluable during the schema evolution process, as it provides the ability to roll back to previous versions, compare schema changes, and validate the impact of schema evolution on existing data and processes.

Techniques for Handling Schema Changes

When managing schema evolution with Delta Lake, following best practices can greatly simplify the process and ensure the integrity and compatibility of your data. Let's explore some key best practices for effective schema evolution as follows:

- **Adding New Columns:** To add new columns to an existing Delta table, you can utilize the **ALTER TABLE** statement in Delta Lake. This statement allows you to specify the new columns and their data types. The new columns will be included when data is subsequently written into the table. Existing data will remain intact, and the new columns will have null values by default.

    Example: To add new columns to an existing Delta table, you can use the **ALTER TABLE** statement with the **ADD COLUMNS** clause. Here's the code syntax for adding the **Discount** and **OrderDate** columns to the **SalesData** table:

```
ALTER TABLE SalesData
ADD COLUMNS (Discount DOUBLE, OrderDate DATE);
```

Figure 2.5: Code to alter table schema by adding more columns

- **Modifying Existing Columns:** In some cases, you may need to modify the properties of existing columns, such as changing the data type, length, or other attributes. Delta Lake provides the **ALTER TABLE** statement with the **CHANGE COLUMN** option to modify the properties of columns. This enables you to adapt the schema to accommodate evolving requirements.

    Example: To modify the properties of existing columns in a Delta table, you can use the **ALTER TABLE** statement with the **CHANGE COLUMN** clause. Here's an example of modifying the data type of the **Quantity** column to **INTEGER** in the **SalesData** table:

```
ALTER TABLE SalesData
CHANGE COLUMN Quantity Quantity INTEGER;
```

Figure 2.6: Code to change the datatype of the column in a table

- **Removing Columns:** If you no longer require certain columns in a Delta table, remove them using the **ALTER TABLE** statement with the **DROP COLUMN** option. This operation will permanently remove the specified columns from the table. It is important to note that this action is irreversible, so exercise caution when removing columns.

Example: To remove columns from a Delta table, you can use the ALTER TABLE statement with the DROP COLUMN clause. Here's an example of removing the "`Discount`" column from the "`SalesData`" table:

```
ALTER TABLE SalesData
DROP COLUMN Discount;
```

Figure 2.7: Code to drop the column name from table

- **Renaming Columns:** Renaming columns can be achieved by creating a new column with the desired name, copying the data from the existing column to the new one, and dropping the old one. This technique allows you to update column names without losing any data.

Example: To rename columns in a Delta table, you can create a new column with the desired name, copy the data from the existing column to the new column, and then drop the old column. Here's an example of renaming the **Quantity** column to **Qty** in the **SalesData** table:

```
ALTER TABLE SalesData
ADD COLUMN Qty INTEGER;

UPDATE SalesData
SET Qty = Quantity;

ALTER TABLE SalesData
DROP COLUMN Quantity;
```

Figure 2.8: Code to alter the name of the column and dropping old column

- **Data Type Evolution:** Schema evolution may involve changing the data type of a column. When performing such changes, it is important to ensure compatibility between the previous and new data types to avoid data loss or inconsistencies. Delta Lake provides built-in data type conversion functions that allow you to perform type conversions during schema evolution.

Example: Let's assume you want to convert the **Price** column from **DOUBLE** to **DECIMAL(10,2)** in the **SalesData** table:

```
ALTER TABLE SalesData
ALTER COLUMN Price TYPE DECIMAL(10,2);
```

Figure 2.9: Code to alter new column in a table

Best Practices for Schema Evolution

- **Plan for Change:** Before making any schema changes, it is important to have a well-defined plan. Understand the reasons behind the schema changes and evaluate the potential impact on data processing workflows, downstream applications, and data consumers. Consider the implications of schema changes on data validation, cleansing, and migration.
- **Maintain Backward Compatibility:** Strive to maintain backward compatibility whenever possible. This allows existing data and applications to continue functioning seamlessly without requiring extensive modifications. Introduce changes in a way that minimizes disruption and provides a smooth transition for data consumers.
- **Versioning and Compatibility:** Implement versioning and compatibility strategies to manage the transition between schema versions. Use version control mechanisms to track changes and maintain a schema evolution history. Document the compatibility requirements for each version, enabling consumers to adapt their applications accordingly.
- **Validate and Cleanse Data:** As part of schema evolution, validate and cleanse existing data to ensure its compatibility with the updated schema. Perform data quality checks, handle missing values, and address inconsistencies or anomalies. Implement data cleansing routines as needed to ensure the integrity and quality of the data.
- **Communicate Changes**: Effective communication is essential during schema evolution. Communicate the schema changes and their impact to stakeholders, data consumers, and downstream systems. Provide documentation, release notes, and data dictionaries to keep everyone informed about the evolving schema and any necessary modifications.
- **Test and Validate:** Thoroughly test and validate the schema changes before deploying them to production. Set up a testing environment that resembles the production environment to simulate real-world scenarios. Validate the compatibility of the new schema with existing data, perform end-to-end testing, and ensure the accuracy and reliability of the data.
- **Plan for Data Migration:** If schema changes require migrating existing data, plan and execute the data migration carefully. Develop data migration scripts or processes that ensure the integrity and completeness of the data during the transition. Perform extensive testing and validation of the migrated data to minimize the risk of data loss or corruption.

Conclusion

In this chapter, we explored the power and capabilities of Delta Lake for efficient data management and processing. We began by understanding the importance of data reliability and consistency in modern data architectures, which led us to introduce Delta tables as a game-changing solution. We discussed the key features and benefits of Delta Lake, highlighting its ACID transactions, scalable performance, unified analytics, and time travel capabilities.

We then delved into the core concepts of Delta Lake, including its architecture, file organization, and transaction log. We explored the Medallion architecture and its role in enabling optimized queries and accelerated data processing.

Next, we focused on schema evolution and table updates with Delta Lake. We learned how Delta Lake handles schema changes, including adding new columns, modifying existing columns, and removing columns, all while maintaining data compatibility and integrity. We discussed the best practices for managing schema evolution, emphasizing the importance of planning, maintaining backward compatibility, and validating data.

Lastly, we discussed techniques such as partitioning, indexing, and caching, which enable faster query performance and improved data processing efficiency.

In the next chapter, we will explore another essential aspect of data engineering with Databricks: data transformation and ETL processes. We will dive into techniques for building scalable data transformation pipelines, applying ETL methodologies, and optimizing data processing and performance using Databricks.

With Delta Lake as our foundation, we are well equipped to tackle the challenges of data engineering and unlock the true potential of data in modern organizations.

Key Terms

- **Medallion Architecture:** A Medallion architecture is a data design pattern used to logically organize data in a lakehouse, with the goal of incrementally and progressively improving the structure and quality of data as it flows through each layer of the architecture (from Bronze ⇒ Silver ⇒ Gold layer tables).
- **ACID Transactions:** Atomicity, Consistency, Isolation, and Durability properties that ensure data integrity and consistency in database operations.

- **Delta Tables:** Tables created and managed using Delta Lake, which provide ACID transactions, reliability, performance optimization, and time travel capabilities.
- **Schema Evolution:** Modifying a database schema to accommodate data requirements and structure changes over time.
- **Delta Lake File Organization:** The structure and organization of Delta Lake data files, including the Delta transaction log and file compaction.
- **Transaction Log:** A log file that records all changes made to a Delta table, enabling consistency and reliability in data operations.
- **Delta Time Travel:** The capability to query and access historical versions of data stored in Delta tables, allowing users to analyze data at different times.
- **Backward Compatibility:** The ability of a system or schema to function properly and accept data created with previous versions.
- **Data Partitioning:** The process of dividing data into logical partitions based on specific criteria, such as date, region, or category, to optimize query performance.
- **Indexing:** Creating indexes on specific columns of a Delta table to improve query performance by enabling faster data retrieval.
- **Caching:** Storing frequently accessed data in memory to speed up query execution and reduce latency.

CHAPTER 3
Data Ingestion and Extraction

"Just as the heart takes in oxygen and releases carbon dioxide, a robust data system inhales raw data and exhales actionable insights."

Introduction

In the rapidly evolving world of data engineering, the ability to efficiently acquire data from various sources and extract valuable insights is crucial for organizations aiming to harness the power of their data. This chapter takes a deep dive into the best practices, techniques, and strategies for effectively handling the data ingestion and extraction processes in Databricks. It explores the significance of proper data ingestion, the implementation of efficient data extraction techniques, and the handling of diverse data formats and sources.

Data ingestion is the critical first step in the data engineering pipeline. It involves acquiring and transferring data from multiple sources into a centralized data platform, such as Databricks. This chapter will discuss the best practices for data ingestion, including data quality considerations, choosing the appropriate method, and implementing efficient ingestion workflows. We will also explore techniques for handling data validation and ensuring data integrity during the ingestion process.

Data extraction, on the other hand, focuses on extracting valuable insights from the acquired data. This process involves retrieving relevant data subsets or aggregations for analysis, reporting, or further processing. This chapter will explore implementing efficient data extraction techniques, including incremental extraction for optimized processing, performance optimization strategies, and ensuring data consistency and integrity during extraction.

Additionally, we will explore the vast landscape of data formats and sources. In today's data-driven world, organizations encounter various structured, semi-structured, and unstructured data formats from multiple sources such as databases, APIs, and files. This chapter will guide you through the intricacies of working with different data formats, handling unstructured data, and transforming it to make it suitable for analysis and decision-making.

By following the best practices, leveraging efficient techniques, and adopting the right strategies for data ingestion and extraction in Databricks, organizations can streamline their data engineering processes, ensure data quality and reliability, and unlock the full potential of their data assets. Let's embark on this journey of data ingestion and extraction to unleash the power of data in Databricks.

Structure

In this chapter, the following topics will be covered:
- Ingesting Data into Databricks
- Implementing Efficient Data Extraction Techniques
- Handling Different Data Formats and Sources

Ingesting Data into Databricks

In data engineering, ingesting data lays the foundation for practical data analysis and decision-making. In this section, we will explore the best practices, considerations, and techniques for acquiring and transferring data into the Databricks platform. We will understand the importance of data ingestion as the initial step in the data engineering pipeline and discover how well-executed data ingestion sets the stage for successful data processing, analysis, and insights. Let's embark on the journey of data ingestion and learn how to optimize this process in Databricks.

Understanding the Importance of Data Ingestion

Data ingestion is crucial in the data engineering process, serving as the foundation for effective data transformation and analysis. It involves bringing data from various sources and systems into a centralized location, often called the ingestion or bronze layer. Understanding the importance of data ingestion is essential for building robust data pipelines and unlocking the full potential of data-driven insights. Here are key reasons why data ingestion is crucial:

- **Consolidating data from multiple sources:**
    - Data ingestion allows organizations to bring data from diverse sources such as databases, data lakes, streaming platforms, or external APIs into a single location.
    - By consolidating data, organizations gain a comprehensive view of their assets, eliminating data silos and enabling cross-functional analysis.
- **Ensuring data availability and accessibility:**
    - Data ingestion ensures that data is readily available and accessible to data engineering and data analytics teams.
    - It provides a centralized repository where data can be easily accessed and utilized for downstream processes such as data transformation, analytics, and machine learning.
- **Enabling data discovery and exploration:**
    - Ingesting data into a centralized location allows for easier discovery and exploration.
    - Data engineers and scientists can efficiently explore, query, and analyze the ingested data, gaining insights and discovering patterns for further analysis.
- **Facilitating data transformation and enrichment:**
    - Data ingestion forms the foundation for data transformation processes, where raw data is refined, cleaned, and prepared for downstream analytics.
    - By ingesting data into the bronze layer, organizations can apply data quality checks, standardize data formats, and enrich the data with additional information.

- **Supporting data governance and compliance:**
  - Centralizing data through ingestion enables organizations to establish data governance practices and ensure compliance with data privacy regulations.
  - It allows for better data lineage tracking, metadata management, and security controls over the ingested data.

In summary, data ingestion is a critical step in the data engineering workflow, bringing data from various sources into a centralized location. It provides the necessary foundation for data transformation, analysis, and decision-making. By understanding the importance of data ingestion and implementing effective strategies, organizations can unlock the full potential of their data assets and drive data-driven insights and innovation.

Choosing the Appropriate Data Ingestion Method

The correct data ingestion method is critical when designing data pipelines in Databricks. Each data ingestion method has strengths, limitations, and suitability for different use cases. Organizations can choose the most appropriate data ingestion method by carefully evaluating the available options and considering specific requirements. Here are critical considerations for selecting the proper data ingestion method:

- **Batch processing:**
  - Batch processing involves ingesting data in large volumes at regular intervals.
  - It is suitable for scenarios where near real-time processing is not required.
  - Batch ingestion is often used for historical data loads or periodic updates.
- **Streaming:**
  - Streaming ingestion enables near real-time or real-time data processing.
  - It is suitable for scenarios requiring low-latency processing and immediate insights.
  - Streaming ingestion is often used for data sources that generate continuous data streams, such as IoT devices, sensor data, or social

Data Ingestion and Extraction 53

   media feeds.
- **Hybrid approach:**
  - In some cases, a hybrid approach that combines batch processing and streaming can be beneficial.
  - This approach allows for storing historical data through batch processing while enabling near real-time updates through streaming.

When choosing the appropriate data ingestion method, consider the following factors:

- **Data characteristics:**
  - Consider the volume, velocity, and variety of data.
  - Evaluate whether the data is best suited for batch processing or streaming.
- **Latency requirements:**
  - Determine the desired latency for data processing and decision-making.
  - If real-time or near real-time insights are crucial, streaming ingestion may be the preferred method.
- **Update frequency:**
  - Assess how frequently the data source generates new or updated data.
  - Batch processing is suitable for periodic updates while streaming is more suitable for continuous data updates.
- **Source system capabilities:**
  - Consider the capabilities and limitations of the data source system.
  - Determine if the source system supports batch or streaming data extraction methods.

By carefully evaluating these factors, organizations can choose the most appropriate data ingestion method for their requirements. This ensures efficient data acquisition and timely processing, enabling organizations to leverage their data assets' power in Databricks.

Identifying Key Considerations for Data Ingestion

When implementing data ingestion processes in Databricks, it is essential to consider various factors to ensure the data ingestion workflows' efficiency, reliability, and scalability. Organizations can optimize their data ingestion strategies by identifying and addressing these key considerations. Here are some essential factors to consider:

- **Data sources and formats:**
    - Identify the data sources to ingest data, such as databases, data lakes, external APIs, or streaming platforms.
    - Understand the formats of the data sources, including structured, semi-structured, or unstructured data formats like CSV, JSON, Avro, Parquet, and more.
    - Determine the compatibility between the data sources and Databricks, ensuring the necessary connectors or libraries are available.
- **Data volume and velocity:**
    - Consider the volume and velocity of the data that needs to be ingested.
    - Assess the scalability requirements of your data ingestion pipelines to handle large data volumes and high data velocities efficiently.
    - Determine the appropriate data ingestion techniques, such as batch processing or real-time streaming, based on the data velocity requirements.
- **Data integration and transformation:**
    - Evaluate the data integration and transformation requirements during the ingestion process.
    - Determine if any data transformations, filtering, aggregation, or enrichment must be performed during ingestion.
    - Choose the appropriate data integration techniques based on your specific needs, such as ETL (Extract, Transform, Load) or ELT (Extract, Load, Transform).
- **Data security and privacy:**
    - Consider data security and privacy aspects during the data ingestion process.
    - Assess the sensitivity of the data being ingested and implement appropriate security measures, such as encryption, access controls, or anonymization techniques.
    - If it's PII data, ensure it has been masked so there is no data policy violation.
    - Ensure compliance with data protection regulations and organizational

policies.
- **Error handling and monitoring**:
  - Implement robust error-handling mechanisms to handle failures during the data ingestion process.
  - Monitor the ingestion pipelines for errors, data quality issues, or performance bottlenecks.
  - Set up logging and alerting mechanisms to proactively identify and address any issues that arise during ingestion.
- **Data governance and metadata management**:
  - Establish data governance practices to ensure data quality, metadata management, and lineage.
  - Define metadata standards, data cataloging techniques, and data governance policies for the ingested data.
  - Implement mechanisms to capture metadata about the data sources, schema information, and transformations.

Organizations can design and implement efficient and reliable data ingestion processes in Databricks by considering these key factors. Considering the data sources, volume, integration needs, security requirements, error handling, and governance aspects enables organizations to build robust and scalable data ingestion pipelines that meet their business needs.

Implementing Data Ingestion Best Practices

Implementing data ingestion best practices is essential for ensuring the reliability, efficiency, and accuracy of the data ingestion process in Databricks. These best practices help organizations optimize data ingestion workflows and minimize potential issues. Here are some essential rules to consider:

- **Data validation and cleansing**:
  - Perform data validation to ensure the integrity and quality of the ingested data. It should validate data at the time of entry of data into the system. Either it should fail the pipeline or store the records in a different queue with a notification sent to the respective team to investigate the matter. This will prevent insufficient data from entering into the system.
  - Use data profiling tools to identify and handle anomalies or missing values during ingestion. It will help maintain the integrity and consistency of the data, making it trustworthy for downstream

processes and jobs.

- **Incremental data loading:**
    - Implement incremental data loading techniques to ingest only the changes or new data since the last ingestion. This will save both time and money and provide a robust solution.
    - Track and maintain metadata or state information to identify delta changes in the data.
    - Utilize efficient data extraction methods, such as Change Data Capture (CDC), to capture and load incremental changes.
- **Error handling and logging:**
    - Establish robust error-handling mechanisms to handle failures during the data ingestion process.
    - Log and track errors, exceptions, and data quality issues for troubleshooting and auditing purposes.
    - Implement alerts and notifications to alert data engineering teams of ingestion failures or anomalies.
- **Metadata management:**
    - Maintain comprehensive metadata about the ingested data, including schema information, lineage, and data source details.
    - Utilize metadata management tools or frameworks to capture and organize metadata effectively.
    - Leverage metadata to ensure data traceability, facilitate discovery, and enable governance processes.
- **Data security and compliance:**
    - Implement security measures to protect sensitive data during the ingestion process.
    - Ensure compliance with data protection regulations and industry standards.
    - Apply encryption techniques for data in transit and at rest to maintain data privacy and integrity.
- **Monitoring and performance optimization:**
    - Establish monitoring mechanisms to track the performance and health of the data ingestion process.
    - Monitor ingestion latency, data volume, and resource utilization to

> identify bottlenecks or performance issues.
> o Optimize data ingestion pipelines by tuning parallelism, optimizing file formats, and leveraging partitioning techniques.

By implementing these best practices, organizations can enhance their data ingestion processes' reliability, efficiency, and effectiveness in Databricks. These practices improve data quality, increase productivity, and better insights from the ingested data.

Implementing Efficient Data Extraction Techniques

As we delve deeper into the world of data engineering, the importance of efficient data extraction becomes increasingly evident. This section will explore the strategies and techniques that empower us to smoothly extract data from diverse sources, setting the stage for meaningful analysis and insights.

Data extraction is the foundation upon which the entire data journey is built. Whether it's streaming in real-time or retrieving from a structured database, the way we extract data shapes the quality and timeliness of our analytics. Join us as we navigate through the intricacies of various extraction methods, ensuring that you are equipped with the knowledge to make informed decisions about the best approach for your projects.

In the following sections, we'll dive into the specifics of data extraction. We'll examine how to seamlessly connect with relational databases, how to tap into cloud storage platforms effortlessly, and how to handle different data formats with finesse. By the end of this section, you'll be well-versed in the art of data extraction and equipped with the tools to bring data into your Databricks environment efficiently.

Now, let's start our journey by understanding the variety of data extraction methods available in the ever-evolving data landscape.

Overview of Data Extraction Methods from Various Sources

In the vast landscape of data engineering, data comes in various shapes, sizes, and sources. Extracting this data efficiently and effectively is a crucial step that lays the groundwork for successful data processing and analysis. This section sheds light on the diverse methods that enable us to extract data from different sources, ensuring that the right data reaches the right destination for further processing.

- **Relational Databases:**

  Relational databases are the bedrock of enterprise data storage. Leveraging connectors, such as Java Database Connectivity (JDBC) or Open Database Connectivity(ODBC), allows us to establish a connection with these databases. By creating a bridge between Databricks and databases like MySQL, PostgreSQL, or SQL Server, we can pull data into our environment for analysis and transformation.

- **Cloud Storage Platforms:**

  Modern data ecosystems often rely on cloud storage platforms like Amazon S3, Azure Blob Storage, or Google Cloud Storage. These platforms offer scalability, flexibility, and accessibility. With the appropriate credentials and configurations, we can seamlessly retrieve data from cloud storage, enabling data engineers to work with the data without the complexities of on-premises setups.

- **Web Scraping:**

  In the age of the internet, data isn't confined to databases alone. Web scraping involves extracting data directly from websites. While this method requires a unique set of skills and tools, it's a valuable approach to gathering real-time data, particularly for tracking competitors, monitoring social media sentiment, or aggregating news articles.

- **API Integration:**

  Application Programming Interfaces (APIs) serve as gateways to access data from various applications or platforms. APIs provide structured endpoints through which we can retrieve specific data sets. Whether it's data from social media platforms, weather services, or financial markets, APIs offer a standardized way to access data programmatically.

- **File-based Extraction:**

  Data often resides in files, be it CSV, JSON, XML, or Parquet. Leveraging file-based extraction techniques allows us to ingest data stored in various formats. Databricks supports multiple file formats, enabling seamless ingestion for analysis and processing.

As we traverse through this chapter, remember that the choice of extraction method depends on the specific requirements of your project. Each method has its strengths and limitations, and understanding these nuances empowers you to select the most suitable approach for your data engineering endeavors. In the subsequent sections, we will explore the intricacies of these methods, equipping you with the insights needed to master data extraction in the Databricks ecosystem.

Extracting Data from Databases Using Connectors and JDBC

Relational databases serve as repositories of structured data crucial for organizations. Efficient and secure extraction of data from these databases is vital for data engineering tasks. The Java Database Connectivity (JDBC) and Open Database Connectivity (ODBC) connectors provide powerful mechanisms to bridge the gap between Databricks and databases such as MySQL, PostgreSQL, or SQL Server.

JDBC and ODBC are industry-standard interfaces that enable applications to interact with databases. In the context of Databricks, they act as gateways for pulling data from databases into the Databricks environment. These connectors streamline the process, allowing data engineers to focus on analysis rather than grappling with complex data retrieval mechanisms.

Working with JDBC Connector

The JDBC connector operates through a driver that communicates with the database. Databricks provides built-in JDBC drivers for various databases. The steps to extract data using the JDBC connector involve establishing a connection, constructing an SQL query, and fetching the data. Databricks notebooks seamlessly integrate SQL and JDBC commands, simplifying data extraction.

Here is a sample code through which you can connect to MySql from Databricks via the JDBC connector:

```python
# Import the required libraries
from pyspark.sql import SparkSession

# Create a Spark session
spark = SparkSession.builder \
    .appName("JDBC Connector Example") \
    .getOrCreate()

# Define the JDBC URL for the MySQL database
jdbc_url = "jdbc:mysql://<hostname>:<port>/<database_name>"

# Define the properties for the connection
connection_properties = {
    "user": "<username>",
    "password": "<password>",
    "driver": "com.mysql.jdbc.Driver"
}

# Define the table name
table_name = "<table_name>"

# Read data from the MySQL database using the JDBC connector
data = spark.read.jdbc(url=jdbc_url, table=table_name, properties=connection_properties)

# Show the retrieved data
data.show()

# Stop the Spark session
spark.stop()
```

Figure 3.1: A sample code

In this example:

- Replace <hostname>, <port>, <database_name>, <username>, <password>, and <table_name> with appropriate values for your MySQL database.
- The JDBC URL specifies the connection details to the MySQL database.
- connection_properties contain the necessary credentials and driver information.
- table_name specifies the name of the table from which you want to extract data.
- Data holds the retrieved data.

Finally, the Spark session is stopped to release resources.

Data Ingestion and Extraction   61

By running this code in a Databricks notebook, you can seamlessly connect to a MySQL database, retrieve data, and perform further analysis. This integration simplifies data extraction, allowing you to concentrate on extracting insights from your data.

Best Practices for Efficient Extraction

Efficient data extraction is crucial for optimizing the performance and reliability of your data engineering workflows. Here are some best practices to consider when implementing data extraction techniques in Databricks:

- **Select Only Necessary Columns:** When extracting data from a source, avoid selecting unnecessary columns. Retrieving only the required columns can significantly reduce the amount of data transferred, leading to improved performance.
- **Filter Data at Source:** Whenever possible, apply filtering conditions directly in the data source query. This reduces the amount of data transferred to Databricks, minimizing network overhead and enhancing extraction speed.
- **Limit the Number of Rows:** Use the LIMIT clause or equivalent methods in your data source query to restrict the number of rows returned. This is particularly useful for testing purposes or when dealing with large datasets during initial development.
- **Leverage Pushdown Queries:** Take advantage of the pushdown query capabilities of connectors. Pushdown queries delegate filtering and transformation operations to the source database, thereby reducing the amount of data that needs to be transferred to Databricks.
- **Use Parallelism:** Distribute data extraction tasks across multiple workers to increase parallelism. This is especially beneficial when dealing with large datasets, as it accelerates the data extraction process.
- **Optimize JDBC Fetch Size:** When extracting data using JDBC connectors, adjust the fetch size to an optimal value. A higher fetch size can reduce the number of round-trips between Databricks and the data source, enhancing data retrieval efficiency.
- **Implement Incremental Loading:** For sources that support it, implement incremental loading. This involves extracting only the new or modified records since the last extraction, thereby reducing the extraction time for subsequent runs.

- **Avoid Using `SELECT` *:** Instead of using `SELECT` * to retrieve all columns, explicitly list the columns you need. This reduces unnecessary data transfer and improves query performance.
- **Monitor Extraction Performance:** Regularly monitor and analyze the performance of your extraction processes. Identify bottlenecks and areas for improvement to ensure optimal data extraction efficiency.
- **Automate Data Extraction:** Implement automation to schedule and trigger data extraction jobs at appropriate intervals. This ensures that the data in your Databricks environment is always up to date.

By adhering to these best practices, you can streamline your data extraction processes, enhance performance, and ensure that the data you're working with is accurate and reliable.

Techniques for Extracting Data from Cloud Storage Platforms

This subsection explores various methods to extract data from cloud storage platforms such as AWS S3 or Azure Blob Storage.

Cloud storage platforms provide scalable and cost-effective solutions for storing and managing large volumes of data. To leverage this data, efficient extraction techniques are essential. Here are several techniques to achieve this:

- **Direct Access:** Cloud storage platforms often provide APIs that allow you to directly access data stored in them. Databricks supports connectors and libraries for direct access, enabling you to read data without the need to download it locally.
- **Delta Lake:** If your data is already stored in Delta Lake format on cloud storage, you can easily read and process it using Databricks. Delta Lake provides ACID transactions and schema enforcement, ensuring data quality during extraction.
- **Cloud-Specific Connectors:** Cloud storage providers offer connectors that simplify data extraction. Databricks supports connectors for AWS S3, Azure Blob Storage, Google Cloud Storage, and others. These connectors provide optimized access to cloud data.

It's crucial to choose the appropriate technique based on factors like data volume, frequency of extraction, and the need for real-time or historical data. By leveraging these techniques, you can efficiently extract data from cloud storage platforms and make it available for further processing and analysis within Databricks.

AWS S3 Connector Sample Code

Efficient data extraction is crucial for optimizing the performance and reliability of your data engineering workflows:

```python
# Import the necessary libraries
from pyspark.sql import SparkSession

# Create a Spark session
spark = SparkSession.builder \
    .appName("S3 Data Extraction") \
    .getOrCreate()

# Set your AWS credentials (Replace 'YOUR_ACCESS_KEY' and 'YOUR_SECRET_KEY'
# with your actual credentials)
spark.conf.set("spark.hadoop.fs.s3a.access.key", "YOUR_ACCESS_KEY")
spark.conf.set("spark.hadoop.fs.s3a.secret.key", "YOUR_SECRET_KEY")

# Define the S3 bucket and path
s3_bucket = "your-s3-bucket"
s3_path = "path/to/your/data"

# Read data from S3 using the defined path
data = spark.read.csv(f"s3a://{s3_bucket}/{s3_path}")

# Show the extracted data
data.show()

# Stop the Spark session
spark.stop()
```

Figure 3.2: AWS S3 Connection Code

In this example, we first import the necessary libraries and create a Spark session. We set the AWS credentials using `spark.conf.set` to authenticate with the S3 bucket. Replace 'YOUR_ACCESS_KEY' and 'YOUR_SECRET_KEY' with your actual AWS credentials.

Then, we define the S3 bucket and path to the data you want to extract. We use the spark.read.csv function to read data from the specified S3 path.

Finally, we show the extracted data using the `data.show()` function and stop the Spark session.

This code demonstrates how to extract data from an AWS S3 bucket using Databricks and the AWS S3 connector. You can adapt this code to your specific use case and customize it based on your data format and structure.

Implementing Efficient Data Extraction Techniques

In the world of data engineering, working with diverse data formats and sources is a common challenge. Modern organizations deal with structured, unstructured, and semi-structured data originating from various systems, applications, and platforms. As data engineers, it's crucial to be well-versed in efficiently extracting, transforming, and integrating these heterogeneous data types into a cohesive ecosystem. This section delves into the intricacies of handling different data formats and sources, providing insights into the tools and techniques required to ensure successful data ingestion and integration.

From structured formats like Parquet, Avro, and ORC that offer high performance and space efficiency to unstructured formats such as JSON, XML, and CSV that capture versatile data, this section explores the nuances of working with each. Additionally, it covers techniques for interfacing with APIs to fetch data and employing web scraping to extract information from websites. By the end of this section, you'll be equipped with the knowledge to efficiently navigate the complex landscape of data formats and sources, enabling you to bring diverse data into your Databricks environment for further processing and analysis.

Working with Structured Data Formats

Structured data formats play a pivotal role in modern data engineering workflows. These formats are designed to efficiently store and manage structured data, providing a balance between performance and storage space. In this section, we'll explore some of the most prominent structured data formats, including Parquet, Avro, and ORC. We'll understand their characteristics, advantages, and how to effectively work with them within the Databricks platform.

Parquet:
- **Characteristics**: Parquet is a columnar storage format optimized for analytical workloads. It's highly efficient for compression and encoding, making it suitable for big data processing.

Data Ingestion and Extraction

- **Advantages**: Parquet reduces I/O and minimizes the data scanned during queries, leading to faster query performance. It's a popular choice for both batch and interactive query processing.
- **Working with Parquet**: Databricks provides native support for Parquet. You can read and write Parquet files directly using the Delta Lake API or Spark DataFrame API. The columnar storage and predicate pushdown in Parquet contribute to optimal query performance.

Avro:
- **Characteristics**: Avro is a compact binary format that supports schema evolution. It includes data schema along with the data, enabling easy changes to the structure without breaking compatibility.
- **Advantages**: Avro's schema evolution makes it adaptable to changes in the data structure over time. It's suitable for scenarios where data schemas might evolve frequently.
- **Working with Avro**: Databricks offers seamless integration with Avro. You can read and write Avro files using Spark's native APIs. Databricks automatically infers the schema from the Avro files, simplifying the data ingestion process.

Optimized Row Columnar (ORC):
- **Characteristics**: ORC is another columnar storage format optimized for Hive and Spark. It's designed to improve performance by using lightweight compression and predicate pushdown.
- **Advantages**: ORC provides excellent compression and supports predicate pushdown, reducing the amount of data read during queries. It is highly efficient for analytics tasks.
- **Working with ORC**: Databricks supports ORC as a storage format. You can read and write ORC files using Spark's native APIs, benefiting from ORC's performance optimizations.

Incorporating structured data formats like Parquet, Avro, and ORC into your data pipelines enhances query performance, reduces storage costs, and simplifies data processing. Understanding the characteristics and benefits of each format empowers you to make informed decisions when designing your data engineering workflows.

Aspect	Parquet	Avro	ORC
Compression	Efficient columnar compression techniques	Compact binary format with built-in compression	Lightweight compression, optimized for both Hive and Spark
Schema Evolution	Limited support for schema evolution	Full support for schema evolution with backward and forward compatibility	Limited support for schema evolution with backward compatibility
Query Performance	Excellent query performance through column pruning and predicate pushdown	Good query performance with schema evolution and predicate pushdown	Excellent query performance with column pruning and predicate pushdown
Data Types	Wide range of supported data types	Supports a variety of data types, although not as extensive as Parquet	Supports a variety of data types, including complex types
Compatibility	Compatible with various big data platforms and tools	Compatible with various big data platforms and tools	Optimized for Hive and Spark, may not work well with non-Hive environments
Use Case Scenarios	Best for scenarios with significant analytical workloads and high compression requirements	Suitable for cases where schema evolution is frequent and compatibility between systems is crucial	Optimal for Hive and Spark environments, especially for read-heavy workloads

Table 3.1: Comparison of Avro Parquet and ORC file format

Keep in mind that the choice between these formats depends on factors such as the specific requirements of your data engineering workflows, the frequency of schema changes, compatibility needs, and the performance characteristics of your queries.

Handling Unstructured and Semi-Structured data

In data engineering, it's common to encounter data in formats that don't neatly fit into traditional structured databases. Unstructured and semi-structured data, such as JSON, XML, and CSV, pose unique challenges and opportunities. Let's explore how to handle these data formats effectively.

JSON (JavaScript Object Notation):

- **Semi-Structured Nature:** JSON is a flexible and semi-structured format commonly used for APIs, configuration files, and documents. It allows nesting of data elements, making it suitable for representing hierarchical structures.
- **Schema Flexibility:** JSON data doesn't require a predefined schema. This flexibility is advantageous when dealing with data sources that might evolve over time.
- **Data Volume:** JSON data can be verbose, leading to larger file sizes compared to more compact formats like Parquet. However, tools like JSON Lines (JSONL) can mitigate this by storing each JSON object on a separate line.
- **Processing JSON:** To process JSON data efficiently, libraries like json in Python can parse JSON strings into structured objects. Data engineers can then transform and load the data into structured formats.

```
# Reading JSON data into a DataFrame
json_df = spark.read.json("path_to_json_file")

# Showing the contents of the DataFrame
json_df.show()
```

Figure 3.3: Read JSON file into a dataframe

XML (eXtensible Markup Language)

- **Hierarchical Structure:** Similar to JSON, XML supports hierarchical data structures. It's commonly used for representing documents and data with nested relationships.
- **Schema Definition:** XML data often adheres to a defined schema using Document Type Definitions (DTD) or XML Schema. This makes it easier to validate and enforce data integrity.
- **Processing XML:** Libraries like `xml.etree.ElementTree` in Python allow you to parse XML documents and extract data. You can then convert the extracted data into structured formats for storage and analysis.

```
# Reading XML data into a DataFrame
xml_df = spark.read.format("xml").option("rowTag", "record").load("path_to_xml_file")

# Showing the contents of the DataFrame
xml_df.show()
```

Figure 3.4: Read XML file into a dataframe

CSV (Comma-Separated Values)

- **Simplicity and Compactness:** CSV is a basic format with simplicity as its advantage. It's compact and easy to generate, making it widely used for tabular data representation.
- **Lack of Schema:** CSV files lack built-in schema information, which can lead to challenges in managing data consistency and quality.
- **Processing CSV:** Python's CSV module provides functionalities to read and write CSV files. Data engineers can preprocess and transform CSV data before converting it into structured formats.

```
# Reading CSV data into a DataFrame
csv_df = spark.read.csv("path_to_csv_file", header=True, inferSchema=True)

# Showing the contents of the DataFrame
csv_df.show()
```

Figure 3.5: Read CSV into a dataframe

Unstructured and semi-structured data often require preprocessing to ensure uniformity and data quality. Techniques like data cleaning, transformation, and enrichment are essential.

Extracted data from JSON, XML, or CSV sources can be integrated with structured data using tools like Databricks Delta Lake. This allows for unified querying and analysis across diverse data formats.

Handling unstructured and semi-structured data involves a combination of preprocessing, transformation, and integration. By converting these data formats into structured formats like Parquet or Avro, data engineers ensure compatibility with analytics tools and enable seamless data analysis.

Aspect	JSON	XML	CSV
Nature	Semi-Structured	Semi-Structured	Structured
Schema Flexibility	Flexible, No Predefined Schema	Defined Schema (DTD, XML Schema)	No Schema
Hierarchical Structure	Yes	Yes	No
Data Volume	Can be Verbose	Variable	Compact
Processing	Parsing Libraries (for example, json)	Parsing Libraries (for example, xml.etree)	CSV Module for Reading/Writing
Integration	Requires Transformation	Integration with Structured Data	Requires Transformation

Table 3.2: Comparison of JSON XML and CSV file format

Techniques for Extracting Data from APIs and Web Scraping

In the world of data engineering, data can come from diverse sources, and Application Programming Interfaces (APIs) and web scraping are valuable techniques for retrieving data from various online platforms and services. APIs provide a structured and controlled way to access and retrieve data from web services, while web scraping involves extracting information directly from web pages.

1. **API Data Extraction**

    APIs allow applications to communicate with external services and retrieve data in a consistent format. Here's how you can perform API data extraction using Python and Spark:

    ```
    import requests

    # Make a GET request to the API endpoint
    response = requests.get("https://api.example.com/data")

    # Extract data from the response
    data = response.json()

    # Convert data into a DataFrame
    api_df = spark.createDataFrame(data)
    api_df.show()
    ```

    Figure 3.6: Get response from API

2. Web Scraping

Web scraping involves extracting information from HTML web pages. Libraries like **BeautifulSoup** and requests in Python facilitate this process. Here's a simple example of web scraping:

```python
from bs4 import BeautifulSoup
import requests

# Make a GET request to the web page
response = requests.get("https://www.example.com")

# Parse the HTML content using BeautifulSoup
soup = BeautifulSoup(response.content, "html.parser")

# Extract specific elements
title = soup.title.text
paragraphs = [p.text for p in soup.find_all("p")]

# Create a DataFrame from extracted data
web_df = spark.createDataFrame([(title, paragraphs)], ["Title", "Paragraphs"])
web_df.show()
```

Figure 3.7: Web Scraping

Note: It's essential to understand the terms of use and legality when performing web scraping, as some websites may have policies against automated data extraction.

Aspect	API Data Extraction	Web Scraping
Data Source	Accesses data directly from an API (structured data)	Extracts data from web pages (HTML content)
Format	Typically provides data in structured formats like JSON or XML	Extracts data as text from HTML elements
Purpose	Designed for programmatic access and data sharing	Used for retrieving information from websites
Data Availability	Offers controlled access to specific data endpoints	Relies on the structure and content of the website
Authentication	Requires API keys, tokens, or authentication mechanisms	No universal authentication method; can be blocked

Aspect	API Data Extraction	Web Scraping
Data Consistency	Usually provides consistent data formats and structures	Prone to inconsistencies due to website changes
Maintenance	API changes may require updates, but generally stable	Prone to breakage if website structure changes
Legal Considerations	Typically respects API terms of use and policies	May face legality issues depending on the website

Table 3.3: Difference between API Web Extraction and Web Scrapping

Remember that while APIs provide a controlled and structured way to access data, web scraping can be more flexible but also more prone to issues if not handled carefully. Always ensure compliance with terms of use and legal considerations when using web scraping techniques.

Conclusion

In this chapter, we embarked on a journey through the crucial phases of data engineering: data ingestion and extraction. We explored the significance of these processes in building a robust data pipeline for your Databricks environment.

In the first section, "*Ingesting Data into Databricks,*" we emphasized the importance of data ingestion as the foundational step. We discussed key considerations, various ingestion methods, best practices, and the significance of ensuring data quality during ingestion. We illustrated how to implement a data ingestion pipeline for an e-commerce platform through a practical case study, highlighting real-world challenges and solutions.

Moving on, "*Implementing Efficient Data Extraction Techniques*" sheds light on data extraction methods from various sources. We walked you through the extraction of data from databases using connectors and JDBC/ODBC, as well as extracting data from cloud storage platforms like AWS S3 and Azure Blob Storage.

The chapter continued with "*Handling Different Data Formats and Sources,*" where we navigated structured, semi-structured, and unstructured data formats. We explained techniques for handling these formats and extracting data from APIs and web scraping, making your data extraction process versatile.

As we conclude this chapter, remember that data ingestion and extraction are the lifeblood of your data engineering efforts. They lay the foundation for subsequent data processing, transformation, and analysis. By mastering these steps and adhering to best practices, you ensure your data is clean, reliable, and readily available for downstream tasks.

This chapter has equipped you with the knowledge and techniques to efficiently bring data into Databricks, extract it from various sources, and handle diverse data formats. It emphasizes the importance of data quality and integrity from the beginning of your data engineering processes, setting the stage for effective data analysis and insights.

In the next chapter, we will explore how to transform this ingested data into meaningful insights with the help of Databricks. We will also learn about the ETL processes and optimizations to handle big data loads.

Key Terms

- **Data Ingestion:** The process of importing or loading data into a data storage system or data lake for analysis and processing.
- **Data Extraction:** The process of retrieving or pulling data from various sources, including databases, APIs, web scraping, and cloud storage.
- **Data Quality:** The measure of the accuracy, completeness, consistency, and reliability of data. High data quality ensures that data is fit for its intended purpose.
- **Data Profiling:** Data analysis to understand its structure, patterns, and quality. It helps identify issues and anomalies in the data.
- **Data Validation:** Ensuring that data meets predefined quality standards and business rules. It includes checks for completeness, accuracy, and consistency.
- **Semi-Structured Data:** Data that does not conform to a rigid structure like traditional relational databases but has some level of structure. Examples include JSON and XML.
- **Unstructured Data:** Data that lacks a specific structure and is not easily queryable. Examples include text documents, images, and videos.
- **Structured Data:** Data that is organized into a specific format or schema, making it easily queryable. Examples include CSV, Parquet, and databases.
- **ETL (Extract, Transform, Load):** The process of extracting data from source systems, transforming it into a suitable format, and loading it into a target system, often a data warehouse.

- **API (Application Programming Interface):** A set of rules and protocols that allows different software applications to communicate with each other. APIs are commonly used for data extraction.
- **Web Scraping:** The automated process of extracting data from websites. It involves fetching web pages, parsing HTML, and extracting specific information.
- **Data Lake:** A centralized repository for storing raw and unprocessed data from various sources. It provides flexibility for data storage and processing.
- **Cloud Storage:** Data storage services provided by cloud providers like AWS S3, Azure Blob Storage, and Google Cloud Storage.
- **Data Transformation:** The process of converting data from one format or structure to another, often to prepare it for analysis or reporting.
- **Data Pipeline:** A series of data processing steps and transformations that move data from source to destination, often involving ingestion, extraction, and transformation.
- **Data Governance:** The set of processes and policies that ensure data quality, security, and compliance throughout its lifecycle.

CHAPTER 4
Data Transformation and ETL Processes

"ETL – Where data finds its purpose, refines its nature, and realizes its potential."

Introduction

In today's data-driven world, the ability to efficiently process, transform, and manipulate data is paramount. Data transformation forms the cornerstone of converting raw data into valuable insights, enabling organizations to make informed decisions. This chapter delves into the art and science of constructing scalable data transformation pipelines using the power of Apache Spark and Databricks.

Effective data transformation involves carefully orchestrated steps that cleanse, reshape, and restructure data into a suitable format for analysis. This chapter will equip you with the tools and knowledge necessary to construct robust data transformation pipelines that can handle large volumes of data, adapt to evolving requirements, and optimize processing performance. From understanding the significance of data transformation to implementing best practices, this chapter is a comprehensive guide to mastering the art of building scalable data transformation pipelines.

Let's explore the techniques, strategies, and considerations essential for designing data transformation workflows that enable organizations to unlock the true potential of their data.

Structure

In this chapter, the following topics will be covered:
- Building Scalable Data Transformation Pipelines
- Applying ETL (Extract, Transform, Load) Methodologies
- Optimizing Data Processing and Performance in Databricks

Building Scalable Data Transformation Pipelines

Data transformation lies at the core of turning raw data into meaningful insights. As organizations gather and accumulate vast amounts of data from diverse sources, the need for efficient and scalable data transformation pipelines becomes increasingly vital. This section will explore the principles, methodologies, and best practices required to construct data transformation pipelines that can seamlessly handle the intricacies of modern data challenges.

In the following sections, we will delve into the fundamental components of a data transformation pipeline, addressing techniques to ensure scalability, reliability, and performance. From the initial stages of data ingestion to the final steps of optimized transformation, we will navigate through the intricacies of creating pipelines that can accommodate current and future data processing needs.

By understanding the concepts and strategies presented in this section, you'll be well-equipped to design and implement data transformation pipelines that empower your organization to derive valuable insights from its data assets efficiently and effectively.

Now, let's dive into the specifics and explore the building blocks of scalable data transformation pipelines.

Understanding the Importance of Data Transformation in Data Engineering

Data transformation is the cornerstone of effective data engineering. It bridges the gap between raw data and valuable insights, playing a pivotal role in various aspects of data processing. Here's a closer look at why data transformation holds such significance:

- **Transforming Raw Data into Insights:**
    - Data transformation shapes, enriches, and refines raw data into a format suitable for analysis.
    - It resolves inconsistencies, missing values, and other data quality issues.
    - By structuring data, it simplifies the process of deriving insights.
- **Creating Consistency and Quality:**
    - Data from diverse sources often have varying formats and structures.
    - Data transformation standardizes formats, resolves discrepancies, and ensures consistency.
    - Enhanced data quality supports accurate reporting and decision-making.
- **Enabling Business Agility:**
    - Rapid adaptation to changing business requirements is crucial.
    - Data transformation facilitates the integration of new data sources and schema changes.
    - Agile data pipelines allow organizations to respond quickly to emerging trends.
- **Extracting Value from Unstructured Data:**
    - Unstructured and semi-structured data are rich sources of insights.
    - Data transformation techniques unlock meaningful information from text, images, and more.
    - It transforms unstructured data into structured formats suitable for analysis.
- **Enhancing Performance:**
    - Data transformation optimizes data for efficient analysis.

- Aggregating data, precomputing metrics, and reducing unnecessary details improve query performance.
- Improved performance leads to quicker analysis and resource savings.
- **Preparing for Advanced Analytics:**
  - Data transformation enriches and labels data for predictive and prescriptive analytics.
  - Effective transformation ensures data meets the requirements of sophisticated applications.
  - Data transformation is a strategic process that empowers organizations to make informed decisions based on accurate, consistent, and well-prepared data.

In the subsequent sections of this chapter, we will explore how to design scalable data transformation pipelines to harness the full potential of data.

Designing Scalable and Efficient Data Transformation Pipelines

Efficient data transformation pipelines are essential for processing large volumes of data accurately and quickly. Here's how to design pipelines that ensure optimal performance and scalability:

- **Define Clear Objcctives:**
  - Understand the specific goals of your data transformation process.
  - Determine the types of transformations required, such as filtering, aggregating, joining, and more.
- **Choose the Right Tools:**
  - Utilize appropriate tools and frameworks, such as Apache Spark, to process data efficiently.
  - Leverage distributed processing to handle big data workloads.
- **Partition and Parallelize:**
  - Divide data into smaller partitions to enable parallel processing.
  - Distribute tasks across a cluster of machines for faster execution.
- **Optimize Data Formats:**
  - Choose storage formats like Parquet, ORC, or Avro for efficient compression and columnar storage.

Data Transformation and ETL Processes 79

- o Optimized formats reduce storage costs and improve query performance.
- **Minimize Data Movement:**
  - o Reduce unnecessary data movement between storage and processing stages.
  - o Use predicates and filters to process only the required data.
- **Use In-Memory Processing:**
  - o Leverage in-memory processing to speed up calculations and transformations.
  - o Utilize data caching for frequently accessed datasets.
- **Monitor and Tune Performance:**
  - o Monitor pipeline performance regularly to identify bottlenecks and inefficiencies.
  - o Profile code execution and optimize resource utilization.
- **Consider Data Partitioning:**
  - o Partition data by relevant attributes to improve query performance.
  - o Prune unnecessary data partitions during processing.
- **Implement Data Quality Checks:**
  - o Include data quality checks to ensure accuracy and reliability.
  - o Identify and handle erroneous or incomplete data gracefully.
- **Apply Incremental Processing:**
  - o Whenever possible, process only the incremental changes since the last transformation.
  - o Incremental processing reduces computation time and resource consumption.

Efficient data transformation pipelines not only enhance data processing speed but also enable data engineers to respond effectively to changing business needs. Following these design principles, you can create reliable and timely results pipelines.

In the subsequent sections, we will delve deeper into specific techniques and tools for building scalable and performant data transformation pipelines.

Techniques for Data Transformation in Databricks

Databricks offers a rich set of features and tools for implementing data transformation pipelines efficiently. Here are some techniques to consider when working with data transformation in Databricks:

- **DataFrames API:**
    - Leverage the DataFrame API, which provides a high-level abstraction for manipulating structured data.
    - Utilize functions like `select`, `filter`, `groupBy`, and more for performing transformations.
- **Spark SQL:**
    - Use Spark SQL to execute SQL queries on distributed datasets.
    - Particularly useful when dealing with data stored in different formats or sources.
- **User-Defined Functions (UDFs):**
- Create custom functions using UDFs to perform specialized transformations.
- UDFs enable you to apply complex logic to data elements.
- **Window Functions:**
- Apply window functions for performing calculations over a sliding window of data.
- Handy for tasks like calculating moving averages or ranking.
- **Aggregations and Joins:**
    - Use aggregations to group data and compute summary statistics.
    - Leverage join operations to combine data from multiple sources.
- **Broadcast Joins:**
    - Implement broadcast joins for smaller datasets that can fit in memory.
    - Broadcast joins reduce the need for shuffling data across the cluster.
- **Caching and Persistence:**
    - Cache intermediate or frequently accessed datasets in memory.
    - Cached data avoids recomputation and speeds up iterative operations.

- **Dynamic Partitioning:**
  - Utilize dynamic partitioning to organize data within a storage system.
  - Enhances query performance by pruning irrelevant partitions.
- **Column Pruning:**
  - Optimize queries by selecting only the necessary columns.
  - Column pruning reduces the amount of data transferred and processed.
- **File Coalescing:**
  - Coalesce small files into larger ones to improve read and write efficiency.
  - Fewer and larger files reduce overhead during processing.

These techniques and Databricks' distributed processing capabilities enable efficient data transformation in large-scale environments. By choosing the right techniques for your specific use case, you can ensure that your data transformation pipelines are both performant and scalable.

Applying ETL Methodologies

In the realm of data engineering, the ETL (Extract, Transform, Load) process stands as a cornerstone for converting raw data into valuable insights. It's the mechanism that underpins the entire data transformation journey. This section delves into the intricate world of ETL methodologies, revealing the strategies and techniques that facilitate the seamless transition from data extraction to transformation and loading.

The ETL process is a structured approach to handling data. It begins by extracting data from various sources such as databases, cloud storage, or APIs. The extracted data then undergoes transformation, where it is cleaned, enriched, aggregated, and molded to fit specific analytical requirements. Finally, the transformed data is located in data warehouses, analytical platforms, or target systems.

This section will explore the essence of ETL, providing an overview of its key components and its pivotal role in modern data engineering. We will unravel the intricacies of each phase, focusing on the importance of structured workflows, data quality assurance, and efficient loading mechanisms. By the end, you'll gain a comprehensive understanding of how ETL methodologies serve as the backbone of successful data transformation, enabling organizations to leverage their data effectively for informed decision-making and valuable insights.

Overview of the ETL Process and Its Key Components

The ETL process embodies a systematic approach to manipulating raw data into a format suitable for analysis. It stands for Extract, Transform, and Load, representing the three essential phases that collectively ensure data quality, consistency, and relevance. Understanding the key components of each phase is paramount for building efficient and robust ETL pipelines.

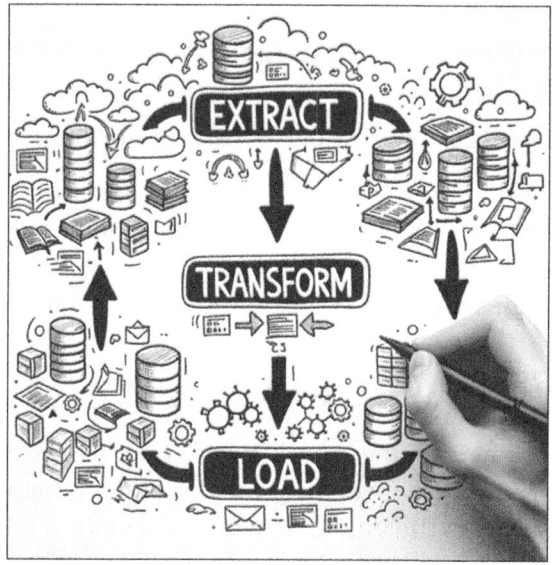

Figure 4.1: ETL

- **Extract**: In this initial phase, data is sourced from various origin points, such as databases, cloud storage, APIs, and external systems. The goal is to retrieve the required data while considering factors like data volume, data velocity (how fast data is generated), and data variety (different data formats). The extracted data might be in the form of structured tables, semi-structured files, or unstructured text.

- **Transform**: The transformation phase is where raw data undergoes a series of operations to convert it into a structured, cleaned, and usable format. Data transformation encompasses tasks like data cleansing, validation, aggregation, and enrichment. This phase plays a crucial role in preparing data for analysis by ensuring accuracy, completeness, and consistency.

- **Load**: After data transformation, the final step is loading the processed data into the target system. This could be a data warehouse, a database, a data lake, or an analytical platform. Loading includes organizing the data in a way that aligns with the data model of the destination system, optimizing it for efficient querying and analysis.

Key Components of the ETL Process:
- **Data Sources:** These are the origin points from which data is extracted. They can range from traditional databases to cloud storage platforms, APIs, logs, and external applications. Selecting the right data sources is crucial for obtaining accurate and relevant information.
- **Data Extraction:** This component involves retrieving data from various sources and converting it into a unified format. Extraction methods can vary depending on the source, and they might include batch processing, real-time streaming, or event-driven triggers.
- **Data Transformation:** Transformation is where data quality, consistency, and structure are established. It encompasses tasks like data cleansing, validation, normalization, enrichment, and aggregation. Complex business logic and rules are applied here to create meaningful insights from raw data.
- **Data Loading:** Loading refers to the process of inserting transformed data into the target system. Efficient loading strategies ensure that data is stored optimally for querying and analysis. Techniques like partitioning, indexing, and compression are often employed for enhanced performance.
- **ETL Workflow Management:** This component orchestrates the entire ETL process. It includes defining the sequence of tasks, handling dependencies, error handling, scheduling, and monitoring. Workflow management tools ensure that the ETL pipeline runs smoothly and reliably.
- **Data Quality Assurance:** Ensuring data quality is a critical component. It involves validating data against predefined rules, identifying and handling anomalies, and conducting data profiling to gain insights into data health.

The ETL process forms the foundation of data transformation, enabling organizations to convert raw data into valuable insights. Its three phases – Extract, Transform, and Load – work in harmony to clean, structure, and deliver data to the right destination. Understanding the key components of this process equips data engineers with the knowledge needed to design robust and efficient ETL pipelines, optimizing data for meaningful analysis.

Extracting Data from Various Sources for Transformation

The process of extracting data from diverse sources sets the stage for its subsequent transformation. Data engineers must navigate through different data structures, access methods, and protocols to gather raw data that will undergo the transformation process. This subsection delves into the intricacies of data extraction and the considerations required to ensure a seamless flow of data into the transformation pipeline.

Data Source Considerations:

- **Data Volume and Velocity:** The volume of data to be extracted and the speed at which it's generated influence the choice of extraction methods. Batch processing is suitable for large volumes, while real-time streaming is ideal for high-velocity data.

- **Data Formats:** Different sources might provide data in varying formats, such as relational databases, CSV files, JSON, XML, and more. Understanding the format is crucial to determine the appropriate extraction technique.

- **Data Access Methods:** Data can be accessed using APIs, connectors, direct queries, or even web scraping. Choosing the right method depends on the data source's capabilities and compatibility with the extraction process.

Common Data Extraction Techniques:

- **Batch Processing:** This involves extracting a large volume of data at regular intervals. Batch processing is efficient for scenarios where data updates occur periodically, such as daily or weekly.

- **Change Data Capture (CDC):** CDC identifies and captures changes in the source data since the last extraction. It's suitable for real-time updates and minimizes the amount of data transferred during extraction.

- **Incremental Loading:** Similar to CDC, this technique extracts only the newly added or modified data since the last extraction. It optimizes extraction times and reduces unnecessary data transfer.

- **Streaming:** Real-time streaming extracts data as it's generated, enabling immediate processing and analysis. Streaming is ideal for scenarios requiring up-to-the-minute insights.

Challenges and Best Practices:
- **Data Consistency:** Ensuring consistent data extraction across sources is challenging. Implementing error handling and retries in case of failures is crucial for maintaining data integrity.
- **Data Security:** Sensitive data must be extracted securely. Implement encryption and authentication methods to safeguard data during extraction.
- **Data Validation:** Verify extracted data for completeness and accuracy. Apply validation rules and checks to identify any anomalies or discrepancies.

Example: Extracting Data from a Relational Database

Consider extracting customer orders from a MySQL database for analysis. The extraction can be performed using a JDBC connector. The connector establishes a connection to the database, executes an SQL query to retrieve the required data, and transfers it to the transformation pipeline.

```python
# Python code using JDBC connector to extract data from MySQL database
from pyspark.sql import SparkSession

# Create a Spark session
spark = SparkSession.builder.appName("DataExtraction").getOrCreate()

# JDBC URL to connect to MySQL database
jdbc_url = "jdbc:mysql://hostname:port/dbname"

# Properties for database connection
connection_properties = {
    "user": "username",
    "password": "password",
    "driver": "com.mysql.jdbc.Driver"
}

# SQL query to extract customer orders
query = "SELECT * FROM orders"

# Extract data using JDBC connector
customer_orders = spark.read.jdbc(url=jdbc_url, table=query, properties=connection_properties)

# Display the extracted data
customer_orders.show()
```

Figure 4.2: Code to Extract Data from Relational Database

Data extraction is the first crucial step in the ETL process. It involves understanding data sources, choosing suitable extraction techniques, and addressing data volume, formats, and security challenges. Extracting data efficiently ensures a smooth transition to the subsequent transformation phase, paving the way for valuable insights from raw data.

Applying Transformations and Business Logic to Prepare Data for Analysis

The transformation phase in the ETL process is where raw data takes on new dimensions. Transformations involve cleansing, structuring, enriching, and aggregating data to align it with the analysis requirements. This subsection explores the significance of data transformations and the techniques employed to mold data into a usable form.

Importance of Data Transformations:

- **Data Cleansing:** Raw data often contains errors, missing values, and inconsistencies. Transformation cleanses the data by removing duplicates, filling in missing values, and correcting inaccuracies.
- **Structuring Data:** Transformation organizes data into a consistent structure, making it easier to analyze. Unstructured or semi-structured data can be converted into structured formats like tables or DataFrames.
- **Enrichment:** Additional information is added to the data through enrichment. This can involve appending data from different sources or calculating derived attributes.
- **Aggregation:** Data is summarized and aggregated to higher levels, reducing the data volume while retaining its essence. Aggregation facilitates faster analysis and reporting.

Common Data Transformation Techniques:

- **Cleaning and Preprocessing:** This involves removing irrelevant data, handling missing values, and standardizing data formats.
- **Data Enrichment:** Data from external sources, like reference tables or APIs, is merged with the existing dataset to enhance its value.
- **Filtering and Selection:** Unnecessary data is filtered out, leaving only the relevant subset required for analysis.
- **Data Mapping and Conversion:** Data fields are mapped to the appropriate format and converted if necessary, such as converting string dates to datetime objects.

- **Aggregation and Grouping**: Data is grouped and aggregated using functions like sum, count, average, and others to generate meaningful insights.

Challenges and Best Practices:
- **Data Consistency**: Ensuring consistent transformations across the dataset is crucial. Implementing reusable transformation functions helps maintain consistency.
- **Scalability**: Transformations must be optimized for scalability as the volume of data increases. Leveraging distributed processing frameworks like Apache Spark ensures efficient transformation even with large datasets.
- **Error Handling**: Implement robust error handling mechanisms to address data issues during transformation, such as missing values or incompatible formats.

Example: Data Transformation with Apache Spark

Consider a scenario where customer data is being transformed for analysis. The transformation includes filtering out inactive customers, calculating the total purchase amount for each customer, and categorizing customers based on their purchase behavior.

```python
# Python code using Apache Spark for data transformation
from pyspark.sql import SparkSession
from pyspark.sql.functions import col, sum, when

# Create a Spark session
spark = SparkSession.builder.appName("DataTransformation").getOrCreate()

# Load the raw customer data
raw_data = spark.read.csv("customer_data.csv", header=True, inferSchema=True)

# Apply transformations
transformed_data = raw_data \
    .filter(col("status") == "active") \
    .groupBy("customer_id") \
    .agg(sum("purchase_amount").alias("total_purchase")) \
    .withColumn("purchase_category", when(col("total_purchase") > 1000, "High").otherwise("Low"))

# Display the transformed data
transformed_data.show()
```

Figure 4.3: *Code to Transform Data via Apache Spark*

Input Data:

customer_id	status	purchase_amount
1	Active	150
2	Inactive	300
3	Active	800
4	Active	1200
5	Inactive	50

Table 4.1: *Input Data*

Output Data:

customer_id	total_purchase	purchase_category
1	150	Low
3	800	Low
4	1200	High

Table 4.2: *Output Data*

In this example, the code filters out inactive customers, calculates the total purchase amount for each active customer, and categorizes them based on their purchase behavior. Customers with a total purchase amount greater than 1000 are categorized as "High," while others are categorized as "Low."

Data transformation is the heart of the ETL process, where raw data is refined, enriched, and structured for analysis. It involves cleaning, aggregating, and shaping data to align with business needs. Effective data transformations ensure that the data is ready for analysis, setting the stage for extracting valuable insights and driving informed decision-making.

Loading Transformed Data into Target Systems or Data Warehouses

Certainly, loading transformed data into target systems or data warehouses is a critical step in the ETL (Extract, Transform, Load) process. Once the data has been extracted, transformed, and prepared, it needs to be loaded into a destination where it can be easily accessed and analyzed. This section focuses on the various techniques and best practices for effectively loading data into

Data Transformation and ETL Processes   89

target systems.

After transforming the data, it's time to load it into a target system or data warehouse. The choice of target system depends on the organization's needs, infrastructure, and tools. Common target systems include data warehouses like Amazon Redshift, Google BigQuery, Snowflake, and traditional relational databases such as MySQL, PostgreSQL, or Microsoft SQL Server.

Key Considerations for Loading Data:
- **Data Warehouse Compatibility:** Ensure that the target system is compatible with the data format and structure of the transformed data. Many modern data warehouses support various data formats like Parquet, ORC, or Avro, which can optimize storage and query performance.
- **Optimal Loading Strategy**: Choose an appropriate loading strategy based on the frequency of updates, data volume, and query patterns. Batch loading is suitable for large volumes of data, while streaming is ideal for real-time analytics.
- **Incremental Loading:** To avoid loading the entire dataset every time, consider implementing an incremental loading strategy. This involves identifying new or changed data since the last load and only loading that data.
- **Data Integrity and Validation:** Implement data validation checks during the loading process to ensure data integrity. This can involve checking for data completeness, accuracy, and conformity to predefined standards.

Loading Techniques:
- **Bulk Loading**: Involves loading large volumes of data in batches. It's efficient for initial data loads and periodic batch updates.
- **Micro-Batching:** Similar to bulk loading, but involves smaller batch sizes, reducing the delay between data transformations and loading.
- **Streaming:** Involves real-time loading of data as it becomes available. Suitable for scenarios requiring up-to-the-moment insights.

Best Practices for Loading Transformed Data:
- **Use Compression and Columnar Storage:** Compress the data and use columnar storage formats to reduce storage costs and improve query performance.
- **Optimize Data Partitioning:** If applicable, partition the data in the target

system to optimize query performance by minimizing the amount of data scanned.
- **Data Quality Checks:** Implement data quality checks during loading to identify and correct errors early in the process.
- **Monitor and Logging:** Set up monitoring and logging to track the loading process's progress, performance, and potential errors.

Case Study: Loading Transformed Data into a Data Warehouse

Imagine an e-commerce platform that transforms customer purchase data into meaningful insights. After applying various transformations, the platform uses an ETL process to load the transformed data into Amazon Redshift, a cloud data warehouse.

- **Loading Strategy:** The platform implements an incremental loading strategy. It identifies new customer purchases since the last load and only loads those new transactions, reducing loading time.
- **Data Validation:** Before loading, the platform performs data validation to ensure that all required fields are present and that purchase amounts are within acceptable ranges.
- **Partitioning:** Data is partitioned in Amazon Redshift based on the purchase date, which helps in optimizing query performance.

Loading transformed data into target systems is a crucial step to make data available for analysis. Careful consideration of loading techniques, compatibility, and optimization strategies ensures that the transformed data is accessible, accurate, and ready for business insights.

In the upcoming sections, we will explore more about other aspects of data transformation and ETL processes.

Optimizing Data Processing and Performance in Databricks

Efficient data processing and query performance are critical factors in any data engineering project. As datasets grow in size and complexity, optimizing the data processing pipelines becomes paramount to ensure timely and accurate insights. Databricks, with its powerful distributed computing capabilities, offers various strategies and tools to enhance data processing performance.

In this section, we will explore techniques and best practices for optimizing data processing and performance within the Databricks platform. From strategic approaches to runtime configurations, data partitioning, and performance tuning, we will delve into the key aspects contributing to smoother, faster, and more efficient data operations.

By implementing these optimization strategies, data engineers and analysts can unleash the full potential of their Databricks environments and ensure that data processing pipelines run seamlessly, providing valuable insights to drive informed decision-making.

Now, let's delve into the specifics of each subsection within this section to uncover how to maximize performance within the Databricks ecosystem.

Strategies for Optimizing Data Processing in Databricks

Data processing optimization is a crucial aspect of maintaining high-performance data pipelines. The efficiency of your data processing directly impacts the speed at which you can derive insights from your data. Databricks offers a range of strategies to optimize data processing, ensuring that your analysis is both accurate and expedient.

- **Understanding Parallelism and Cluster Scaling**:

    Databricks leverages Apache Spark's distributed processing capabilities to execute tasks in parallel across a cluster of machines. By appropriately configuring the cluster's size and resources, you can effectively manage the level of parallelism. This allows for faster execution of data transformation and analysis tasks.

- **Caching and Persistence:**

    Databricks enables caching of intermediate results using in-memory storage. By caching frequently accessed or computationally intensive datasets, you reduce the need to recompute them repeatedly, significantly improving query performance. You can persist DataFrames, tables, or even intermediate computations, optimizing data retrieval and transformation operations.

- **Pipeline Optimization Techniques:**

    Databricks supports pipeline optimization techniques such as predicate pushdown and column pruning. Predicate pushdown involves pushing filtering conditions closer to the data source, reducing the amount of data transferred and processed. Column pruning involves selecting only the necessary columns, further minimizing the data processed during transformations.

- **Utilizing Parquet and Delta Lake:**

    Parquet is a columnar storage format optimized for analytic queries. Leveraging Parquet as the storage format for your data can lead to significant performance improvements in query processing. Additionally, Delta Lake's capabilities, such as data skipping and compaction, enhance query performance by minimizing the amount of data that needs to be processed.

- **Applying Indexes and Statistics:**

    Databricks allow you to create indexes and gather statistics on your data, enhancing query performance by enabling the query engine to make informed decisions about execution plans. These optimizations are especially valuable for large datasets where efficient query execution becomes critical.

By employing these strategies for optimizing data processing in Databricks, you can effectively reduce processing times, enhance query performance, and ensure that your data pipelines operate efficiently. Each of these strategies contributes to making the most of Databricks' powerful distributed computing capabilities and enables you to harness insights from your data quickly and effectively.

In the upcoming sections, we will explore further aspects of optimizing data processing and performance within the Databricks environment.

Leveraging Databricks Runtime Configurations for Performance Improvements

Databricks offers a range of runtime configurations that allow you to fine-tune the behavior of your clusters and jobs to achieve optimal performance. These configurations provide you with control over memory allocation, parallelism, caching, and more. By carefully configuring these settings, you can optimize your data processing workflows and enhance the overall performance of your data pipelines.

- **Cluster-Level Configuration:**

Databricks allows you to configure cluster-level settings that impact the behavior of all jobs running on that cluster. This includes parameters like the number of worker nodes, the amount of memory allocated to each node, and the type of instance used. By scaling the cluster resources according to the workload's demands, you can ensure that your data processing tasks are executed efficiently.

- **Spark Configuration:**

  Databricks allows you to set various Apache Spark configurations at runtime. These configurations govern aspects such as memory usage, parallelism, and data shuffle behavior. Tuning these settings can significantly impact the performance of Spark jobs. For example, you can adjust the memory allocated to various Spark components, such as executor memory and heap size, to avoid out-of-memory errors.

- **Optimizing for Data Shuffling:**

  Shuffling large amounts of data during join or aggregation operations can be resource-intensive. Databricks provide configurations to control the behavior of data shuffling, such as the size of data to be shuffled before spilling to disk. Efficient shuffling minimizes the overhead associated with moving data across the cluster and enhances job performance.

- **Garbage Collection Tuning:**

  Garbage collection is a critical aspect of memory management in Spark applications. Databricks lets you configure garbage collection settings, such as heap size and frequency of collection cycles. Tuning garbage collection can prevent long pauses that might impact job performance and cluster stability.

- **Fine-Tuning Data Caching:**

  Caching data in memory can significantly accelerate query performance. Databricks enables you to configure the caching behavior, specifying whether to store data in memory, on disk, or both. By judiciously choosing which datasets to cache and how to manage cached data, you can avoid unnecessary memory consumption and improve query response times.

- **Dynamic Allocation and Autoscaling:**

  Databricks supports dynamic allocation, allowing clusters to automatically scale the number of worker nodes based on the workload. This feature optimizes resource utilization by adding or removing nodes as required. Autoscaling ensures that you pay only for the resources you need while maintaining efficient job execution.

By leveraging Databricks runtime configurations, you can optimize your clusters and jobs for peak performance. Careful adjustment of these settings in accordance with your specific data processing needs can lead to faster execution times, reduced resource wastage, and enhanced overall efficiency of your data transformation pipelines. It's essential to monitor the impact of these configurations on job performance and adjust them as necessary to achieve the desired results.

Performance Tuning for Data Transformation Operations in Databricks

Performance tuning is a critical aspect of data engineering to improve the speed and efficiency of data transformation operations. In Databricks, you can leverage various strategies and optimizations to enhance the performance of your data processing workflows, ensuring that your transformations are executed as efficiently as possible.

- **Caching and Persistence:**

    Caching involves storing intermediate or frequently accessed data in memory to avoid recomputation. By caching DataFrames or tables, you reduce the need to recompute the same transformations repeatedly, resulting in significant time savings. You can also use different storage levels based on your data access patterns.

- **Broadcasting Small Data:**

    Broadcasting is a technique where smaller datasets are replicated and distributed across all worker nodes in a cluster. This is particularly useful when joining a large dataset with a relatively small one. Broadcasting prevents data shuffling and reduces network traffic, leading to faster join operations.

- **Using the Catalyst Optimizer:**

    Apache Spark's Catalyst optimizer optimizes query plans by applying various rules and transformations to optimize the execution plan. While the Catalyst optimizer works automatically in Spark, you can also influence optimization by structuring your code in a way that allows the optimizer to make better decisions.

- **Data Skew Handling:**

    Data skew occurs when the distribution of data across partitions is highly uneven. This can lead to some partitions taking longer to process than others, causing performance bottlenecks. Techniques to handle data skew include repartitioning, aggregating on skewed keys separately, or using techniques like salting to distribute data more evenly.

- **Parallelism and Resource Allocation:**

  Adjusting the level of parallelism and resource allocation can significantly impact performance. You can control the number of partitions, adjust the memory allocation per executor, and fine-tune the number of concurrent tasks. Optimizing these parameters based on the available cluster resources can lead to better resource utilization and improved performance.

- **Hardware Considerations:**

  The underlying hardware on which your Databricks cluster is deployed also plays a crucial role in performance. Consider factors like CPU, memory, and storage speed when provisioning your cluster. Utilizing instances with higher CPU and memory specifications can lead to faster data transformation operations.

- **Profiling and Monitoring:**

  Databricks provides built-in tools for profiling and monitoring your jobs' performance. You can use the Spark UI to analyze the execution plan, identify bottlenecks, and optimize resource usage. Regularly monitoring and profiling your jobs can help you identify areas for improvement.

By implementing these performance-tuning strategies, you can ensure that your data transformation operations run smoothly and efficiently, optimizing resource usage and reducing processing times. Careful consideration of each technique in the context of your specific data and query patterns can result in significant performance improvements for your data engineering pipelines.

Conclusion

Throughout this chapter, we have discussed the key components involved in transforming raw data into structured and actionable information, emphasizing the importance of data enrichment and feature engineering.

Furthermore, we've dived deep into ETL methodologies, shedding light on the Extract, Transform, and Load phases. We've explored how to extract data from various sources, apply transformations and business logic, and load the transformed data into target systems or data warehouses.

We have discussed strategies for optimizing data processing within the Databricks environment. Leveraging Databricks partitioning data and performance tuning techniques are essential for achieving high-quality, high-performance data transformation pipelines.

This chapter has equipped you with the knowledge, strategies, and best practices to design, build, and optimize data transformation pipelines.

In the next chapter, we will explore the critical aspects of data quality and validation, ensuring that the data used in your analyses and models is accurate, reliable, and consistent.

Key Terms

- **DataFrames API:** A high-level tool for manipulating structured data in platforms like Databricks.
- **User-Defined Functions (UDFs):** Custom functions created by users for specialized data transformations.
- **Dynamic Partitioning:** Organizing data into partitions based on specific attributes to enhance query performance.
- **ETL Workflow Management:** The orchestration tool oversees the entire ETL process, handling task sequencing, dependencies, error responses, scheduling, and monitoring.
- **Change Data Capture (CDC):** A method that identifies and captures alterations in source data since the last extraction, facilitating real-time updates.
- **Incremental Loading:** A technique that extracts only newly added or modified data since the previous extraction, minimizing unnecessary data transfers.
- **ETL Workflow Management:** The orchestration tool oversees the entire ETL process, handling task sequencing, dependencies, error responses, scheduling, and monitoring.

CHAPTER 5
Data Quality and Validation

"Quality in data is not an act, it's a habit."

— Adapted from Aristotle

Introduction

In the world of data engineering, the quality and reliability of data play a pivotal role in making informed decisions and driving meaningful insights. Data quality and validation ensure that the data you're working with is accurate, consistent, complete, and trustworthy. As organizations increasingly rely on data-driven strategies, maintaining high data quality and effectively validating data become crucial steps to success.

This chapter focuses on the essential aspects of data quality and validation within the context of Databricks. We will explore the significance of data quality, the design of validation processes, techniques for identifying and rectifying data quality issues, and the implementation of monitoring mechanisms. Additionally, we will delve into the application of data validation techniques, methods to ensure data completeness, consistency, and accuracy, and the strategies to handle data anomalies and outliers.

By understanding and implementing these practices, data engineers can lay the foundation for a solid data infrastructure that supports accurate insights, enhances decision-making, and fosters trust in data-driven processes. Let's embark on this journey to delve into the techniques and methodologies that elevate data quality and validation to new heights within the realm of Databricks and beyond.

Structure

In this chapter, the following topics will be covered:
- Ensuring Data Quality and Integrity in Databricks
- Implementing Data Validation Techniques and Rules
- Handling Data Anomalies and Outliers

Ensuring Data Quality and Integrity in Databricks

Data quality and integrity form the bedrock of any successful data-driven organization. Data accuracy, consistency, and reliability are imperative for informed decision-making, meaningful insights, and building trust in data-driven processes. As data engineering continues to evolve, ensuring data quality and integrity becomes a fundamental aspect of data management.

This section of the chapter will provide a comprehensive understanding of data quality and integrity within the context of Databricks. We will explore the significance of maintaining data quality, designing robust data quality checks and validation processes, techniques for identifying and addressing data quality issues, and the implementation of effective data profiling and monitoring strategies.

By mastering the techniques presented in this section, data engineers can elevate the quality of the data they work with, ensuring that it aligns with organizational goals, enhances data-driven initiatives, and empowers stakeholders with reliable insights. Let's now delve deeper into the nuances of maintaining data quality and integrity within the Databricks environment.

Importance of Data Quality

Here are some of the key points underscoring the importance of data quality practices in an organization:

- **Informed Decision-Making:** Data quality is the cornerstone of effective decision-making. Accurate, consistent, and reliable data ensures that business leaders base strategies on factual insights, reducing the risk of misguided decisions and enhancing overall outcomes.
- **Trustworthy Insights:** High-quality data generates trustworthy insights. These insights guide stakeholders in making informed choices, optimizing processes, and confidently identifying growth opportunities.
- **Operational Efficiency:** Data quality directly impacts operational efficiency. Accurate data eliminates redundant manual validation and correction efforts, streamlining processes and allowing teams to focus on value-added activities.
- **Regulatory Compliance and Reputation:** Inaccurate data can lead to regulatory non-compliance and damage an organization's reputation. Ensuring data quality ensures adherence to regulations, fostering trust and credibility with stakeholders.
- **Customer Experience Enhancement:** Quality data improves customer experiences by enabling personalized interactions and tailored services. It leads to higher customer satisfaction and stronger customer relationships.

By understanding and implementing these key points, organizations can elevate their data quality practices, effectively driving decisions, optimizing operations, and enhancing overall business performance. Within Databricks, a focus on data quality ensures that transformations and analyses are built on a foundation of accurate and reliable data. This proactive approach positively impacts every aspect of data engineering endeavors.

Designing Data Quality Checks and Validation Processes

In this section, let's see how we can define data quality checks and validation rules to ensure we have good data in place:

- **Define Business Rules:** Begin by defining business rules that your data should adhere to. These rules will be the basis for designing validation processes. For instance, when dealing with sales data, you might establish rules for minimum and maximum sales amounts or require certain fields to be non-null.

Example: The e-commerce platform establishes a business rule that the transaction amount cannot be negative. This rule helps maintain the integrity of financial records and prevents errors in financial reporting.

- **Identify Critical Fields:** Identify the most critical fields for your analysis. These are the fields that have a significant impact on decision-making or are frequently used in reporting. Focus your validation efforts on these fields to ensure their accuracy and reliability.

  Example: In this case, critical fields include customer information, product details, and transaction amounts. They directly impact order processing, inventory management, and financial calculations.

- **Select Validation Techniques:** Choose appropriate validation techniques based on your data and business rules. Techniques can include data type validation, range validation, uniqueness checks, pattern matching, and more. Selecting the right technique for each field ensures accurate data quality checks.

  Example: For the transaction amount, the platform uses range validation to ensure that the amount falls within reasonable limits. This prevents unrealistic or fraudulent transactions from being processed.

- **Implement Automated Checks:** Implement automated data quality checks as part of your ETL pipeline. This ensures that data is validated consistently each time it's ingested or transformed. Automation reduces the risk of human errors and saves time.

  Example: As new orders are placed, the platform's ETL pipeline automatically validates the transaction amount against the defined range. If an order violates the range, an alert is raised, and the order is flagged for manual review.

- **Handle Data Anomalies:** Design validation processes to handle data anomalies gracefully. Implement strategies for missing data, outliers, and inconsistencies. For example, you could impute missing values based on averages or exclude outliers from calculations.

  Example: The platform incorporates data imputation techniques to handle missing customer information. If a customer's contact number is missing, the system might automatically fill it with a placeholder value or request the customer to provide the missing information before processing the order.

By adhering to these design considerations, you'll establish a robust framework for data quality checks and validation processes in Databricks. This ensures that your data is accurate, consistent, and reliable, forming a solid foundation for further analysis and decision-making.

Techniques for Identifying and Handling Data Quality Issues

Let's delve into the topic of techniques for identifying and handling data quality issues:

- **Data Profiling:** Data profiling involves analyzing the data to understand its structure, patterns, and quality. In our e-commerce platform example, data profiling might reveal anomalies like orders with extremely high transaction amounts or customers with unusually high purchase frequency.
- **Statistical Analysis:** The platform can identify data inconsistencies by applying statistical methods. For instance, if the average order amount suddenly deviates significantly from historical averages, it could indicate data entry errors or fraud.
- **Cross-validation:** This technique involves comparing data from different sources to identify discrepancies. The e-commerce platform might cross-validate customer addresses between order records and shipping records to ensure accuracy.
- **Outlier Detection:** Outliers are data points that significantly differ from others. The platform can use outlier detection algorithms to spot anomalies like orders with unusually high quantities of products or transactions that deviate from normal patterns.
- **Data Cleansing:** Cleansing involves correcting or removing erroneous data. For instance, if a product price is listed as negative due to a data entry error, the platform can apply data cleansing to correct the price to a valid value.
- **Data Enrichment:** Sometimes, incomplete data can be enriched with additional information. For instance, the platform can use external data sources to fill in missing customer details such as city or postal code.

- **Rule-Based Validation:** Business rules define acceptable values and relationships between data. The e-commerce platform can use rule-based validation to check if orders with high quantities are justified based on historical buying patterns.
- **Timeliness Validation:** Ensuring that data is up-to-date is crucial. The platform can implement validation checks to identify stale or outdated data.
- **Feedback Loop:** When data quality issues are detected, it's important to have a feedback loop for correction. In the case of our e-commerce platform, if a customer's address is incomplete, the system could prompt the customer to provide the missing information.

By applying these techniques, the e-commerce platform maintains the quality and integrity of its data. This prevents errors and inaccuracies and ensures that the business decisions and analytics insights drawn from the data are reliable and trustworthy.

Implementing Data Profiling and Monitoring in Databricks

Let's delve into the topic of implementing data profiling and monitoring in Databricks:

- **Data Profiling Tools:** Databricks provides built-in functions and libraries like PySpark for data profiling. For instance, you can use describe() and summary() functions to analyze data statistics such as mean, standard deviation, and quartiles. Let's say you're working with a sales dataset. By using data profiling, you can identify that the average order value is $150 with a standard deviation of $30, helping you spot outliers.
- **Automated Data Quality Checks:** Automating data quality checks ensures ongoing monitoring. You can schedule notebook runs to perform regular checks on critical data metrics. If you're dealing with customer data, you can set up a daily job to verify that the number of new customer records matches expectations. If the count deviates, an automated alert can notify the data team for investigation.

- **Data Monitoring Dashboards:** With Databricks' visualization capabilities, you can create interactive dashboards. Consider an example of monitoring website user activity. You can visualize user engagement metrics like page views, bounce rates, and session durations. If the bounce rate suddenly spikes, it could indicate an issue with the website's performance or content.
- **Alerts and Notifications:** Let's say you have a financial dataset containing transaction details. You can set up an alert to trigger when the sum of transactions for a day exceeds a certain threshold, indicating possible fraud. This alert can be sent to the fraud detection team, allowing them to investigate promptly.
- **Data Quality Reports:** Databricks allow you to generate detailed data quality reports using markdown or HTML in notebooks. For instance, you can create a report on a retail inventory dataset, highlighting the percentage of missing values for each product. This report can be shared with stakeholders to drive discussions about data cleansing strategies.
- **Data Lineage Tracking:** In a healthcare dataset, you can use data lineage tracking to understand how patient records are transformed. Tracing the transformations allows you to identify the source of inconsistencies in medical records. This aids in ensuring the accuracy and reliability of patient data.

By implementing data profiling and monitoring in Databricks, any user, like the e-commerce platform in our example, can effectively monitor data quality, promptly respond to anomalies, and maintain trustworthy data for their analytics and decision-making processes.

Practical Example:

For a practical example of data profiling in Databricks using PySpark, let's consider a scenario where you have a sales dataset and you want to perform basic profiling to understand its statistical characteristics. The dataset is assumed to have columns like `OrderValue`, `OrderDate`, `CustomerID`, and more. Here's a sample PySpark code that you can use in a Databricks notebook:

```
from pyspark.sql import SparkSession
from pyspark.sql.functions import col

# Initialize Spark session
spark = SparkSession.builder.appName("DataProfilingExample").getOrCreate()

# Load your sales data into a DataFrame (assuming data is in a CSV format for
this example)
df = spark.read.csv("/path/to/your/sales_data.csv", header=True, infer-
Schema=True)

# Show the schema to understand what the data looks like
df.printSchema()

# Perform basic statistics profiling
basic_stats = df.describe(["OrderValue"]).show()

# Advanced profiling - calculate additional statistics like skewness and kur-
tosis
from pyspark.sql.functions import skewness, kurtosis

advanced_stats = df.select(
    skewness(col("OrderValue")).alias("Skewness_OrderValue"),
    kurtosis(col("OrderValue")).alias("Kurtosis_OrderValue")
).show()

# Example of custom profiling - Find the average order value per customer
avg_order_per_customer = df.groupBy("CustomerID").avg("Order-
Value").alias("AverageOrderValue").show()
```

Figure 5.1: *Data Profiling*

In this code:

- A Spark session is initiated, which is essential for any data processing in PySpark.
- The sales data is read into a DataFrame. This should be replaced with the actual path to your dataset.
- **df.printSchema()** is used to print the schema of the dataset, giving you an idea of the data columns.
- **describe()** is used to compute basic statistics like count, mean, standard deviation, min, and max for the **OrderValue** column.
- For more advanced statistics, functions like skewness and kurtosis are used. These can provide insights into the distribution of **OrderValue**.
- As an example of custom profiling, the average order value per customer is calculated using **groupBy** and **avg**.

Implementing Data Validation Techniques and Rules

Data validation is a crucial aspect of maintaining data quality and ensuring the accuracy of analytical results. It involves applying predefined rules and constraints to verify whether data meets certain criteria. This section will delve into various methodologies and techniques to implement effective data validation in Databricks.

Data validation is like quality control for your data. Just as a manufacturing process needs checks to ensure the product's quality, data validation ensures the quality of data entering your analytics pipeline. This is especially important when dealing with diverse data sources and data transformations.

In this section, we will explore:

- **Overview of Data Validation Methodologies:**

  Understanding the fundamental approaches to data validation, such as rule-based validation, pattern matching, referential integrity checks, and outlier detection.

- **Applying Data Validation Rules and Constraints:**

  Implementing rules that align with the nature of your data. For example, in a retail dataset, you might enforce that the price of a product cannot be negative.

- **Techniques for Validating Data Completeness, Consistency, and Accuracy:**

  Exploring how to ensure that data is complete (no missing values), consistent (conforms to defined formats), and accurate (reflects reality).

- **Implementing Automated Data Validation Processes in Databricks:**

  Leveraging Databricks' automation capabilities to establish systematic data validation workflows. For instance, you can set up scheduled jobs to run validation checks on a daily basis.

- **Case Study: Data Validation in a Financial Transaction System:**

  We'll take a practical example of a financial institution's transaction records. We'll design and implement data validation checks to ensure that all transactions have valid dates, amounts, and account references.

Overview of Data Validation Methodologies

Data validation methodologies encompass a range of techniques and strategies to ensure the integrity and reliability of your data. These methodologies form the cornerstone of data quality assurance, helping organizations identify and address data anomalies before they propagate downstream. Let's explore the key methodologies that are commonly employed for data validation:

- **Rule-based Validation:**

    Rule-based validation involves defining a set of explicit rules that data must adhere to. These rules can encompass various aspects, such as data type checks, range validations, and format requirements. For instance, in a customer database, you could have a rule that ensures the email addresses are in a valid format.

- **Pattern Matching:**

    Pattern matching involves verifying whether data matches predefined patterns or regular expressions. This is useful for validating complex formats like phone numbers, addresses, or credit card numbers. For example, you can use pattern matching to ensure that phone numbers are in the correct format.

- **Referential Integrity Checks:**

    Referential integrity checks ensure that relationships between different datasets or tables are maintained. This is particularly important in databases where data is linked through foreign key relationships. For instance, in a database containing orders and products, referential integrity checks would ensure that every order references an existing product.

- **Statistical Analysis:**

    Statistical analysis involves using statistical methods to detect outliers, anomalies, and trends in the data. This can be useful for identifying data points that deviate significantly from the norm. For instance, in a sensor data stream, statistical analysis can help identify unusual readings that may indicate equipment malfunctions.

- **Business Logic Validation:**

    Business logic validation involves applying domain-specific rules and logic to validate data. These rules are often unique to each organization and reflect the business processes and requirements. For example, in a healthcare system, business logic validation could ensure that patient records have accurate medical codes.

Understanding these methodologies provides a foundation for establishing effective data validation processes. The choice of methodology depends on the nature of the data, the industry, and the specific use case. Organizations often combine multiple methodologies to create a comprehensive data validation strategy that ensures data quality and accuracy throughout the analytics lifecycle.

Applying Data Validation Rules and Constraints

Data validation rules and constraints play a pivotal role in maintaining the quality and integrity of your data. These rules define the permissible values and conditions that data must adhere to. By enforcing these rules during data processing, organizations can identify and address issues that could impact downstream analysis. Here are some key practices for applying data validation rules and constraints effectively:

- **Establish Clear Rules:**

  Begin by defining clear and comprehensive rules that data must adhere to. These rules can encompass a wide range of criteria, such as data type constraints, value ranges, uniqueness requirements, and more. For example, you could establish a rule that ensures every customer record has a unique `customerID`.

- **Implement Data Type Checks:**

  Validate that data conforms to the expected data types. This prevents issues arising from mismatched data types that could cause errors during analysis. For instance, you can ensure that a 'Date of Birth' field contains valid date values.

- **Define Range Validations:**

  Specify allowable ranges for numerical data to ensure accuracy. For instance, in a dataset containing product prices, you could define a rule that flags prices falling outside a specified price range.

- **Enforce Format Requirements:**

  For data with specific formats, like email addresses or phone numbers, enforce format requirements using regular expressions or pattern matching. This guards against input errors that might lead to inaccurate analysis results.

- **Ensure Referential Integrity:**

    When working with relational databases, establish referential integrity constraints. This guarantees that relationships between different tables are maintained, preventing orphaned or inconsistent data. For instance, if you have a `'Customer'` table linked to an `'Orders'` table, referential integrity ensures that every order belongs to an existing customer.

- **Allow Nulls with Care:**

    Decide carefully where null values are permitted. While nulls can indicate missing or unknown data, their misuse can lead to confusion or inaccurate analysis results. Define rules for when nulls are acceptable and when they're not.

By applying these practices, organizations can ensure that data entering their systems is of high quality and adheres to predefined standards. This lays the foundation for accurate and reliable analytics and decision-making processes downstream.

Techniques for Validating Data Completeness, Consistency, and Accuracy

Ensuring data quality involves more than just verifying data against predefined rules. It requires evaluating the completeness, consistency, and accuracy of the data. Here are techniques to achieve these goals:

- **Profiling Data Completeness:**

    Data completeness refers to the extent to which all expected data points are present. Profile the data to identify missing values in critical fields. For instance, you could profile customer records to find out how many of them lack contact information. This provides insights into data gaps that might impact analysis outcomes.

- **Cross-Field Consistency Checks:**

    Validate data consistency across related fields. For instance, if you have data about product quantities and their prices, ensure that the total revenue is consistent with the calculated values. Such checks can identify anomalies that might indicate errors or data entry issues.

- **Referential Integrity Verification:**

  In relational databases, ensure that foreign keys and references between tables are consistent. This verification guarantees that relationships between data entities are maintained correctly, preventing data inconsistencies.

- **Data Profiling for Accuracy:**

  Use data profiling techniques to identify potential accuracy issues. For example, if you're dealing with temperature data, profiling might reveal extreme values that could be outliers. Detecting and addressing inaccuracies at an early stage prevents misleading analysis results.

- **Data Matching and Deduplication:**

  When working with data from multiple sources, employ data matching and deduplication techniques. These methods help identify and merge duplicate records, improving data quality and preventing redundant information.

- **Time-Series Data Validation:**

  For time-series data, verify the chronological order and intervals between data points. This ensures data consistency over time and helps identify gaps or irregularities in the temporal sequence.

- **Domain-Specific Validation:**

  Different types of data require unique validation techniques. For instance, textual data might undergo spell-checking, while geographical data could be verified against known geographical boundaries. Custom validation methods tailored to specific data domains enhance accuracy.

- **Data Profiling for Statistical Measures:**

  Profile data to calculate statistical measures like mean, median, and standard deviation. Comparing these measures against expectations can uncover data discrepancies that warrant further investigation.

- **User-Defined Rules and Custom Validation:**

  Incorporate user-defined rules and custom validation logic specific to your organization's requirements. This flexibility allows you to address domain-specific data quality challenges that standardized techniques might overlook.

Data engineers and analysts can comprehensively validate data for completeness, consistency, and accuracy by employing these techniques. This ensures that data-driven insights are built on a solid foundation of reliable information.

Implementing Automated Data Validation Processes in Databricks

Automating data validation is crucial to maintain data quality efficiently, especially in large-scale and rapidly changing environments. Implementing automated processes ensures that data validation is consistent, timely, and scalable. Here's how to achieve this within Databricks:

- **Automated Workflow Triggers:**

  Set up automated triggers that initiate data validation workflows based on predefined schedules or event-driven conditions. For instance, you can schedule daily validation of sales data to ensure its accuracy for daily reporting.

- **Continuous Monitoring:**

  Leverage Databricks' automation capabilities to continuously monitor incoming data. As new data arrives, automated validation checks can be triggered immediately to detect issues in real-time.

- **Integration with CI/CD Pipelines:**

  Integrate data validation processes into your continuous integration and continuous deployment (CI/CD) pipelines. This ensures that data quality checks are performed as part of the deployment process, preventing the release of erroneous data.

- **Custom Validation Jobs:**

  Create custom validation jobs using Databricks notebooks or scripts. These jobs can be scheduled to run at specific intervals, validating data against predefined rules. Any discrepancies can trigger alerts or notifications for immediate attention.

- **Integration with Alerting Systems:**

  Integrate automated data validation with alerting systems such as email notifications or messaging platforms. When data quality issues are detected, relevant stakeholders can be notified promptly for corrective actions.

- **Logging and Reporting:**

  Implement comprehensive logging and reporting mechanisms to capture the results of data validation runs. This historical record helps in auditing and identifying patterns of data quality issues over time.

- **Dynamic Validation Rules:**

  Design data validation rules in a dynamic way, allowing for rule configuration changes without manual intervention. This is particularly useful when dealing with evolving data sources and changing business requirements.

- **Remediation Workflows:**

  Integrate automated remediation workflows alongside validation processes. For example, if an anomaly is detected, an automated process can be triggered to cleanse or correct the data before it is used downstream.

- **Collaborative Validation Workflows:**

  Enable collaboration between data engineers, analysts, and domain experts in designing and implementing automated validation processes. This ensures that the validation logic remains aligned with business requirements.

- **Version Control for Validation Logic:**

  Use version control systems to manage changes to validation logic. This ensures that modifications to validation rules are tracked and can be rolled back if unintended consequences arise.

Automating data validation processes in Databricks empowers organizations to maintain high-quality data consistently and efficiently. By minimizing manual effort and ensuring timely validation, data engineers and analysts can focus on generating insights rather than grappling with data quality issues.

Case Study

Scenario:

A leading bank named "**FinTrust**" operates globally with hundreds of branches across different regions. Every day, the bank's centralized system receives millions of transaction records from these branches. Each record comprises the transaction ID, transaction date, transaction amount, account number, and the respective branch code.

The bank uses Databricks to process and analyze this enormous amount of data. Since this data comes from diverse sources (branches located in different countries with different operational standards and technologies), there are often inconsistencies and errors.

These inconsistencies could be due to:
- Human errors during data entry
- System glitches or bugs
- Varied data entry formats across branches
- Communication issues during data transfer

Problem Statement:

FinTrust has identified several issues with its incoming transaction data:
- **Missing Values**: Some records are missing essential data such as transaction date or account number.
- **Inconsistent Formats**: Transaction dates might be in different formats, depending on the region. For example, MM/DD/YYYY in the US and DD/MM/YYYY in Europe.
- **Invalid Data**: Some transaction amounts are recorded as negative values or extremely large numbers that do not make sense.
- **Referential Issues**: Account numbers mentioned in some transactions do not match any account in the bank's primary account database.

To maintain its reputation and ensure accurate financial reporting, FinTrust needs a robust data validation system to identify and rectify these anomalies before they impact its analytics and reporting.

Solution:

To address the issues faced by FinTrust, we will implement a series of data validation checks using Databricks and Apache Spark.

Data Quality and Validation

Setting up the Environment:

```python
from pyspark.sql import SparkSession

# Create Spark session
spark = SparkSession.builder.appName("DataValidation").getOrCreate()

# Sample data for the case study
data = [
    {"transaction_id": 1, "date": "01/15/2023", "amount": 100, "account_number": "A123"},
    {"transaction_id": 2, "date": "16/01/2023", "amount": -50, "account_number": "A124"},
    {"transaction_id": 3, "date": "", "amount": 200, "account_number": "A125"},
    {"transaction_id": 4, "date": "01/20/2023", "amount": 1_000_000, "account_number": "A126"},
    {"transaction_id": 5, "date": "02/01/2023", "amount": 150, "account_number": "XYZ123"}
]

df = spark.createDataFrame(data)
```

Figure 5.2: Creating Sample Data

Data Validation Checks:

```python
from pyspark.sql.functions import col, count, when, regexp_replace

# Count missing values for each column
missing_values = df.select([count(when(col(c).isNull() | (col(c) == ""), c)).alias(c) for c in df.columns])
missing_values.show()

# Convert DD/MM/YYYY to MM/DD/YYYY
df = df.withColumn("date", regexp_replace("date", r'(\d{2})/(\d{2})/(\d{4})', r'\2/\1/\3'))

# Filter out transactions with negative or overly large amounts
invalid_amounts = df.filter((df["amount"] < 0) | (df["amount"] > 500_000))
invalid_amounts.show()

# List of valid account numbers (sample)
valid_accounts = ["A123", "A124", "A125", "A126", "A127"]

# Filter out transactions with invalid account numbers
invalid_accounts = df.filter(~df["account_number"].isin(valid_accounts))
invalid_accounts.show()
```

Figure 5.3: Performing Data Validation Checks

Data validation is paramount in ensuring that analytical processes yield accurate and reliable results. Through our financial transaction system case study, we have showcased the importance of a systematic approach to data validation using Databricks and PySpark.

Key takeaways:

- **Relevance of Data Validation**: In any data pipeline, particularly in sensitive sectors like finance, ensuring data quality is essential. Even minor inaccuracies can lead to significant discrepancies in analytical outcomes.
- **Comprehensive Checks**: It's crucial to perform diverse validation checks, from handling missing values and standardizing formats to applying business-specific rules (like checking for negative transaction amounts or validating account references).
- **Automation and Regular Monitoring**: With platforms like Databricks, one can automate these validation processes, ensuring that data is consistently checked and validated without manual intervention.
- **Proactive Error Handling**: By identifying potential issues proactively through validation checks, organizations can address and rectify errors promptly, thereby maintaining the trustworthiness of their data.
- **Continuous Iteration**: As business rules and data evolve, so should validation processes. Regular reviews and updates to validation rules are necessary to adapt to changing data landscapes.

In conclusion, while the tools and technologies can facilitate efficient data validation, the underlying principle remains constant: a commitment to data quality and integrity. By investing in robust validation processes, organizations can make data-driven decisions with confidence and precision.

Handling Data Anomalies and Outliers

Data anomalies and outliers are data points that deviate significantly from the rest of the dataset. These deviations can stem from various factors, such as measurement errors, sensor malfunctions, or even genuine rare events. Understanding anomalies and outliers is crucial for maintaining data quality and making informed decisions based on accurate insights.

- **Anomalies vs. Outliers:**
    - **Anomalies**: These are data points that deviate significantly from the expected pattern. They might indicate errors, fraud, or rare

occurrences. Anomalies can be indicative of issues that require investigation.
- ○ **Outliers**: Outliers are observations that fall far away from the majority of data points. While they might be anomalies, they can also be valid data points that reflect genuine variations in the data.
- **Importance of Identifying Anomalies:**
  - ○ **Data Quality**: Anomalies can compromise the quality of the entire dataset. Detecting and addressing them improves data accuracy.
  - ○ **Business Decisions**: Erroneous data can lead to poor decision-making. Identifying anomalies helps ensure decisions are based on reliable insights.
  - ○ **Operational Efficiency**: Detecting anomalies in real-time, such as equipment malfunctions, can prevent disruptions and downtime.
- **Causes of Anomalies:**
  - ○ **Errors**: Data entry errors, sensor malfunctions, or equipment glitches can lead to erroneous data points.
  - ○ **Fraud**: Anomalies might represent fraudulent activities that deviate from regular patterns.
  - ○ **Rare Events**: Genuine rare events like a once-in-a-lifetime event or extreme weather conditions can cause anomalies.
  - ○ **Data Transformation**: Data transformations can sometimes introduce anomalies due to rounding errors or transformation algorithms.
- **Detecting Anomalies:**
  - ○ **Visual Inspection**: Graphs, scatter plots, and histograms can help visualize data patterns and identify potential outliers.
  - ○ **Statistical Methods**: Z-Score, IQR, and Grubbs' Test are statistical techniques to quantify how far a data point deviates from the mean.
  - ○ **Machine Learning**: Algorithms like Isolation Forest and One-Class SVM can learn the normal data distribution and flag deviations.
- **Business Impact of Unaddressed Anomalies:**
  - ○ **Financial Loss**: Fraudulent anomalies can result in financial losses.
  - ○ **Safety Concerns**: Anomalies in critical systems (like manufacturing) can pose safety risks.
  - ○ **Reputation Damage**: Poor data quality due to unaddressed anomalies can harm an organization's reputation.

- **Identifying Contextual Anomalies:**
  - **Historical Analysis**: Comparing current data with historical trends to identify deviations.
  - **Domain Expertise**: Involving subject matter experts helps distinguish between valid outliers and anomalies.
  - **Pattern Recognition**: Developing models that understand regular patterns and identify deviations.
- **Business Use Cases:**
  - **Financial Services**: Detecting fraudulent transactions by identifying anomalous spending patterns.
  - **Healthcare**: Identifying unusual vital signs that might indicate a health issue.
  - **Manufacturing**: Detecting anomalies in machinery to prevent breakdowns and optimize maintenance.

In conclusion, understanding data anomalies and outliers is a fundamental aspect of ensuring data quality and integrity. By recognizing the causes of anomalies, employing various detection techniques, and involving domain expertise, organizations can ensure that their data remains accurate and reliable for making informed decisions.

Strategies for Managing and Correcting Data Anomalies and Outliers

Once anomalies and outliers are detected, it's essential to determine the appropriate strategy for handling them. Databricks offers various methods to manage and correct data anomalies and outliers, ensuring the accuracy and reliability of downstream analyses.

- **Data Imputation:**

  Data imputation involves replacing missing or outlier-affected values with estimated or imputed values. Simple methods include mean, median, or mode imputation, while more advanced techniques involve predictive modeling to infer missing values.

- **Transformation:**

  Transforming the data can help make it more compatible with the rest of the dataset. For example, applying logarithmic transformation can help mitigate the impact of extreme values.

- **Removal:**

  In some cases, outliers can be removed from the dataset if they are genuine errors or anomalies. However, careful consideration is needed, as removing valid outliers can lead to biased results.

- **Binning or Discretization:**

  Binning involves grouping data points into bins or discrete ranges. This can help mitigate the impact of outliers by reducing their effect on the overall analysis.

- **Capping or Flooring:**

  Capping involves setting a threshold beyond which values are capped, while flooring sets a minimum value. This approach can help bring extreme values within a certain range.

- **Transformation Functions:**

  Applying transformation functions, such as the Winsorizing method, involves replacing extreme values with values closer to the mean or median. This approach can help preserve the overall distribution while minimizing the impact of outliers.

- **Robust Statistical Methods:**

  Using robust statistical methods, like the Median Absolute Deviation (MAD), can help calculate statistics that are less affected by outliers.

- **Contextual Analysis:**

  Understanding the context of the data can provide insights into whether an outlier is valid or erroneous. For example, a sudden temperature spike might be a sensor malfunction rather than a real event.

Business Use Case: Sales Forecasting with Outliers

Consider a retail company using historical sales data for forecasting. Outliers in the sales data could be caused by promotions, holidays, or other factors. By employing outlier correction strategies, the company can ensure that the forecasting models are based on accurate and representative data, leading to more reliable predictions.

Conclusion

In the ever-evolving landscape of data engineering, the quest for high-quality and reliable data remains unyielding. This chapter has taken you on a journey through the intricacies of data quality and validation, shedding light on their paramount importance in the realm of data-driven decision-making.

We began our exploration by emphasizing the indispensable role of data quality and integrity in data engineering. Understanding the significance of clean and accurate data is the foundation upon which informed decisions are made. Designing meticulous data quality checks and validation processes is not just a best practice; it's a necessity.

We delved into the methodologies and techniques for identifying and addressing data quality issues. Whether it's data completeness, consistency, or accuracy, this chapter equipped you with the knowledge to tackle these challenges effectively. Moreover, we explored the implementation of data profiling and monitoring within the Databricks environment, ensuring that data quality remains an ongoing, proactive endeavor.

Moving forward, we ventured into the realm of data validation techniques and rules. By providing an overview of various validation methodologies, we offered a comprehensive toolkit for enforcing data quality standards. The application of validation rules and constraints, coupled with techniques to ensure data completeness and accuracy, paved the way for robust data validation processes. Automation, a key theme in modern data engineering, also found its place in data validation, simplifying and streamlining the quality assurance process.

Lastly, we confronted the enigmatic world of data anomalies and outliers. Armed with statistical approaches and strategies for detection and correction, we tackled the challenges posed by irregular data patterns. By mastering the art of handling data anomalies, you are better prepared to maintain data quality and integrity throughout your data transformation journey.

In closing, this chapter has not only underscored the paramount importance of data quality and validation but has also provided practical insights, techniques, and methodologies to uphold these standards. As you continue your data engineering endeavors, remember that data quality is not a destination; it's a continuous journey that requires vigilance, diligence, and the knowledge you've gained through this chapter.

With this foundation, you are better equipped to harness the true potential of your data, unlocking insights that drive innovation and informed decision-making in the data-driven world.

Multiple Choice Questions

1. Why is data quality important in data engineering?
   a. To increase data volume
   b. To enhance data integrity
   c. To reduce data diversity
   d. To simplify data processing

2. What aspect of data quality encompasses variations in data format, structure, or encoding?
   a. Data accuracy
   b. Data completeness
   c. Data diversity
   d. Data consistency

3. What does ETL stand for in data engineering?
   a. Extract, Tag, Load
   b. Extract, Test, Load
   c. Extract, Transform, Load
   d. Execute, Transform, Load

4. Which data validation approach focuses on ensuring that data adheres to a specific format or structure?
   a. Data completeness
   b. Data consistency
   c. Format validation
   d. Data profiling

5. What is one of the primary steps in the data validation process?
   a. Data extraction
   b. Data transformation
   c. Identifying data quality issues
   d. Data loading

6. Which type of data often requires specialized outlier detection techniques?
   a. Categorical data
   b. Numerical data
   c. Structured data
   d. Time-series data

7. Which statistical method is commonly used for detecting outliers in data?
   a. Mean method
   b. Range method
   c. Z-Score method
   d. Median method

8. What is the advantage of continuous monitoring in data quality management?
   a. Lower implementation cost
   b. Decreased data volume
   c. Continuous monitoring
   d. Increased data diversity

9. Which action is typically not a part of data cleansing?
   a. Correcting
   b. Standardizing
   c. Deleting
   d. Validating

10. Which strategy for handling data anomalies focuses on removing outliers from the dataset?
    a. Correcting
    b. Ignoring
    c. Deleting
    d. Treating

Answers

1. b
2. c
3. c
4. c
5. c
6. d
7. c
8. c
9. c
10. c

CHAPTER 6
Data Modeling and Storage

"The art of data is in its modeling; the strength of data is in its storage."

Introduction

In the modern data-driven landscape, businesses and organizations are constantly inundated with vast amounts of data from a multitude of sources. Effective data modeling and storage are imperative to harness the true potential of this data and transform it into actionable insights. In this chapter of our journey through Databricks, we explore these vital components of data engineering, shedding light on designing, managing, and optimizing data models and storage solutions for analytical workloads.

Data modeling, often referred to as the blueprint of data analysis, is the process of structuring and organizing data to make it meaningful and usable. Within the realm of Databricks, understanding the importance of data modeling is the first step toward constructing robust and efficient data pipelines. We delve into the significance of data modeling in Databricks data engineering, emphasizing its role in shaping the foundation for all downstream analytical processes. We explore the principles of effective data modeling, offering insights into how to create models tailored to analytical workloads. Additionally, we delve into techniques for designing schema-on-read and schema-on-write models, helping you choose the right approach for your data.

Structured and unstructured data abound in the data ecosystem. While structured data follows a well-defined format, unstructured data can take various forms, from text and images to sensor readings and social media posts. In this chapter, we provide an overview of structured and unstructured data storage options within Databricks, discussing the utilization of data lakes and data warehouses for different use cases. We explore the nuances of choosing the appropriate storage format for different data types, enabling you to make informed decisions about how to store and retrieve your data effectively. We also investigate strategies for seamlessly integrating structured and unstructured data in the Databricks environment.

Data optimization is another crucial aspect covered in this chapter. We uncover the benefits of data partitioning in Databricks and elucidate techniques for partitioning data based on various criteria. By optimizing data storage and query performance through partition pruning, you'll learn how to make your analytical workloads more efficient. We round off the chapter with data compaction and optimization strategies, ensuring your data storage remains streamlined and cost-effective.

As we journey through this chapter, we'll equip you with the knowledge and tools to navigate the intricate world of data modeling and storage in Databricks. From understanding the core principles to practical implementation, this chapter is your guide to architecting data solutions that drive value and insights from your data assets.

Structure

In this chapter, the following topics will be covered:
- Designing Effective Data Models
- Utilizing Structured and Unstructured Data Storage Options
- Data Partitioning and Optimization Strategies

Designing Effective Data Models

Effective data modeling is a pivotal step in the data engineering process. It is the foundation upon which analytical workloads are built, determining the ease of data access, processing efficiency, and the quality of insights derived. In the context of Databricks, a cloud-based platform known for its prowess in big data analytics and AI, understanding how to craft data models that align with its capabilities is paramount.

In this section, we embark on a journey to explore the intricacies of data modeling within Databricks. We begin by highlighting the significance of data modeling, shedding light on why it's a critical component of Databricks data engineering. Understanding its role in shaping the entire data pipeline is essential for anyone looking to harness the power of Databricks for data processing and analysis.

We then delve into the principles of effective data modeling for analytical workloads. These principles serve as guiding lights, helping you make informed decisions when structuring your data. Whether you're dealing with massive datasets or real-time streaming data, these principles will empower you to create models that optimize query performance, facilitate data integration, and ensure data quality.

Additionally, we explore the concept of schema-on-read and schema-on-write data models. These two approaches have distinct advantages and use cases, and understanding when to use each is vital for designing efficient data pipelines in Databricks. You'll gain insights into the trade-offs and benefits associated with each approach, allowing you to tailor your data modeling strategy to your specific needs.

Lastly, we provide a comprehensive overview of best practices for designing data models that meet technical requirements and align with your business objectives. Effective data models serve not just data engineers and scientists; they empower the entire organization to make data-driven decisions and uncover valuable insights.

As we navigate this section, you'll gain the knowledge and skills needed to architect data models that are efficient, scalable, and agile enough to adapt to the evolving data landscape. Let's embark on this journey to master designing effective data models for Databricks.

Importance of Data Modeling

Data modeling is the process of defining the structure, organization, and relationships within your data. In the context of Databricks data engineering, it plays a pivotal role in ensuring that data is stored, processed, and analyzed efficiently. Let's explore the importance of data modeling in Databricks and why it's a fundamental aspect of data engineering:

- **Structure and Organization:** Data modeling provides the blueprint for structuring data within Databricks. It defines the tables, columns, and data types, ensuring data is organized logically and consistently. This structure simplifies data access, making it easier for data engineers, analysts, and scientists to work with the data.
- **Query Performance:** Well-designed data models optimize query performance. In Databricks, where large volumes of data are processed, efficient querying is crucial. Properly modeled data reduces query execution times, enabling faster insights and more responsive analytics.
- **Data Integration:** Databricks often deal with data from diverse sources, such as databases, data lakes, and streaming platforms. Data modeling allows for the integration of these disparate data sources. By defining a unified schema, data engineers can harmonize data from different origins, ensuring a consistent view for analysis.
- **Data Quality and Consistency:** Data modeling includes specifying data validation rules, constraints, and data quality checks. This ensures that data entering Databricks meets predefined standards. Enforcing data quality at the modeling stage prevents data inconsistencies and errors downstream.
- **Scalability:** Databricks are designed to handle large-scale data processing. Effective data modeling considers scalability, allowing your data pipeline to grow seamlessly as your data volume increases. It ensures that your system can handle the ever-expanding demands of big data.
- **Flexibility and Adaptability:** Data models in Databricks should be adaptable to changing business requirements. As businesses evolve, data needs change. A well-designed data model allows you to add new data sources, modify existing structures, and implement schema changes without disrupting data pipelines.
- **Cost Efficiency:** Efficient data models optimize storage and processing costs. You can reduce infrastructure expenses by eliminating redundant data and optimizing storage formats. This cost efficiency is particularly crucial when working with cloud-based platforms like Databricks.

Data modeling in Databricks is the foundation for your entire data engineering and analytics efforts. It ensures data is structured, processed, and utilized effectively, enabling organizations to extract valuable insights and drive informed decision-making. The next sections will delve deeper into the principles and techniques for effective data modeling within the Databricks environment.

Types of Data Modeling

Data modeling is a critical aspect of database and data management. There are several data modeling techniques, each serving a specific purpose. Here are some of the key types:

- **Conceptual Data Modeling**
    - **Purpose**: It focuses on defining high-level concepts and relationships between data entities without delving into technical details.
    - **Representation**: Often represented using Entity-Relationship Diagrams (ERD).
    - **Use Cases**: Useful for initial discussions with stakeholders to understand data requirements.
- **Logical Data Modeling**
    - **Purpose**: This type defines the data structure without specifying how it will be physically implemented. It bridges the gap between conceptual and physical models.
    - **Representation**: Typically represented using Entity-Relationship Diagrams (ERD) or Unified Modeling Language (UML) diagrams.
    - **Use Cases**: Helps design databases and data warehouses, ensuring data is organized logically.
- **Physical Data Modeling**
    - **Purpose**: It deals with physically implementing data structures in a database system, including tables, columns, indexes, and storage details.
    - **Representation**: Often represented using Data Definition Language (DDL) scripts.
    - **Use Cases**: Essential for database administrators and developers when setting up the actual database.
- **Dimensional Data Modeling**
    - **Purpose**: Primarily used in data warehousing, dimensional modeling focuses on creating structures like star and snowflake schemas for efficient querying and reporting.
    - **Representation**: Star schema diagrams are common in dimensional modeling.
    - **Use Cases**: Ideal for designing data warehouses optimized for analytical queries.

- **Relational Data Modeling**
  - **Purpose**: This type models data in a tabular format with tables, rows, and columns, emphasizing relationships between entities.
  - **Representation**: Typically represented using Entity-Relationship Diagrams (ERD) with primary and foreign keys.
  - **Use Cases**: Commonly used in relational database management systems (RDBMS) like MySQL, PostgreSQL, and Oracle.
- **NoSQL Data Modeling**
  - **Purpose**: NoSQL databases, like MongoDB and Cassandra, require a different modeling approach. It focuses on defining data structures compatible with NoSQL databases.
  - **Representation**: Varies based on the NoSQL database type, including document-based, key-value, column-family, and graph-based models.
  - **Use Cases**: Suitable for applications requiring high scalability, flexibility, and schema-less data storage.
- **Hierarchical Data Modeling**
  - **Purpose**: Used for organizing data in a hierarchical structure, where each element has a parent-child relationship.
  - **Representation**: Often visualized as tree diagrams.
  - **Use Cases**: Useful for representing structured data like file systems or organizational structures.
- **Object-Oriented Data Modeling**
  - **Purpose**: It extends the principles of object-oriented programming to data modeling, defining data entities as objects with attributes and methods.
  - **Representation**: Utilizes object-oriented diagrams and notations.
  - **Use Cases**: Common in object-oriented databases and applications where data is closely tied to software objects.

These are some of the key types of data modeling techniques, and the choice of which to use depends on the specific requirements of your data management and analysis projects.

Principles of Effective Data Modeling for Analytical Workloads

Effective data modeling is essential for creating data structures well-suited for analytical workloads in Databricks. Here are some key principles to consider when designing data models:

- **Business Understanding**

    Objective Clarity: Before designing a data model, it's crucial to understand the business's goals and objectives clearly. Engage with business stakeholders to determine what questions the data should answer and what insights are required for decision-making.

    Data Relevance: Identify the most relevant data for analysis. Not all available data may be pertinent to the analytics objectives, so focus on data that directly contributes to addressing business challenges.

- **Simplicity and Clarity**

    Avoid Over-Engineering: While meeting analytical requirements is essential, avoid over-complicating the data model. An excessively complex model can lead to difficulties in maintenance and understanding.

    Clear Naming Conventions: Use clear and consistent naming conventions for tables, columns, and relationships. This aids in comprehensibility and reduces the likelihood of errors during querying.

    Documentation: Document the data model comprehensively. Explain the purpose of each table and the relationships between them. This documentation is a reference point for data users and future data engineers.

- **Normalization/Denormalization Balance**

    Normalization: Normalize the data to eliminate redundancy and maintain data integrity. It involves organizing data into separate tables to minimize data duplication. This is crucial for transactional systems.

    Denormalization: In cases where query performance is critical, consider denormalization. It involves combining data from multiple tables into one to reduce the complexity of queries. Denormalized structures are suitable for analytical and reporting databases.

- **Data Integrity Enforcement**

    Constraints: Implement data constraints such as primary keys, foreign keys, unique conditions, and check conditions. Primary keys enforce uniqueness, foreign keys maintain referential integrity, and special restrictions prevent duplicate data.

Validation Rules: Define validation rules to ensure that data entered into the system adheres to predefined criteria. These rules help maintain data quality and consistency.

- **Scalability**

    Horizontal Scaling: Plan for scalability from the outset. Consider horizontal scaling techniques like data sharding or partitioning. These methods divide data into smaller, manageable chunks distributed across servers, enhancing storage capacity and query performance.

    Indexes: Implement appropriate indexes on columns frequently used in queries. Indexes significantly accelerate data retrieval and are essential for large datasets.

By adhering to these detailed principles, data engineers can design data models that support analytical workloads effectively and ensure data quality, maintainability, and scalability in the Databricks environment.

Schema-on-Read and Schema-on-Write models

Let's explore the methods for creating schema-on-read (SoR) and schema-on-write (SoW) data models in more detail.

Schema-on-Read

Schema-on-Read (SoR) is an approach to data modeling where data is ingested as-is without a predefined schema. This means that the structure of the data is not enforced during ingestion. Here are the key aspects of SoR:

- **Late Binding:** In SoR, data is ingested without imposing a structure upfront. The schema is applied during data access or analysis rather than during ingestion.
- **Flexibility:** SoR allows for flexibility in handling unstructured and semi-structured data. It's well-suited for scenarios where data formats change frequently, or you must explore the data before applying a schema.
- **Storage Efficiency:** Data is stored in its raw format, which can be more storage-efficient than schema-on-write. There's no need for data transformation during ingestion.

- **Data Exploration:** SoR is ideal for data exploration and discovery. Analysts and data scientists can analyze the data without worrying about predefined structures.

Schema-on-Write

Schema-on-Write (SoW) is an approach where data is ingested with a predefined schema, and data that doesn't conform to the schema is rejected or transformed to fit the schema. Here are the key aspects of SoW:

- **Predefined Structure:** SoW enforces a predefined schema during data ingestion. Data that doesn't adhere to the schema is either rejected or transformed to fit the schema.
- **Data Validation:** SoW ensures data quality by validating incoming data against predefined rules. It prevents incorrect or incomplete data from entering the system.
- **Query Performance:** Structured data models (for example, relational databases) are typically schema-on-write. They are optimized for query performance since the schema defines how data is organized and indexed.
- **Data Integrity:** SoW provides strong data integrity, as data adheres to a fixed schema. This reduces the risk of inconsistent or invalid data.

Hybrid Approaches

Many modern data platforms, including Databricks, support hybrid approaches. You can initially ingest data as schema-on-read for exploration and then transform it into a schema-on-write format for optimized querying and reporting. One example of a hybrid approach is Delta Lake, which combines the benefits of SoR and SoW by providing ACID transactions on data lakes.

Best Practices for Designing Data Models

Let's focus on the first eight points, providing more detailed insights into best practices for creating data models aligned with business requirements:

- **Understand Business Requirements**

    In the initial phase of data modeling, prioritize understanding the specific data needs of the business. Engage with stakeholders and subject matter experts to gather requirements. This deep understanding will inform your data modeling decisions.

- **Choose the Right Data Model**

  Carefully select a data model that aligns with your use case. Common options include:
  - **Relational Model:** Suitable for structured data with well-defined relationships.
  - **Star Schema:** Ideal for data warehousing and analytics, simplifying complex queries.
  - **Snowflake Schema:** A variation of star schema that further normalizes data.
  - **NoSQL:** Suited for unstructured or semi-structured data and flexible schemas.
  - **Graph Database:** Effective for managing highly interconnected data.

- **Normalize or Denormalize Wisely**

  In relational databases, consider normalization to minimize data redundancy and maintain data integrity. However, denormalization might be necessary for analytical workloads that require quick query performance. Find the right balance based on your specific needs.

- **Define Clear Data Types**

  Assign appropriate data types to each column in your data model. This not only ensures data accuracy but also optimizes storage space. Avoid using generic data types when more specific ones are available. For instance, use 'INTEGER' instead of 'NUMERIC' if the column only stores whole numbers.

- **Establish Naming Conventions**

  Set up clear and consistent naming conventions for database objects, including tables, columns, indexes, and constraints. Meaningful and consistent names enhance understanding, maintainability, and collaboration among team members.

- **Document Your Model**

  Comprehensive documentation is indispensable. Document the data model with schema definitions, relationships, data transformation logic, and any business rules associated with the data. Such documentation aids in onboarding new team members and maintaining data lineage.

- **Consider Data Governance**

  Implement robust data governance practices. This includes defining access controls, data lineage tracking, and auditing mechanisms. Ensure compliance with data regulations and industry standards relevant to your domain.

- **Optimize for Performance**

    Design your data model with performance optimization in mind to achieve efficient query performance. Key considerations include:
    - **Indexing:** Use appropriate indexing techniques to speed up query execution.
    - **Partitioning:** Implement data partitioning strategies, especially for large datasets, to minimize the amount of data scanned during queries.
    - **Data Types:** Choose the most efficient data types for your data storage engine.
    - **Query Optimization:** Regularly review and optimize queries based on data model changes and query performance.

By implementing these detailed best practices, you'll be well-equipped to design data models that meet business requirements and enhance data usability, performance, and maintainability.

Utilizing Structured and Unstructured Data Storage Options

Organizations deal with various data types in today's data-driven landscape, from well-structured databases to unstructured text and multimedia files. Managing and storing these diverse data forms is crucial for data engineering and analytics. This chapter delves into the world of data storage within the Databricks environment, exploring how to make strategic decisions regarding where and how to store data.

Structured data often resides in relational databases, while unstructured data can be anything from log files to social media posts. To harness the full potential of your data, it's essential to understand the storage options available in Databricks, ranging from data lakes to data warehouses, and to select the most appropriate storage formats.

We'll explore the nuances of these storage solutions, learn when to utilize each, and understand how to integrate them seamlessly within the Databricks ecosystem. Moreover, we'll delve into choosing the right storage format, optimizing data organization, and laying the groundwork for efficient data analysis.

As we venture further into this chapter, we'll uncover the principles that govern data storage in Databricks, guiding you toward informed decisions that align with your organization's data requirements and goals. So, let's embark on a journey through the intricacies of data storage within the Databricks platform, where data is not just information but a valuable asset driving insights and innovation.

Overview of Structured and Unstructured Data Storage Options

In modern data engineering, having the right storage strategy is critical to harness data's power effectively. Databricks provides a versatile platform for processing and analyzing data, and understanding the storage options it offers is fundamental.

Structured Data Storage

Structured data often originates from relational databases or structured files like CSV or Parquet. In Databricks, you have several storage options for structured data:

- **Data Lakes:** Databricks integrates seamlessly with data lakes like AWS S3, Azure Data Lake Storage, and Google Cloud Storage. Data lakes are well-suited for storing structured data due to their scalability and cost-effectiveness.
- **Data Warehouses:** While traditionally used for structured data, data warehouses like Snowflake and Delta Lake provide robust solutions for storing and querying structured data. They are ideal when you need strong data consistency and optimized query performance.

Unstructured Data Storage

Unstructured data encompasses various information, such as text documents, images, audio, and video. Databricks accommodates unstructured data through different storage options:

- **Object Storage:** Unstructured data often finds a home in object storage systems like AWS S3, Azure Blob Storage, or Google Cloud Storage. These platforms are well-suited for handling large binary objects like images and multimedia.

- **Data Lakes:** Unstructured data, such as log files or JSON documents, can also be stored in data lakes alongside structured data. This approach allows for unified data storage and processing.

Hybrid Approaches

In practice, organizations often work with both structured and unstructured data. Databricks enables hybrid storage approaches, using data lakes and warehouses to manage structured data and object storage for unstructured content.

Understanding these storage options is crucial for optimizing data management in Databricks. It allows data engineers and analysts to decide where to store their data based on the data's type, access patterns, and analytical requirements. The versatility of Databricks' storage solutions empowers organizations to efficiently handle both structured and unstructured data within a unified platform.

Utilizing Data Lakes and Data Warehouses

In data engineering, the choice between data lakes and data warehouses plays a pivotal role in shaping data storage and processing strategies. Each has its strengths and best-suited use cases within the Databricks ecosystem.

Data Lakes

Data lakes are well-known for their flexibility and scalability. They are essentially large repositories that can store vast amounts of structured and unstructured data, making them ideal for various use cases:

- **Data Ingestion:** Data lakes are excellent for raw data ingestion, allowing you to ingest data without a predefined schema. This flexibility is valuable when dealing with diverse data sources.
- **Data Exploration:** Data scientists and analysts often use data lakes for exploratory data analysis. They can quickly access raw data and experiment with various transformations and calculations.
- **Big Data Processing:** Data lakes naturally fit big data processing frameworks like Apache Spark. They enable distributed processing of large datasets, making them suitable for tasks like machine learning and data transformation.

- **Cost-Effective Storage:** Data lakes are more cost-effective for long-term storage than data warehouses, making them a preferred choice when budget constraints are a concern.

Data Warehouses

Data warehouses are designed for structured data and are optimized for querying and reporting. They excel in specific scenarios as follows:

- **Business Intelligence:** Data warehouses are the go-to solution for business intelligence (BI) and reporting. They provide fast, efficient querying capabilities for structured data.
- **Structured Data Analytics:** When your data primarily consists of structured information, such as sales transactions or customer records, data warehouses offer superior performance for complex SQL queries.
- **Data Consolidation:** Data warehouses often consolidate data from various sources into a structured format, ensuring data consistency and integrity.
- **Data Governance:** Data warehouses provide strong features, including access controls and auditing, making them suitable for compliance-sensitive industries.

Hybrid Approach

In practice, organizations often employ a hybrid approach, using both data lakes and data warehouses to complement each other. Data lakes can act as a landing zone for raw data, while data warehouses are structured data repositories for analytical purposes.

Understanding when to leverage data lakes and data warehouses in Databricks is essential for creating an efficient and cost-effective data storage and processing strategy. The choice depends on your data's characteristics, your specific use case, and the analytical requirements of your organization. Databricks' integration with both storage options offers flexibility and empowers data engineers to make informed decisions.

Choosing the Appropriate Storage Format

In Databricks and data engineering, selecting the right storage format for your data is crucial. The storage format impacts storage costs and affects query performance, data processing, and compatibility with various tools and frameworks. Here, we'll explore the considerations for choosing storage formats tailored to different data types:

Parquet for Structured Data

- **Data Type**: Parquet is an excellent choice for structured data, including tabular data with well-defined schemas.
- **Benefits**: Parquet is columnar storage, which stores data column-wise instead of row-wise. This format is highly efficient for analytical queries, as it allows for column pruning, which reads only the necessary columns, reducing I/O operations and enhancing query performance. Parquet is also a highly compressed format, saving storage costs.
- **Use Cases**: Use Parquet for structured data like CSV files and log files or data from relational databases.

ORC for Optimized Hive Integration

- **Data Type**: ORC (Optimized Row Columnar) format is ideal when you require compatibility with Hive, as it's optimized for Hive.
- **Benefits**: ORC is similar to Parquet but is optimized specifically for Hive. It provides excellent compression and query performance, making it suitable for analytical workloads. It also supports predicate pushdown, further enhancing query efficiency.
- **Use Cases**: Use ORC when your data engineering workflow heavily relies on Hive integration or when working with Hive tables.

Avro for Schema Evolution

- **Data Type**: Avro is a suitable choice when schema evolution is considered, as it supports schema evolution without requiring schema modifications on write.
- **Benefits**: Avro is a row-based format that stores data with its schema, making it self-descriptive. This flexibility makes it easy to evolve schemas over time, a valuable feature when dealing with changing data sources.
- **Use Cases**: Use Avro when dealing with semi-structured or schema-less data that may change frequently.

JSON for Semi-Structured Data

- **Data Type**: JSON (JavaScript Object Notation) is the go-to format for semi-structured data due to its flexibility.

- **Benefits**: JSON is human-readable and highly flexible, allowing you to store data with varying structures within the same dataset. It's widely used for web services, logs, and NoSQL databases.
- **Use Cases**: Use JSON for data sources where the schema is not well-defined or varies significantly across records.

Binary Formats for Serialization
- **Data Type**: Binary formats like Apache Avro and Apache Thrift are efficient choices for data serialization.
- **Benefits**: Binary formats are highly efficient in storage and processing. They are commonly used in scenarios where you need to serialize and deserialize data rapidly, such as in data streaming or inter-process communication.
- **Use Cases**: Use binary formats for high-speed data serialization and deserialization.

Aspect	Parquet	ORC	Avro	Difference
Data Type Suitability	Best for structured data	Ideal for Hive integration	Suitable for schema evolution	Parquet and ORC are optimized for structured data, with ORC having a specific advantage in Hive ecosystems. Avro excels in scenarios requiring schema evolution
Storage Model	Columnar storage	Columnar storage	Row-based storage	Both Parquet and ORC are columnar, optimizing for analytical queries. Avro's row-based model is better for scenarios where each record carries its schema
Query Performance	High efficiency in read-heavy analytical workloads	Similar to Parquet but optimized for Hive	Good for read/write operations, less for analytics	Parquet and ORC are superior in query performance for analytics, with ORC being Hive-optimized. Avro offers balanced read/write performance but lags in analytics

Aspect	Parquet	ORC	Avro	Difference
Compression and I/O Efficiency	Highly compressed, less I/O during reads	High compression, efficient I/O	Compressed but typically less than Parquet/ORC	Parquet and ORC provide better compression and I/O efficiency, crucial for large datasets. Avro's compression is good but not at the same level for large-scale analytics
Schema Evolution	Supports to an extent	Supports to an extent	Designed for easy schema evolution	Avro is the clear choice for evolving schemas without rewriting data. Parquet and ORC support schema evolution but are not as flexible as Avro
Interoperability	Widely supported in data processing tools	Optimized for Hive, supported in many tools	Strong in scenarios requiring data interchange	Parquet and ORC have broad support, especially in analytics. Avro stands out in data interoperability and integration scenarios
Use Cases	Analytical workloads, BI tools, data warehousing	Hive queries, Hive-centric data processing	Data with frequently changing schemas	Parquet is general-purpose for analytics, ORC is Hive-focused, and Avro is for data that undergoes frequent schema changes

Table 6.1: Comparison of Popular Formats: A Handy Reference Table

Choosing the right storage format for different data types in Databricks ensures optimal performance, efficient storage utilization, and compatibility with your data processing and analytical tools. Understanding the characteristics of each format empowers data engineers to make informed decisions based on their specific use cases and requirements.

Data Partitioning and Optimization Strategies

In the realm of big data processing, optimizing data storage and query performance is of paramount importance. This section delves into the techniques and strategies employed for efficient data partitioning and optimization within Databricks. Whether dealing with massive datasets, real-time analytics, or complex queries, understanding data partitioning and optimization can significantly enhance your data engineering workflows.

Data partitioning involves dividing datasets into smaller, more manageable subsets based on specific criteria. When implemented effectively, it can substantially improve query performance, reducing the amount of data that needs to be scanned or processed. Additionally, optimizing data storage and query performance goes beyond just partitioning; it encompasses various strategies for enhancing the efficiency of data storage and retrieval.

By the end of this section, you'll have a comprehensive understanding of data partitioning and optimization strategies in Databricks. You'll be equipped with the knowledge and tools necessary to make data engineering decisions that enhance the performance and efficiency of your data pipelines and analytical processes. Whether you're dealing with structured or unstructured data, real-time or batch processing, these strategies are essential for maximizing the potential of Databricks in your data engineering workflows.

Understanding Data Partitioning

Optimizing query performance is a top priority in big data, where datasets can grow into petabytes and beyond. This is where data partitioning comes into play. Data partitioning is a database design technique that divides large datasets into smaller, more manageable pieces known as partitions. Each partition contains a subset of the data, making it easier and faster to query specific portions of the dataset. In Databricks, understanding data partitioning and its benefits is crucial for efficient data processing.

Key Concepts of Data Partitioning:

- **Partition Key:** The partition key is the column or set of columns used to divide the dataset into partitions. Selecting an appropriate partition key that aligns with your query patterns is essential. Common partition keys include date, time, location, or any attribute frequently used in your queries.

- **Partition Pruning:** One of the significant advantages of data partitioning is partition pruning. When executing a query, Databricks can intelligently skip reading entire partitions irrelevant to the question, dramatically reducing the amount of data scanned. This leads to faster query execution times.

Benefits of Data Partitioning in Databricks:

- **Improved Query Performance:** By dividing data into partitions and employing partition pruning, queries become significantly faster. Databricks only scan the relevant sections, reducing the query's execution time.
- **Efficient Data Storage:** Data partitioning can also lead to efficient storage. You can store data in a columnar format within partitions, compressing and storing data more efficiently, saving storage costs.
- **Scalability:** As your data grows, partitioning allows for horizontal scaling. You can add new partitions, ensuring your data infrastructure remains scalable and responsive.
- **Ease of Maintenance:** Managing and maintaining smaller partitions is more manageable than handling a monolithic dataset. It simplifies tasks like data archiving, retention policies, and data lifecycle management.

Considerations for Effective Data Partitioning

It's essential to consider various factors like query patterns, data volume, and storage costs to harness the benefits of data partitioning effectively. Selecting an appropriate partition key that aligns with your queries is critical. Additionally, monitoring and optimizing partitioning strategies as your data evolves is ongoing.

In summary, data partitioning is a fundamental technique in Databricks for optimizing query performance and managing large datasets efficiently. Understanding how and when to employ it is essential for designing robust data engineering workflows in Databricks.

Different Techniques for Partitioning Data

Data partitioning is a powerful technique to enhance query performance and manage large datasets efficiently in Databricks. While the previous section discussed the benefits and key concepts of data partitioning, this section focuses on partitioning data based on various criteria using the following techniques:

- **Time-Based Partitioning**

    One of the most common partitioning strategies is time-based partitioning. In this approach, data is partitioned based on timestamps or date attributes. For example, you can partition data by year, month, day, or even at a finer granularity like hours or minutes. Time-based partitioning is highly effective for time-series data such as logs, sensor readings, or financial transactions.

- **Location-Based Partitioning**

  Location-based partitioning is valuable for geospatial data or data with a strong geographic component. You can partition data based on geographic attributes like country, state, city, or coordinates (latitude and longitude). This partitioning method facilitates efficient spatial queries and analysis.

- **Hash-Based Partitioning**

  Hash-based partitioning involves applying a hash function to a specific column to determine the partition assignment. This method evenly distributes data across partitions based on the hash value. It can be useful for load balancing and ensuring an even data distribution, especially when no clear partitioning key exists.

- **Range-Based Partitioning**

  In range-based partitioning, data is partitioned based on specified ranges or intervals of a particular attribute. For instance, if you have sales data, you could partition it by revenue ranges such as low, medium, and high. Range-based partitioning is suitable when data distribution doesn't follow a natural hierarchy but can be categorized by intervals.

- **Custom Criteria Partitioning**

  In some cases, you might have unique partitioning criteria specific to your business or use case. Custom criteria partitioning allows you to define partition keys based on your requirements. For example, if dealing with product data, you could partition it by product categories, custom tags, or any attribute that suits your analysis.

- **Combination Partitioning**

  Often, a single partitioning criterion may not be sufficient. In such cases, combining multiple criteria for partitioning can be beneficial. For example, you might partition data by time and location, creating partitions for each month within each geographic region.

Benefits of Tailored Data Partitioning

- **Optimized Query Performance**: Partitioning data based on relevant criteria ensures that queries are executed more efficiently. It reduces the amount of data scanned, leading to faster query results.

- **Improved Data Organization**: Tailored partitioning enhances data organization, making it easier to manage and maintain. It also aligns with your specific analytical needs.

- **Cost Efficiency**: By scanning only relevant partitions, you can save on processing costs and reduce query execution time, resulting in cost-efficient data operations.

Considerations for Data Partitioning

While data partitioning offers substantial benefits, it's crucial to carefully select partition keys and strategies based on your data and query patterns. Regular monitoring and adjusting partitioning schemes as your data evolves are essential to maintaining optimal performance.

In summary, data partitioning in Databricks provides flexibility to tailor your partitioning strategy according to the nature of your data and analytical requirements. Understanding these techniques enables you to design efficient data partitioning schemes that enhance query performance and data management.

Strategies for Data compaction and Optimization in Databricks

Data compaction and optimization are essential to managing your data in Databricks effectively. These strategies aim to reduce storage costs, enhance query performance, and maintain data quality over time. This section will explore strategies and best practices for compacting and optimizing your data in Databricks:

- **Data Compaction Overview**

    Data compaction refers to reducing the volume of stored data while retaining essential information. Compaction can involve techniques like compression, aggregation, and data summarization.

- **Benefits of Data Compaction**
    - **Cost Reduction**: Compacted data occupies less storage space, reducing storage costs, especially in cloud-based storage environments where prices are based on data volume.
    - **Improved Query Performance**: Compact data requires fewer I/O operations, leading to faster query execution and reduced query costs.
    - **Data Quality**: Compaction can help maintain data quality by reducing redundancy and ensuring consistency in your datasets.

- **Data Aggregation and Summarization**
  - **Aggregation**: Aggregating data involves combining multiple records into a single, summarized form. For example, hourly data points can be aggregated into daily or monthly summaries. This reduces the overall volume of data.
  - **Summarization**: Summarizing data entails creating compact representations of the original data, such as calculating statistical measures (for example, averages, totals) or extracting essential features.
- **Data Compression**
  - Compression techniques reduce data size by encoding it in a more efficient format. Common compression algorithms include gzip, snappy, and Parquet's built-in compression.
  - Columnar Storage: Storing data in columnar formats like Parquet inherently provides compression benefits because similar data values are stored together, allowing for efficient encoding.
- **Data Retention Policies**

  Implement data retention policies to remove or archive data that is no longer needed for analysis automatically. This helps keep storage costs in check and ensures you work with relevant data.
- **Data Lifecycle Management**

  Define clear data lifecycle management practices, including when to archive, delete, or transform data. Regularly assess data storage and access patterns to refine these practices.
- **Data Cleaning and Deduplication**

  Periodically clean and deduplicate your datasets to remove redundant or erroneous records. This not only reduces data volume but also improves data quality.
- **Indexing and Metadata**

  Use indexing and metadata to locate and retrieve specific data points within large datasets efficiently, reducing the need for full scans.
- **Data Pruning**

  Prune older or less frequently accessed data to reduce storage costs. Ensure you have efficient mechanisms for accessing archived or historical data when needed.

- **Data Partitioning**

    Partition your data optimally to ensure that queries and operations only target relevant partitions, reducing the amount of data scanned.

Data compaction and optimization strategies are crucial for maintaining efficient and cost-effective data storage and processing in Databricks. By implementing these strategies and adapting them to your specific use cases, you can balance storage costs, query performance, and data quality, ensuring that your data assets remain valuable and manageable over time.

Conclusion

In today's data-driven landscape, effective data modeling and storage strategies are the cornerstones of any successful data engineering endeavor. This chapter has provided a deep dive into the intricacies of designing data models and managing data storage in the context of Databricks, equipping you with the knowledge and tools necessary to handle data efficiently and effectively.

We began by exploring the critical aspects of data modeling, emphasizing its significance in Databricks data engineering. Understanding the principles of effective data modeling for analytical workloads was a key takeaway, and we delved into techniques for designing schema-on-read and schema-on-write models. Best practices were highlighted, ensuring data models aligned seamlessly with business requirements.

Moving forward, we examined the rich landscape of structured and unstructured data storage options within Databricks. The comprehensive overview helped you grasp the versatility of data lakes and warehouses and how to choose the appropriate storage format for varying data types. Strategies for integrating structured and unstructured data were discussed, enabling you to harness the full potential of your data assets.

The final section delved into data partitioning and optimization, illuminating the benefits and techniques involved. Understanding the principles of data partitioning, optimizing storage and query performance through partition pruning, and implementing strategies for data compaction rounded off this section. These strategies ensure that your data remains cost-effective, query-efficient, and high-quality.

In conclusion, this chapter equips you with the knowledge and practical insights needed to design effective data models, make informed storage decisions, and optimize data management within Databricks. By applying these principles and practices, you can leverage the full potential of your data assets, enabling your organization to confidently make data-driven decisions.

As you continue your journey in data engineering, these skills will prove invaluable in managing and extracting actionable insights from the ever-growing volumes of data in the modern digital landscape. In the next chapter, we will explore the Orchestrating and monitoring these workflows.

Key Terms

- **Data Modeling:** Creating an abstract representation of data structures and their relationships, focusing on how data is organized and accessed.
- **Schema-on-Read (SoR):** A data modeling approach where data is stored in its raw form, and the structure is applied when it is read or queried. It offers flexibility in handling diverse data types.
- **Schema-on-Write (SoW):** A data modeling approach where data is pre-structured before storage, ensuring consistency and efficiency but potentially limiting flexibility.
- **Data Lake:** A storage repository that can hold vast amounts of raw data in its native format, offering cost-effective and scalable storage.
- **Data Warehouse:** A centralized repository for structured data, optimized for querying and reporting, typically used for business intelligence and analytics.
- **Storage Format:** How data is encoded and stored, such as Parquet, Avro, or ORC, affects storage efficiency and query performance.
- **Data Partitioning:** Dividing large datasets into smaller, manageable parts based on specific criteria, often improving query performance.
- **Partition Pruning:** An optimization technique that allows the query engine to skip reading irrelevant partitions, reducing query processing time.
- **Data Compaction:** Reducing storage space usage by removing unnecessary data or optimizing storage formats.
- **Data Optimization:** Strategies to enhance data storage, access, and query performance while minimizing costs.

CHAPTER 7
Data Orchestration and Workflow Management

"Workflow is the rhythm of progress; orchestration is the choreography of data."

– Adapted from Michael Bierut

Introduction

In the world of data engineering, the ability to process, transform, and analyze data is crucial. However, as data volumes grow and processing tasks become more complex, manual execution and management of data workflows become increasingly impractical. This is where the importance of workflow automation and orchestration shines.

This chapter explores the realm of Data Orchestration and Workflow Management – a domain critical for streamlining data engineering processes, enhancing efficiency, and ensuring the timely delivery of insights. Whether you are dealing with massive datasets, intricate data pipelines, or a combination of both, this chapter will equip you with the knowledge and tools needed to conquer the challenges of modern data engineering.

The journey begins with an understanding of workflow automation's significance. We delve into the advantages it brings to the data engineering landscape, enabling teams to save time, reduce errors, and expedite data processing. The chapter introduces Databricks Jobs and Notebooks, revealing how they serve as the foundation for workflow automation. Practical insights and best practices for designing and deploying automated data pipelines are provided, with real-world examples illustrating the substantial efficiency gains that automation can deliver.

Managing dependencies between tasks and pipelines becomes paramount as workflows become more complex. This chapter explores strategies for understanding, managing, and resolving dependencies in Databricks workflows. It provides a comprehensive guide to scheduling and orchestrating data pipelines using Databricks Jobs, along with best practices for handling the complexities of intricate workflows.

The final section delves into monitoring and error handling – an essential aspect of ensuring the reliability and robustness of automated workflows. It outlines practical strategies for monitoring workflow execution, including tools and techniques for gaining progress visibility. Implementing logging and alerting mechanisms for error detection is discussed in detail, alongside proactive procedures for handling failures and retries. The chapter concludes by demonstrating how to utilize Databricks' built-in monitoring and debugging tools to optimize workflow performance and resource utilization.

Whether you're new to workflow automation or seeking to enhance your existing practices, this chapter will provide a comprehensive understanding of data orchestration and workflow management in Databricks. From automating data pipelines to handling complex dependencies and ensuring error-free execution, the knowledge and insights offered in this chapter will empower you to become a proficient data orchestrator and workflow manager.

Structure

In this chapter, the following topics will be covered:
- Implementing Workflow Automation with Databricks
- Managing Dependencies and Scheduling Data Pipelines
- Monitoring and Error Handling in Workflow Execution

Implementing Workflow Automation with Databricks

In the realm of data engineering, efficiency and accuracy are paramount. Manual execution and management of data workflows can be time-consuming and prone to errors. This is where workflow automation with Databricks takes center stage. In this section, we'll explore workflow automation's fundamental concepts and practices – a game-changer in data engineering.

Workflow automation involves orchestrating various data-related tasks and processes, ensuring they run seamlessly and efficiently. It enables data engineers to streamline work, reduce manual intervention, and accelerate data processing. Within the Databricks ecosystem, automation is made accessible through Databricks Jobs and Notebooks, powerful tools designed to simplify and enhance the management of data workflows.

This section serves as your gateway to understanding the significance of workflow automation, its impact on data engineering, and how Databricks empowers you to harness its potential. We'll delve into the principles, techniques, and real-world examples that showcase the transformative power of automating data pipelines. By the end of this section, you'll have a solid foundation in implementing workflow automation within the Databricks environment, setting the stage for efficient and timely data processing.

Overview of Workflow Automation

Workflow automation is the systematic orchestration of data-related tasks, allowing for the seamless execution of complex processes. Its essence lies in automating and streamlining repetitive or intricate workflows, liberating data engineers from manual execution. The result? Enhanced efficiency, accuracy, and scalability in data processing – a trifecta that is indispensable in the contemporary data landscape.

Within the expansive arsenal of data engineering tools, Databricks stands out as an automation champion. Databricks Jobs and Notebooks emerged as the vanguard of this movement, offering a cohesive platform to design and execute automated data pipelines. This subsection serves as your compass in navigating the landscape of workflow automation, focusing on Databricks as a vehicle for transformation.

In the labyrinth of modern data engineering, the orchestration of tasks has become a linchpin for success. The following are some benefits of it:

- **Efficiency Boost:** Workflow automation is like having a helpful robot that can perform many data-related tasks for you. It is super handy because it makes your work faster and easier. You do not have to do all the boring or complicated stuff yourself.
- **Fewer Mistakes:** When people do things manually, they can make mistakes. Automation is like a careful robot that doesn't make mistakes. This means your data stays correct and trustworthy.
- **Handles Big Jobs:** Nowadays, we deal with massive amounts of data. Automation can handle big data tasks without breaking a sweat. So, no matter how much data you have, it covers you.
- **On Time, Every Time:** Automation ensures things happen when they should. This is crucial for using data to make decisions. You can't wait around for data – you need it on time.
- **Saves Resources:** Think of automation as an intelligent manager. It uses your computer and people's time wisely, helping you save money and get more done with less effort.

So, in simple terms, workflow automation is like having a helpful, mistake-free, fast, and efficient assistant for your data tasks. It makes your data work a breeze!

Introduction to Databricks Jobs and Notebooks for Workflow Automation

Let us dive into Databricks Jobs and Notebooks, like the magic wands for workflow automation.

- **Databricks Jobs:** These are like the task manager for your data jobs. Just like you have a to-do list, Databricks Jobs keeps track of all the things your automation needs to do. They make sure everything runs on time, so you do not have to babysit your data tasks.
- **Notebooks:** Think of these as your digital workbenches. Notebooks are where you create, test, and run your data magic. It's like your playground for coding and analyzing data. With Databricks Notebooks, you can write code, see results, and ensure your data behaves as expected.

Databricks, Jobs, and Notebooks are a powerful team. You create your data transformations and analysis in Notebooks, and then Jobs takes care of running them automatically. It's like telling your assistant what needs to be done, and they handle the rest.

- **Easy to Use:** The best part is you don't need to be a computer whiz to use them. Databricks makes it user-friendly, so even if you're new to this, you'll get the hang of it quickly.
- **Super Productive:** Jobs and Notebooks save you tons of time. You set them up, and they do the work while you can focus on other things. It's like having extra hours in your day.
- **Collaborative:** They're also fantastic for teamwork. Multiple people can work on Notebooks, and Jobs can run them for everyone. So, your whole team can benefit from automation.

So, in a nutshell, Databricks Jobs and Notebooks are your dynamic duo for workflow automation. They make your data tasks easier, save time, and are surprisingly easy to use. You'll wonder how you ever managed without them!

Designing and Implementing Automated Data Pipelines in Databricks

Data pipelines serve as the backbone of modern data engineering. They are the pathways through which data flows from source to destination. To comprehend their significance, think of them as orchestrators of a data symphony. A data pipeline's primary objective is to ensure that raw data, often scattered across various sources, is collected, transformed, and delivered in a format ready for analysis.

Data pipelines consist of three essential components:

- **Data Extraction:** This is where the journey begins. Data is collected from disparate sources such as databases, cloud storage, APIs, and so on. Understanding how to extract data efficiently is crucial, as it sets the stage for the entire pipeline.
- **Data Transformation:** Once the data is collected, it rarely arrives in the ideal format. It might be messy, unstructured, or incomplete. This phase involves cleaning, reshaping, and enriching the data to make it worthwhile. Transformations can range from simple operations like filtering and aggregation to complex machine-learning models.
- **Data Loading:** After the data is transformed, it needs a home where it can be easily accessed and analyzed. Data loading involves storing the processed data in a suitable repository, such as a data lake, data

warehouse, or database. The choice of storage depends on factors like data volume, query performance, and cost considerations.

Automation is a game-changer in the world of data pipelines. It offers several advantages:

- **Efficiency:** Automated pipelines run consistently and can handle large volumes of data without manual intervention. This frees valuable time for data engineers to focus on more critical tasks.
- **Consistency:** Automation ensures that every data processing step is executed the same way every time. This consistency reduces the risk of errors and data inconsistencies.
- **Timeliness:** Automated pipelines can be scheduled to run at specific intervals, ensuring that data is always up to date and readily available for analysis.

Real-world Use Cases: To understand the practical applications of automated data pipelines, let's consider some real-world scenarios:

- **E-commerce Optimization:** Retailers use automated pipelines to collect and process sales data in real time. This enables them to optimize supply chains, manage inventory, and make data-driven decisions.
- **Healthcare Analytics:** Healthcare providers leverage automated pipelines to gather patient data from diverse sources. This data aids in improving patient care, predicting disease outbreaks, and streamlining operations.
- **Financial Analysis:** In the finance sector, automated pipelines aggregate and analyze market data, supporting investment decisions, risk management, and fraud detection.

Best Practices: Designing efficient and reliable data pipelines requires adhering to best practices. Some fundamental principles include:

- **Modularity:** Break down your pipeline into modular components for easier maintenance and scalability.
- **Error Handling:** Implement robust error handling mechanisms to identify and rectify issues promptly.
- **Monitoring:** Set up monitoring and alerting systems to track pipeline performance and detect anomalies.
- **Documentation:** Thoroughly document your pipeline design, transformations, and data sources for future reference.

By mastering these concepts, you'll be well-prepared to effectively design, implement, and orchestrate automated data pipelines in Databricks.

Managing Dependencies and Scheduling Data Pipelines

In data engineering, managing complex workflows is like conducting an orchestra. The key to harmonious data processes lies in effectively managing dependencies. Dependencies are the threads that connect different tasks within your data pipelines, orchestrating their execution logically and efficiently. In this section, we embark on a journey to explore the intricate art of managing dependencies and scheduling data pipelines within Databricks.

Imagine a symphony orchestra where each musician plays their part, and the conductor ensures the performance flows seamlessly. Similarly, in data engineering, tasks, and data pipelines depend on each other to create a symphony of data processing. Understanding these dependencies is akin to deciphering the musical score and ensuring that charges are correctly orchestrated.

Dependencies in data engineering can take various forms, each with unique characteristics. There are task dependencies, where one task relies on the successful completion of another. For instance, before performing data analysis, data cleansing must be executed. Data dependencies come into play when one dataset depends on another, like a sales report relying on daily sales data. Time dependencies dictate when specific tasks should be executed, such as daily data backups or weekly report generation.

Effectively managing dependencies is not just about maintaining order; it's about optimizing your data processes. One powerful way to grasp dependencies is through visualization.

As we venture further into this section, we will explore techniques and best practices for effectively managing dependencies, enabling you to orchestrate your data workflows like a maestro, creating a symphony of data processing that resonates with efficiency and precision.

Understanding Dependencies Between Data Pipelines and Tasks

In the world of data engineering, dependencies are the invisible threads that connect different tasks and data pipelines, forming a web of relationships. Understanding these dependencies is akin to mapping out a complex road network before embarking on a cross-country journey. This subsection focuses on the critical aspect of comprehending the intricate dependencies that exist within your data workflows.

What are Dependencies?

At its core, a dependency is a relationship between tasks or data sources where the execution of one task relies on the successful completion of another. In simple terms, it answers questions like *What needs to be done before this task can start?* or *Which data source must be ready before we proceed?* Dependencies ensure that your data workflows flow logically, efficiently, and without errors.

Dependencies can take various forms:

- **Task Dependencies:** These involve one task relying on the output of another task. For example, data cleansing must occur before data analysis can commence.
- **Data Dependencies:** These occur when one data source or dataset depends on another. For instance, a sales report might depend on daily sales data being available.
- **Time Dependencies:** Some tasks must be executed at specific times or intervals, creating time-based dependencies. Regular data backups are an example.

Why Understanding Dependencies Matters:

- **Error Prevention:** By understanding dependencies, you can identify potential bottlenecks or conflicts in your workflow, reducing the likelihood of errors and data inconsistencies.
- **Efficiency:** Knowing dependencies helps optimize task scheduling, ensuring that tasks are executed efficiently.
- **Resource Management:** Properly managing dependencies allows you to allocate resources effectively. For instance, you can ensure that the right computing resources are available when needed.

Consider a scenario in e-commerce: To generate daily sales reports, several tasks must be completed sequentially. Data must be extracted, cleansed, aggregated, and finally analyzed. Completing each task relies on the successful execution of the previous one. Understanding these dependencies is crucial to ensuring timely and accurate sales reports.

In the following sections, we will explore techniques for managing these dependencies effectively, enabling you to orchestrate your data workflows seamlessly.

Techniques for Managing Dependencies in Databricks Workflows

In the grand symphony of data orchestration, managing dependencies effectively is akin to ensuring that each musical note plays in harmony. Databricks offers a range of techniques and tools to help data engineers master this art. Following are key techniques for managing dependencies within Databricks workflows:

- **Workflow Automation Tools:** Databricks provides features like Jobs and Notebooks that orchestrate tasks and manage their dependencies. Databricks Jobs allows you to schedule and automate the execution of Notebooks, making it easier to manage tasks and their order of execution.
- **Task Sequencing:** To handle task dependencies, organize your workflow by creating a sequence of tasks. Start with tasks that have no dependencies and progressively add tasks that rely on the completion of previous ones. This way, you can ensure tasks are executed in the correct order.
- **Dependency Annotations:** Within Databricks Notebooks, you can annotate cells with dependency information. For instance, you can indicate that a specific cell depends on the successful execution of another cell. This simple yet effective technique helps in visualizing and tracking dependencies directly within your Notebooks.
- **Notebook Versioning:** Databricks allows you to version your Notebooks, providing a history of changes made over time. This feature is invaluable for tracking changes in dependencies, ensuring that your workflow remains consistent and error-free.
- **Job Scheduling:** Databricks Jobs offers advanced scheduling options. You can specify when and how often a job should run. Leveraging this scheduling flexibility, you can ensure that tasks dependent on external factors, like data availability, are executed at the right time.

- **Trigger-Based Execution:** Databricks allow you to trigger the execution of tasks based on specific events or conditions. For example, you can set up a trigger to initiate a data processing job when new data is ingested into a storage location, ensuring that your pipeline responds dynamically to changing data.
- **Error Handling:** While managing dependencies, it's crucial to consider error scenarios. Databricks provide mechanisms for error detection and handling. You can set up alerts and notifications to be informed of any task failures. Additionally, you can configure automated retries for robust error recovery.
- **Workflow Testing:** Before deploying complex workflows into production, it's advisable to conduct thorough testing. Databricks facilitates testing by allowing you to create test clusters, ensuring that your dependencies and workflows function as expected.
- **Monitoring and Logging:** Databricks provides monitoring and logging capabilities to track the progress of your workflows. You can gain insights into task execution times, resource utilization, and error logs, allowing for proactive management of dependencies.
- **External Dependency Management:** In some cases, tasks in your workflow might depend on external systems or data sources. Databricks allows you to manage these dependencies by integrating with external services and APIs, ensuring seamless data exchange.

As you delve into managing dependencies within Databricks workflows, remember that the goal is to create a well-orchestrated data processing pipeline. By employing these techniques, you can ensure that your data processes play in harmony, producing valuable insights and analytics efficiently and precisely.

Scheduling and Orchestrating Data Pipelines Using Databricks Jobs

Scheduling and orchestration form the backbone of efficient data engineering workflows. Databricks provides a robust set of features for scheduling and orchestrating data pipelines. Let's explore the key techniques and best practices in this area:

- **Databricks Job Scheduling:** Databricks Jobs are instrumental in scheduling tasks within your data pipelines. You can create Jobs through the Databricks UI or use the REST API for programmatic scheduling. Jobs allow you to specify when and how often a task should run, making it possible to automate repetitive tasks and ensure timely data processing.

- **Cron-Style Scheduling:** Databricks supports cron-style scheduling, which provides fine-grained control over task execution times. Using cron expressions, you can define schedules down to the minute, hour, day, week, or month. This flexibility is especially useful for handling time-sensitive tasks and ensuring that data processing aligns with business needs.
- **Dependency Management:** Effective orchestration requires careful management of task dependencies. Databricks allows you to define dependencies between tasks, ensuring that they are executed in the correct order. You can specify that a task should only run after the successful completion of its prerequisite tasks, ensuring a smooth workflow.
- **Parameterization:** Databricks Jobs supports parameterization, allowing you to create dynamic and reusable workflows. You can pass parameters to your Jobs, making it easy to customize task behavior without the need for separate Job definitions. This parameterization simplifies workflow maintenance and reduces duplication of effort.
- **Trigger-Based Execution:** In addition to scheduled execution, Databricks supports trigger-based execution. This means tasks can be triggered to run in response to specific events or conditions. For example, you can set up a trigger that initiates data processing when new data is ingested into a storage location, ensuring real-time data processing.
- **Concurrency Control:** Databricks provide concurrency control options to manage the execution of multiple tasks concurrently. You can set concurrency limits to prevent overloading your clusters and ensure optimal resource utilization. This feature is particularly useful in multi-tenant environments.
- **Error Handling and Retries:** When orchestrating data pipelines, it's essential to consider error scenarios. Databricks allows you to configure error handling and automatic retries for tasks. You can set up alerts and notifications to be informed of task failures, enabling timely intervention and error recovery.
- **Workflow Visualization:** Databricks offers visualization tools that allow you to gain insights into your workflow's execution. You can track task progress, execution times, and resource utilization. Visual

representations of your workflows help in identifying bottlenecks and optimizing performance.

- **Monitoring and Logging:** Comprehensive monitoring and logging capabilities in Databricks provide visibility into the execution of your data pipelines. You can access logs, metrics, and job run history to troubleshoot issues, ensure compliance, and track workflow performance over time.
- **Integration with External Systems:** Databricks supports integration with external systems and services, enhancing your orchestration capabilities. You can trigger tasks based on events from external sources or integrate with third-party workflow orchestration tools, ensuring seamless data flow across your ecosystem.

By mastering these scheduling and orchestration techniques within Databricks, you can design and manage data pipelines that operate efficiently, meet business requirements, and adapt to changing data needs. Effective scheduling and orchestration are vital components of a well-structured data engineering ecosystem, ensuring data processes run smoothly and deliver actionable insights.

Best Practices for Handling Complex Workflows and Task Dependencies

Handling complex workflows with numerous task dependencies can be a challenging yet crucial aspect of data orchestration. To ensure smooth and efficient execution, consider these best practices:

- **Workflow Modularity:** Break down complex workflows into modular components or sub-workflows. This modular approach simplifies management, testing, and debugging. Each module can focus on a specific task or set of related tasks, making identifying and resolving issues easier.
- **Dependency Mapping:** Create a clear and comprehensive dependency map for your workflow. Visualize the relationships between tasks and their dependencies. Tools, such as directed acyclic graphs (DAGs), can help illustrate the flow of data and ensure that tasks are executed in the correct order.
- **Error Handling Strategies:** Develop robust error handling strategies. Define how the workflow should respond to task failures. You can implement actions such as retries, sending notifications, or triggering alternative paths within the workflow. Effective error handling reduces the risk of data pipeline failures.

- **Parameterization:** Parameterize your workflows to make them more adaptable. Instead of hardcoding values, use parameters that allow you to configure task behavior dynamically. Parameterization simplifies workflow customization and reduces the need for creating multiple similar workflows.
- **Testing and Validation:** Prioritize testing and validation at various stages of workflow development. Test individual tasks, sub-workflows, and the complete workflow to identify and address issues early. Use test data that represents real-world scenarios to validate the workflow's behavior.
- **Documentation:** Maintain thorough documentation for your workflows. Document the purpose of each task, its input and output data, dependencies, and any specific configurations. Well-documented workflows are easier to understand, maintain, and troubleshoot.
- **Version Control:** Implement version control for your workflows. Use a version control system (VCS) like Git to track changes and revisions. Version control ensures that you can roll back to previous versions if issues arise and help in collaborative development.
- **Monitoring and Alerting:** Set up robust monitoring and alerting mechanisms. Continuously monitor workflow execution, task statuses, and resource utilization. Configure alerts to notify you of any anomalies or deviations from expected behavior. Proactive monitoring minimizes downtime and ensures timely intervention.
- **Scalability Planning:** Consider scalability from the beginning. Anticipate future data growth and workload increases. Design workflows to scale horizontally or vertically as needed. Ensure that your orchestration system can handle higher volumes of data and tasks without performance degradation.

Following these best practices, you can effectively manage complex workflows and task dependencies within Databricks. These strategies promote workflow reliability, maintainability, and scalability, ensuring your data engineering processes operate seamlessly, even in intricate scenarios.

Monitoring and Error Handling in Workflow Execution

In the realm of data orchestration and workflow management, effective monitoring and error handling are like the vigilant guardians of your data processes. This section will delve into the critical aspects of ensuring your orchestrated workflows run smoothly, detect and address issues promptly, and maintain the integrity of your data operations.

Monitoring encompasses continuously surveilling your workflows, task statuses, and resource utilization. It's about keeping a watchful eye on the health of your data pipelines in Databricks. With proper monitoring, you gain insights into the performance and behavior of your workflows, allowing you to identify bottlenecks, anomalies, and opportunities for optimization.

On the flip side, error handling is your safety net against unexpected hiccups in the execution of tasks or workflows. It involves defining how your workflow should react when things are unplanned. Robust error-handling strategies can include automatic retries, alert notifications, or alternative pathways within the workflow. These mechanisms ensure that even when errors occur, your data processes can recover gracefully and continue their operations, preventing costly downtime and data loss.

This section will guide you through the strategies and techniques for efficient workflow monitoring, error detection, and handling within Databricks. From setting up monitoring systems to configuring alerting mechanisms and implementing error-handling workflows, you'll gain the knowledge and skills needed to maintain the reliability and resilience of your data orchestration efforts. Let us explore the tools and practices that will help you keep your data workflows on track.

Strategies for Monitoring Workflow Execution

Effective monitoring of workflow execution is essential for maintaining the health and performance of your data pipelines. In Databricks, you can access various tools and techniques to closely monitor how your orchestrated tasks and workflows are progressing. Here, we'll explore the strategies and best practices for monitoring workflow execution in Databricks.

- **Logging and Metrics:** Implement comprehensive logging and metric collection within your Databricks workflows. Logging allows you to capture important events, errors, and performance indicators. Metrics provide quantitative data on resource utilization, execution times, and task statuses. Tools like Databricks Unified Logging and Apache Spark

metrics can be invaluable.
- **Dashboarding and Visualization:** Leverage Databricks' built-in capabilities for dashboarding and data visualization. Services like Databricks Workspace enable you to create custom dashboards that display real-time metrics and execution statuses. Visualization tools help you quickly identify trends, anomalies, or areas needing optimization.
- **Alerting and Notifications:** Implement alerting mechanisms to receive timely notifications when issues arise. Databricks allows you to set up alerts based on predefined thresholds or conditions. You can configure notifications via email, SMS, or integration with collaboration tools like Slack. Timely alerts empower you to respond swiftly to potential problems.
- **Resource Monitoring:** Keep monitoring resource utilization closely to prevent bottlenecks or overloads. Databricks provides resource monitoring features to track CPU, memory, and storage usage. Monitoring these metrics allows you to proactively allocate resources where needed and ensure efficient workflow execution.
- **Custom Monitoring Scripts:** Consider developing custom scripts or using third-party monitoring solutions for more advanced monitoring needs. Databricks supports the execution of custom scripts within workflows, allowing you to integrate with external monitoring systems or perform specialized checks tailored to your requirements.
- **Logging for Troubleshooting:** Effective monitoring isn't just about real-time insights; it's also about providing a historical record for troubleshooting. Ensure that your logging captures sufficient detail for post-mortem analysis. This historical data can be invaluable when investigating past issues or optimizing workflows.

By applying these monitoring strategies in Databricks, you can maintain visibility into your workflow execution, promptly detect anomalies, and take proactive measures to ensure the reliability and efficiency of your data orchestration processes. Monitoring is not just about observing; it's about empowering you to take control of your data workflows and keep them running smoothly.

Implementing Logging and Alerting Mechanisms for Error Detection

In any data engineering workflow, especially when dealing with large volumes of data, it's crucial to have a robust system in place for detecting and handling errors. Error detection mechanisms help identify issues promptly and enable you to take corrective actions. This section will explore the strategies for implementing logging and alerting mechanisms in Databricks to enhance error detection and response.

- **Comprehensive Logging:** Logging is your first line of defense against errors. Implement logging at critical junctures in your workflows, such as data extraction, transformation, and loading stages. Databricks provides built-in logging functionality, allowing you to capture detailed information about each step's execution, including input data, transformations applied, and output results.
- **Error Handling Framework:** Develop an error handling framework defining how different errors should be handled. Categorize errors based on severity and establish predefined actions for each category. For example, minor data validation errors might trigger automatic retries, while critical pipeline failures might necessitate immediate notifications to the data engineering team.
- **Alerting Rules:** Create alerting rules based on predefined error scenarios. Databricks allows you to configure alerting rules that trigger notifications when specific errors occur. For instance, you can set up alerts for data ingestion failures, data quality issues, or workflow execution timeouts. These rules ensure that the right individuals or teams are promptly informed of errors.
- **Integration with Collaboration Tools:** Integrate your alerting system with collaboration tools like Slack or Microsoft Teams. This streamlines communication when an error is detected. Notifications are sent directly to relevant channels, enabling cross-functional teams to collaborate on issue resolution.
- **Automatic Error Recovery:** Design your workflows to include automatic error recovery mechanisms whenever possible. For example, if a data extraction job fails, consider implementing retry logic to reattempt the extraction after a brief delay. This can significantly reduce the impact of transient failures.
- **Logging Enrichment:** Enrich your logs with contextual information. Include timestamps, job IDs, and data lineage details in log entries. This contextual information simplifies troubleshooting by providing a clear picture of the workflow's execution path.
- **Testing and Simulation:** Regularly test error scenarios and responses in a

controlled environment. Databricks allows you to simulate errors during workflow development and testing. This proactive approach helps you fine-tune error detection and response mechanisms.
- **Documentation and Runbooks:** Maintain documentation that outlines common error scenarios and their resolution steps. Create runbooks to guide data engineers through the troubleshooting and resolution process. Clear documentation ensures consistent error-handling practices across your team.

Implementing these logging and alerting mechanisms in Databricks can enhance your workflow's resilience to errors. Early detection and efficient error response minimize downtime and contribute to the overall reliability and robustness of your data orchestration processes.

Techniques for Handling Workflow Failures and Retries

Handling workflow failures and implementing effective retry strategies is a critical aspect of data orchestration and workflow management in Databricks. Failures can occur due to various reasons, including infrastructure issues, data source unavailability, or transient errors. In this section, we'll delve into techniques for gracefully handling workflow failures and designing robust retry mechanisms.

- **Error Classification:** Begin by categorizing errors based on their nature and impact. Common categories include transient errors (temporary issues that may resolve on retry), data-related errors (for example, schema mismatches), and infrastructure failures. By classifying errors, you can tailor your retry strategies accordingly.
- **Retry Policies:** Define retry policies for different error categories. For transient errors, consider implementing exponential back-off strategies. This means that if a task fails, the system waits for a short duration before retrying, gradually increasing the wait time between retries. This approach helps avoid overloading resources during temporary downtimes.
- **Max Retries and Timeouts:** Establish maximum retry limits for tasks to prevent endless retry loops in the event of persistent issues. Additionally, set timeouts for each task to limit the time spent on retries. If a task consistently fails, it's essential to mark it for manual intervention rather

than continuously retrying.

- **Failure Handling Hooks:** Implement failure handling hooks that execute custom logic when a task fails. Depending on the error type, you can trigger actions such as notifying the data engineering team, capturing additional diagnostic information, or automatically adjusting data ingestion rates.
- **Stateful Retry:** In scenarios where maintaining state is critical, employ stateful retry mechanisms. This means recording the execution state of a failed task before retrying it. Stateful retry ensures that the task resumes from the point of failure, preventing data inconsistencies.
- **Monitoring and Alerting:** Continuously monitor workflow execution and track the number and types of retries. Set up alerts to notify relevant teams when tasks repeatedly fail or when retry counts exceed predefined thresholds. This proactive monitoring allows for quick responses to persistent issues.
- **Dead Letter Queues:** Implement dead letter queues (DLQs) for tasks that repeatedly fail. DLQs capture failed task inputs and metadata, allowing for in-depth analysis and debugging. DLQs also prevent data loss by preserving failed task data for later examination.
- **Incremental Backfill:** In cases where retrying an entire workflow is not feasible, consider incremental backfill strategies. Identify the point of failure and design workflows to rerun only the affected tasks and their downstream dependencies.
- **Documentation and Incident Response:** Maintain detailed documentation of error handling and incident response procedures. Create incident response runbooks that outline steps for diagnosing, resolving, and documenting issues. This documentation ensures consistency in handling failures.
- **Post-Mortem Analysis:** Conduct post-mortem analyses to identify root causes and preventive measures after resolving a workflow failure. Use this information to improve error handling and prevent similar issues in the future.

Handling workflow failures and retries is critical to ensuring the reliability and robustness of data orchestration in Databricks. By implementing these techniques, you can minimize disruptions, enhance system resilience, and maintain data pipeline integrity.

Utilizing Databricks Monitoring and Debugging Tools for Workflow Optimization

Effective monitoring and debugging are indispensable for maintaining the health and performance of data orchestration workflows in Databricks. Databricks provides tools and features designed to simplify these tasks and optimize workflow execution. This section explores how to leverage Databricks monitoring and debugging capabilities for workflow optimization.

- **Databricks Monitoring Console:** The Databricks Monitoring Console offers a centralized dashboard for tracking the execution of jobs, clusters, and notebooks. It provides real-time insights into the performance of running workflows, allowing you to monitor resource utilization, identify bottlenecks, and detect anomalies.
- **Cluster Logs and Metrics:** Dive into cluster-specific logs and metrics to better understand cluster behavior. These logs provide information about cluster initialization, resource allocation, and task execution. By analyzing cluster logs, you can fine-tune cluster configurations to align with workflow requirements.
- **Notebook Execution Insights**: For workflows implemented using notebooks, Databricks offers execution insights. You can review execution details, code execution order, and the duration of each code cell's execution. This feature helps identify long-running code segments and optimize notebook performance.
- **Structured Streaming Metrics:** If your workflows involve real-time data processing using structured streaming, Databricks provides metrics for monitoring stream progress, input rates, and processing times. Monitoring structured streaming metrics is crucial for identifying bottlenecks and ensuring timely data processing.
- **Alerting and Notifications:** Set up custom alerts and notifications based on predefined thresholds or anomalies detected during workflow execution. Databricks can notify relevant teams or individuals via email, messaging platforms, or integration with external alerting systems.
- **Debugging with Visualizations:** Leverage Databricks' interactive debugging capabilities, which include data visualizations and debugging notebooks. These tools help you identify data quality issues, anomalies,

or logic errors in your workflows.
- **Job Cloning and Reproduction**: Databricks allows you to clone and reproduce jobs and notebooks easily. This feature is valuable for replicating and testing workflows, especially when diagnosing and resolving complex issues.
- **Logging and Auditing**: Implement comprehensive logging practices within your workflows. Databricks provides logging capabilities that allow you to capture detailed execution logs, audit changes, and monitor user activities for compliance and security.
- **Integration with Third-Party Tools**: Databricks seamlessly integrates with third-party monitoring and observability tools. Consider leveraging these integrations to gain additional insights into workflow performance and resource utilization.
- **Workflow Optimization Iteration**: Use the insights gained from monitoring and debugging to iteratively optimize your workflows. Continuously review and refine code, cluster configurations, and resource allocations to enhance performance and reliability.
- **Collaborative Debugging**: Foster collaboration within your data engineering team by sharing debugging insights and findings. Databricks notebooks support collaborative editing and commenting, making it easier to collectively debug and improve workflows.

By effectively utilizing Databricks' monitoring and debugging tools, data engineers can proactively identify and address issues, optimize workflows for efficiency, and ensure the reliable execution of data orchestration tasks. These capabilities play a pivotal role in maintaining data pipeline integrity and achieving optimal performance.

Conclusion

In this chapter, we explored the key components and principles that underpin the effective automation of data workflows, from the essential concept of workflow automation to the intricate details of managing dependencies, scheduling, monitoring, and error handling.

We began by recognizing the paramount importance of workflow automation in modern data engineering. We delved into techniques for managing these dependencies, often the lifeline of complex data workflows. We learned how Databricks Jobs offers scheduling capabilities and orchestration features to streamline data pipeline execution.

To ensure the robustness and reliability of data orchestration, we examined strategies for monitoring and handling errors in workflow execution. The art of debugging was also a significant facet of our exploration, with Databricks' interactive debugging tools and visualization capabilities providing valuable support

Lastly, we highlighted the iterative nature of workflow optimization, reinforcing the idea that continuous improvement is the hallmark of effective data orchestration. As we conclude this chapter, we have equipped ourselves with the knowledge and tools to navigate the intricate landscape of data orchestration and workflow management.

In the next chapter, we will dive deep into the performance optimization section, a mandated feature for a robust pipeline in production.

Key Terms

- **Workflow Automation:** The process of designing, scheduling, and executing a series of data-related tasks and processes in an automated manner to streamline data engineering operations.
- **Databricks Jobs:** Databricks Jobs are a feature that allows you to schedule notebooks or Spark jobs to run at specified intervals or in response to triggers.
- **Dependency Management:** In workflow management, interdependencies between tasks and processes are managed to ensure they are executed correctly.
- **Scheduling:** Setting up a predefined timetable or schedule for running data-related tasks and processes.
- **Orchestration:** Coordinating and managing various data-related tasks, processes, and workflows to achieve a specific goal efficiently.
- **Alerting:** The process of setting up notifications or alerts to inform stakeholders of specific events or issues, such as workflow failures.
- **Cluster Logs:** Logs generated by Databricks clusters can provide valuable insights into cluster performance, errors, and debugging.
- **Reproduction:** In the context of workflow management, creating copies or replicas of workflows to ensure they can be recreated if needed.

- **Compliance:** Adherence to regulatory and industry standards and best practices in data handling, storage, and processing.
- **Metrics:** Measurable data points used to monitor and assess the performance and efficiency of workflows, such as execution times, resource utilization, and error rates.

CHAPTER 8
Performance Tuning and Optimization

"The essence of performance tuning is not about making things run faster, but making them run just right."

– Adapted from Alan Kay

Introduction

While Databricks provides many functionalities out of the box, leveraging its maximum potential requires a deep understanding of its performance tuning and optimization techniques. This chapter delves into that critical domain.

We will start by understanding the essence of performance optimization in data engineering and discussing various techniques and best practices tailored for Databricks. Next, we will dissect how Databricks manages resources in its clusters and understand the art of cluster configuration. In the final section, we will navigate the world of performance bottlenecks - identifying, analyzing, and mitigating these bottlenecks are skills every Databricks enthusiast should master.

Structure

In this chapter, the following topics will be covered:
- Techniques for Optimizing Databricks Performance
- Resource Management and Cluster Optimization
- Identifying and Resolving Performance Bottlenecks

Techniques for Optimizing Databricks Performance

Performance optimization is not just a technical requirement; it's a vital pillar that underpins the success of any data engineering endeavor. As data volume, variety, and velocity grow, the need for optimized data processing pipelines becomes more pronounced. Before diving into the specifics, let's enumerate the top reasons underscoring the importance of performance optimization in data engineering:

- **Enhanced Data Processing Speed:** In today's fast-paced digital environment, businesses can't afford delays. Optimizing performance ensures that data pipelines can handle large datasets without lag, providing outputs at the speed of business needs. This acceleration is critical, especially for industries like finance or healthcare, where real-time data processing can make a significant difference.

- **Cost Efficiency:** Performance optimization impacts the bottom line beyond the evident time savings. Businesses can save substantially on infrastructure and operational costs by streamlining operations and reducing the need for additional resources or extended processing times.

- **Improved Resource Utilization:** Every data engineering platform, Databricks included, operates within the confines of available resources. Optimized processes ensure that memory, CPU, or storage resources are used judiciously. This prevents resource wastage and ensures that the system remains responsive and agile.

- **Ensuring Timely Data Insights:** In the age of data-driven decision-making, delays in data processing can lead to missed opportunities. Whether it's a retailer adjusting prices in real time based on demand or a manufacturer tweaking production based on supply chain data, timely insights can be a game-changer. Performance optimization ensures that these insights are delivered promptly.

- **Higher User Satisfaction:** For end-users, whether they are data scientists running queries or business analysts accessing reports, efficiency is key. Performance optimization translates to reduced wait times, faster query executions, and a smoother overall user experience. This boosts user satisfaction and increases trust in the system's capabilities.
- **Future-Proofing Systems:** As businesses grow and evolve, so do their data needs. An optimized system today is better prepared to handle the challenges of tomorrow. Whether scaling to accommodate more data or adapting to new data types and sources, performance-optimized systems have the agility to evolve as requirements change.

In conclusion, performance optimization in data engineering isn't just about speed or efficiency; it's about ensuring data operations align with current and future business goals. It's a critical component in the data engineering toolkit, driving value across multiple facets of an organization efficiently.

Overview of Key Performance Optimization Techniques in Databricks

Databricks, built upon the robust foundation of Apache Spark, offers many features designed to optimize performance. For anyone looking to elevate their Databricks experience, it's imperative to be familiar with these techniques. Here's an overview of some of the fundamental performance optimization techniques specific to Databricks:

- **Data Partitioning:** One of the most impactful techniques is data partitioning, which involves dividing your dataset into smaller, more manageable chunks. By doing so, when a query is run, Databricks can scan only the relevant partitions, thus speeding up the process. This is especially beneficial for large datasets where scanning the entire dataset can be time-consuming.
- **Caching and Data Skipping:** Databricks offers a feature called Delta Cache that allows frequently accessed data to be stored in memory. This reduces the need to read data from storage repeatedly. Alongside caching, data skipping is another technique where Databricks avoids scanning irrelevant data blocks. These two combined can drastically reduce query times.
- **Optimized Data Shuffling:** Data shuffling is the process of redistributing data across the partitions. While this is sometimes necessary, it can also be resource-intensive. Databricks offers optimizations like the

Z-Ordering of data and adaptive query execution, which minimize the need for shuffling and ensure that it's as efficient as possible when it's done.

- **Data Serialization:** Serialization, the process of converting data into a format that can be easily stored or transmitted, plays a vital role in distributed data processing. Databricks supports efficient serialization formats like Parquet, compressing data and ensuring faster read/write operations.
- **Adaptive Query Execution (AQE):** AQE is a feature in Databricks that allows the engine to adjust query plans on the fly based on real-time statistics from the data. This dynamic adjustment can lead to more efficient query execution, especially when the data distribution differs from initial estimates.
- **Cluster Configuration:** While not a direct data processing technique, correctly configuring your Databricks cluster is paramount. Selecting the right type and number of nodes, determining the right auto-scaling settings, and other cluster configurations can directly impact how efficiently tasks are executed.

Incorporating these techniques into your Databricks workflows can bring about substantial performance improvements. It's worth noting that the effectiveness of each technique can vary based on specific use cases and datasets. Therefore, a thorough understanding and occasional experimentation are recommended to determine the best combination of techniques for any given scenario. As Databricks continues to evolve, staying updated with the latest optimization features will ensure you're always leveraging its full potential.

Utilizing Caching and Data Skipping for Faster Query Execution

Databricks, with its Delta Engine, provides advanced capabilities for caching and data skipping, enabling significantly faster query executions. These optimizations are particularly crucial for dynamic business environments, where timely insights can differentiate between opportunities seized and missed. Let's dive deep into the practical applications and benefits of these techniques:

Understanding Delta Cache:
- **What it is**: Delta Cache is an in-memory caching layer that stores parquet data for rapid access. When a user runs a query, Delta Cache checks if

the relevant data is available in the cache before accessing the underlying storage.
- **Use Case**: Consider a scenario where a data analyst frequently runs queries on the latest month's sales data. Instead of repeatedly reading this data from disk, which can be slow, Databricks with Delta Cache keeps the most accessed data in memory for quicker retrievals.

Benefits of Data Skipping:
- **What it is:** Data skipping is an intelligent way to bypass unnecessary data. When data is written to Databricks, statistics about the data (like min/max values) are also stored. Using these statistics, queries can avoid scanning irrelevant data blocks.
- **Use Case:** Let's say you're querying for sales records above a certain threshold. With data skipping, Databricks can bypass data files where the maximum sales value is below your query's threshold, resulting in faster query execution.

Combining Caching and Data Skipping:
- **Synergistic Effect**: Caching and data skipping can dramatically accelerate query performance when used together. Data skipping narrows down the dataset, and caching ensures rapid data retrieval.
- **Use Case**: A retailer analyzing Black Friday sales might run several ad-hoc queries on the same dataset throughout the day. By leveraging caching and data skipping, the retailer can quickly get insights without heavily taxing the system.

Databricks' Auto Caching:
- **What it is:** Databricks has an auto-caching feature that automatically caches frequently accessed datasets. This ensures optimal performance without manual intervention.
- **Use Case:** In an organization where multiple departments access a common dataset, such as a customer database, Databricks can recognize the frequent access patterns and auto-cache the dataset for faster future queries.

Practical Tips:
- **Manual Cache Management:** While Delta Cache is efficient, there might be instances where you would want to proactively cache specific datasets. Databricks allows you to manually cache data using the **CACHE TABLE** command.

- **Cache Monitoring:** Monitoring cache usage is crucial to ensure efficiency. If the cache becomes too full, it may evict some datasets. Using Databricks' built-in monitoring tools can help manage and optimize cache usage.
- **Understanding Data Patterns:** The more you understand the access patterns of your datasets, the better you can optimize caching and data skipping. Analyzing query logs and understanding peak usage times can provide insights.

In conclusion, caching and data skipping are theoretical concepts and practical tools in Databricks that can offer tangible performance improvements. By understanding their mechanisms and knowing when to use them, data professionals can ensure that their Databricks environment remains agile, responsive, and efficient.

Practical Use Case: E-commerce Sales Analysis

Imagine an e-commerce company with a large dataset containing sales records for the past five years. The company frequently analyses sales data from the past 30 days to adjust its marketing strategies. The dataset is updated daily with new sales records.

Running queries on the entire dataset to extract a month's worth of data can be slow and resource-intensive, especially given the vastness of the dataset. Here is the solution with Caching and Data Skipping:

Caching

The company decided to cache the most recent sales data to speed up queries on the latest month:

```sql
-- Caching the last month's data
CREATE OR REPLACE TEMPORARI VIEW recent_sales AS
SELECT * FROM sales WHERE sale_date > current_date() - 30;
CACHE TABLE recent_sales;
```

Figure 8.1: Data Caching

When analysts query the `recent_sales` view, the data is fetched from the cache, resulting in faster query execution.

Data Skipping

The company's sales dataset has been saved in the Delta format, which inherently supports data skipping. When the dataset was written, min/max statistics for the `sale_date` column were saved. When querying for a specific date range, Databricks will skip files where the date range doesn't match the min/max statistics.

As a result of these optimizations:
- Queries on recent sales data are significantly faster, allowing real-time insights.
- The system is less taxed, as unnecessary data reads are minimized, leading to cost savings and better resource utilization.

Monitoring

The company monitors cache usage to ensure the cache doesn't become overloaded:

```
-- Monitoring cache usage
DESCRIBE DETAIL recent_sales;
```

Figure 8.2: Describing Table

The DESCRIBE DETAIL command provides information about cache usage and can be used to decide if data needs to be uncached or if other datasets should be cached.

In conclusion, combining caching and data skipping helped the e-commerce company achieve near real-time performance for its most frequent and critical analyses. The marketing team could adapt their strategies swiftly, responding to recent trends, leading to better-targeted campaigns and increased sales.

This use case exemplifies the tangible benefits of caching and data skipping in Databricks and showcases how simple commands can lead to significant performance improvements.

Techniques for Optimizing Data Shuffling and Data Serialization

Data shuffling and serialization are integral processes in distributed data processing. These aspects play pivotal roles, especially in Databricks, which leverage the power of Apache Spark. When managed correctly, they can considerably expedite the processing of large datasets. Conversely, if not handled well, they can become performance bottlenecks. Let's delve into ways to optimize these aspects in Databricks:

Understanding Data Shuffling:
- **What it is:** Data shuffling refers to the process of redistributing data across the partitions of a Spark cluster. It occurs during operations that require data reorganization, such as **groupBy**, join, or repartition.
- **Impact:** Excessive shuffling can lead to data being transferred across nodes in the cluster, leading to network overhead and slower processing times.

Minimizing Shuffling:
- **Salting Technique:** For operations like joins where one table has skewed data (few keys with exceptionally high values), we can use salting. This involves adding a random number (or salt) to the key and distributing its rows more evenly across partitions.
- **Using Broadcast Joins:** Using broadcast joins when joining a large data frame with a much smaller one. It sends the smaller data frame to all worker nodes, eliminating the need to shuffle the larger data frame.

```
from pyspark.sql.functions import broadcast
result = largeDF.join(broadcast(smallDF), on="common_column")
```

Figure 8.3: Broadcast Join

Optimizing Serialization:
- **What it is:** Serialization converts an object into a byte stream, facilitating storage or transmission. In Spark, this is important when data or tasks are sent across nodes.
- **Use Kryo Serialization:** Spark's default Java serialization can be slow and bulky. Switching to Kryo serialization can lead to better performance and a more compact format. In Databricks, you can set this via the Spark configuration:

```
spark.conf.set("spark.serializer", "org.apache.spark.serializer.KryoSerializer")
```

Figure 8.4: Kryo Serialization

Tuning Shuffle Partitions:
- **Default Partitions:** By default, Spark creates 200 shuffle partitions. While this may be fine for smaller datasets, it could lead to too many small partitions for larger ones.
- **Adjusting Partitions:** Base the number of partitions on the dataset's size and the cluster's resources. You can set the number using:

```
spark.conf.set("spark.sql.shuffle.partitions", "desired_number_of_partitions")
```

Figure 8.5: *Adjusting Partitions*

Monitoring and Diagnosing Shuffling Issues:
- **Spark UI:** Databricks integrates with Spark UI, an invaluable tool for monitoring shuffling and serialization metrics. Regularly checking the Stage tab can help identify stages with excessive data shuffling.
- **Avoid Repartitioning Unless Necessary:** While repartitioning can help balance out skewed data, unnecessary repartitioning can lead to increased shuffling. Only repartition when you have a clear understanding of the data's distribution.

In conclusion, data shuffling and serialization are essential processes in distributed computing that, when optimized, can lead to notable improvements in performance. With the aforementioned techniques, Databricks users can ensure efficient data processing, even with vast datasets.

Resource Management and Cluster Optimization

In the world of distributed computing, the effective utilization and management of resources are critical. This is especially true in Databricks, an environment that thrives on efficiently balancing computational demands. Resource management is not just about having vast resources at your disposal; it's about how adeptly you allocate and utilize them based on the tasks. When handled precisely, it ensures that every computation, no matter how complex or data-intensive, is executed seamlessly.

A closely related aspect is cluster optimization. Databricks clusters, the heart of its processing capability, must be tailored according to the nature of the workload. This involves choosing the cluster's right type, size, and configuration. Imagine wearing shoes - the right fit ensures comfort and agility, while an ill fit can hinder movement. Similarly, a well-configured cluster boosts performance, while a poorly set one can slow down processes and escalate costs.

Furthermore, it's not just about setting up the cluster. We also delve into strategies for its continuous optimization. How do we ensure that a cluster, once set, remains efficient in the face of evolving workloads? The key lies in dynamically scaling and adapting based on demand, ensuring optimal utilization without wasting resources. Techniques like auto-scaling come into play, automatically adjusting resources based on the workload's needs. Alongside this, we will explore the concept of workload isolation, a method to ensure tasks do not interfere with each other, leading to a harmonious and efficient computational environment.

As we traverse this section, we'll equip you with insights and tools to master resource management and cluster optimization in Databricks, setting the foundation for superior performance and streamlined operations.

Understanding Resource Management in Databricks Clusters

Databricks, built atop Apache Spark, inherently harnesses the power and challenges of distributed computing. One of the primary challenges in such an environment is effective resource management. Let's delve into the nuances of how Databricks manages its resources:

- **Distributed Nature:** Databricks clusters comprise multiple nodes. Each node has its CPU, memory, and storage. Resource management, in essence, is about effectively allocating tasks to these nodes, ensuring they run efficiently without overwhelming the system or wasting resources.

- **Dynamic Resource Allocation:** Databricks support dynamic resource allocation. This means that based on the workload, it can automatically adjust the number of executors, helping in efficiently using resources and improving cluster performance. For instance, during periods of lighter loads, executors can be reduced to save costs, and during intense workloads, they can be increased for better performance.

- **Executor Memory and Cores:** Some executors carry out tasks within each node. Configuring the memory and cores for these executors is crucial.

Too little memory can lead to frequent garbage collection slowing down processes, while too much can lead to wasted resources.

- **Resource Pools:** Databricks allow the creation of resource pools. These are essentially allocations of a cluster's resources to specific tasks or users. Segmenting resources ensures that important tasks get the resources they need, and it prevents one heavy task from hogging all available resources.
- **Resource Overheads:** It's also important to account for overheads. Apart from the memory allocated to executors, there's a small overhead memory for system processes. Ensuring this overhead is correctly configured prevents out-of-memory errors.
- **Monitoring and Feedback Loop:** Databricks provides various monitoring tools, like the Spark UI, to gauge how resources are utilized. Regular monitoring helps identify bottlenecks or wastages, and the feedback can be used to fine-tune resource configurations.

Understanding and optimizing resource management is like mastering the mechanics of a well-oiled machine. Every component, from the smallest cog to the largest gear, plays a vital role. In Databricks clusters, ensuring each node, executor, and task gets the resources it requires while maintaining the system's balance is the essence of effective resource management.

Best Practices for Cluster Configuration and Sizing

Configuring and sizing your Databricks cluster is akin to setting up the engine of a race car. The right adjustments can lead to peak performance, while misconfigurations can hinder efficiency and drive up costs. Let's explore some best practices to ensure your Databricks cluster is primed for optimal operation:

- **Understand the Workload:** Before diving into configurations, it's essential to understand the nature of your workload. Is it CPU-intensive, memory-intensive, or IO-bound? This knowledge will guide many of the subsequent configuration decisions.
- **Choose the Right Instance Type:** Databricks supports various cloud-based virtual machine types. Choose an instance that aligns with your workload's requirements, balancing between CPU, memory, and storage.
- **Leverage Spot Instances:** If you want to cut costs without compromising performance, consider using spot instances. They're often cheaper but

can be pre-empted based on demand. Ensure your workload can handle potential interruptions.

- **Dynamic Allocation:** Enable dynamic allocation, which allows Databricks to dynamically add or remove Spark executors based on the workload. This ensures you're not over-provisioning or under-utilizing resources.
- **Set Appropriate Executor Sizes:** Configure the executor memory and cores based on your task requirements. Avoid the temptation to allocate maximum memory, as this might lead to inefficiencies. Instead, strike a balance based on the dataset size and processing needs.
- **Cluster Autoscaling:** Use Databricks' autoscaling feature, which adjusts the number of nodes in a cluster based on the workload. This ensures optimal performance while keeping costs in check.
- **Limit Shuffle Partitions:** Shuffle operations can be expensive. By default, Spark sets the number of shuffle partitions to 200. Depending on your data volume, consider adjusting this number to optimize performance.
- **Avoid Oversubscription:** Ensure that the total number of cores across all executors does not exceed the total number of cores available in the cluster. Oversubscription can lead to context switching and reduced performance.
- **Optimal Storage Configuration:** Ensure your storage is configured for high throughput and low latency, especially using external storage systems like S3 or Azure Blob Storage. Use techniques like data locality to enhance performance.
- **Regularly Monitor and Adjust:** Cluster needs can change over time as workloads evolve. Regularly monitor performance metrics and be prepared to adjust configurations based on observed bottlenecks or inefficiencies.

In essence, cluster configuration and sizing in Databricks is both an art and a science. While best practices and guidelines exist, the optimal setup often emerges from understanding workloads, experimentation, and regular monitoring.

Techniques for Optimizing Cluster Utilization and Cost Efficiency

Ensuring the optimal utilization of Databricks clusters leads to enhanced performance and efficient use of financial resources. It's about maximizing output for every dollar spent. Here are some techniques to strike that balance between performance and cost:

- **Terminate Idle Clusters**: One of the simplest ways to optimize cost is to ensure that clusters aren't running when not needed. Databricks provides an auto-termination feature that can automatically shut down clusters after a specified period of inactivity.
- **Use Spot/Preemptible Instances:** These instances are often available at a fraction of the price of on-demand instances. However, they can be terminated if the cloud provider needs them. This can be a cost-effective choice if your workload can tolerate potential interruptions.
- **Opt for Auto-scaling**: Auto-scaling automatically adjusts the number of nodes in your cluster based on the current workload. It helps optimize resources and ensures you do not pay for unused capacity.
- **Implement Workload Prioritization:** If running multiple tasks, prioritize them. Critical jobs can be given more resources, while less important tasks can run with fewer resources or during off-peak times.
- **Consolidate Workloads:** Instead of running multiple smaller clusters, consider consolidating workloads onto fewer, larger clusters. This can lead to better resource utilization and can sometimes be more cost-effective.
- **Optimize Data Storage**: Efficiently storing data can lead to quicker access times and reduced data transfer costs. Techniques like partitioning, data compaction, and columnar formats like Parquet can save costs.
- **Caching Strategically:** Cache frequently accessed data in memory. While this increases memory usage, it can significantly speed up access times, reducing the compute resources needed for repeated operations.
- **Analyze Spend with Cost Management Tools:** Utilize cloud provider-specific cost management tools to analyze and track your spending on Databricks. Insights from these tools can help identify areas of inefficiency.
- **Optimize Job Scheduling:** Schedule jobs strategically, perhaps running non-critical, resource-intensive jobs during off-peak times when compute resources might be cheaper.
- **Review and Clean Old Data and Jobs:** Review stored data and jobs periodically. Clean up old datasets, logs, and job outputs that aren't needed, reducing storage costs.

Mastering cluster utilization and cost efficiency is akin to running a tight ship. It's about ensuring every resource, be it computation or storage, is used judiciously and every expenditure is justified. Blending the right techniques and ongoing monitoring ensures that Databricks clusters are high-performing and cost-effective.

Strategies for Managing Cluster Auto-Scaling and Workload Isolation

Databricks clusters are dynamic entities. Their power lies in the ability to scale based on the moment's needs, ensuring that resources match the demands without wastage. Additionally, isolating workloads becomes crucial in a multi-user or multi-task environment to prevent interference and ensure consistent performance. Let's delve deeper into strategies for managing these two critical aspects:

- **Understanding Auto-Scaling**: At its core, auto-scaling in Databricks adjusts the number of nodes in a cluster based on current workload demands. You can control the scaling range by setting minimum and maximum limits, ensuring that your cluster scales according to predefined boundaries.

- **Reacting to Workload Peaks**: Ensure that your maximum node limit in auto-scaling is set to handle peak loads. This ensures that during sudden spikes in demand, the cluster scales up quickly to accommodate the increased workload without causing performance degradation.

- **Avoid Overprovisioning**: While setting a high maximum limit is tempting, overprovisioning can lead to unnecessary costs. Monitor historical workloads and set a realistic maximum that balances performance needs with cost considerations.

- **Scale-Down Considerations**: Auto-scaling isn't just about scaling up; scaling down when the demand subsides is equally important. Configure the cool-down period wisely so that nodes aren't terminated prematurely, especially if a new surge in workload is anticipated soon.

- **Isolating Workloads with Resource Pools**: Databricks allows you to create resource pools, which are partitions of a cluster's resources. By allocating specific resources to different tasks or users, you ensure that one heavy task doesn't monopolize all available resources.

- **User-Based Isolation:** If multiple users are working on the same cluster, allocate separate resource pools to each user. This ensures that one user's intensive tasks don't hinder another user's performance.
- **Task-Based Isolation:** You can create dedicated resource pools for tasks or jobs, such as ETL operations versus machine learning workloads. This ensures that each task type gets resources optimized for its specific needs.
- **Monitoring and Alerting:** Set up monitoring and alerts for auto-scaling events. Notifying when the cluster scales up or down can provide insights into workload patterns and help fine-tune auto-scaling configurations.
- **Testing Auto-Scaling:** Periodically, it's wise to simulate heavy loads and test how your cluster's auto-scaling responds. This helps identify potential bottlenecks and ensure that scaling happens smoothly during actual demand spikes.
- **Review and Adjust:** As with many configurations in Databricks, auto-scaling and workload isolation settings aren't *set and forget*. Regularly review the performance and adjust based on evolving needs and observed patterns.

By effectively managing auto-scaling and isolating workloads, you can ensure that your Databricks cluster operates like a finely tuned orchestra, with each component playing its part in harmony, delivering optimal performance without stepping on each other's toes.

Identifying and Resolving Performance Bottlenecks

In data processing and analytics, performance bottlenecks can act as unseen adversaries, covertly hindering the potential of your workflows and elongating execution times. These bottlenecks can stem from a myriad of sources - from the way data is ingested to the intricacies of transformation logic or even how resources are allocated within clusters. Identifying and resolving these bottlenecks is akin to a detective's work: you seek clues, diagnose the root causes, and then implement corrective measures to restore efficiency.

In this section, we embark on a journey to uncover the typical performance bottlenecks in Databricks environments and devise strategies to alleviate them. We will begin by exploring techniques to profile performance and methods to pinpoint where slowdowns occur. Once we've identified these potential hurdles, we will delve deeper into the world of query execution plans, a vital tool in understanding the sequence and efficiency of operations, highlighting any potential areas of concern.

Beyond that, we will navigate the intricate realm of complex transformations and joins. As datasets grow and transformations become multifaceted, there's an increased potential for performance degradation. By mastering optimization techniques specific to these scenarios, you can ensure swift data processing even in the most complex tasks. Lastly, the challenge of data skew and skewness will be brought to the fore. Unbalanced data distribution can be a silent performance killer, and recognizing and rectifying such imbalances can result in substantial performance gains.

By the end of this section, you'll be equipped with a comprehensive toolkit of strategies and techniques to ensure your Databricks workflows remain at the pinnacle of efficiency, irrespective of the challenges thrown their way. Let's dive in and demystify the world of performance bottlenecks in Databricks.

Techniques for Performance Profiling and Bottleneck Identification

Performance profiling is the systematic observation and analysis of a system to determine where time and resources are spent, allowing for the identification of bottlenecks. In the context of Databricks, understanding where slowdowns are occurring is pivotal for optimization. Here are some techniques and tools to help you pinpoint these performance roadblocks:

- **Spark UI:** Integral to Apache Spark, the Spark UI provides a visual console to monitor detailed performance metrics of your active Spark applications. Within it, the `'Stages'` tab can offer insights into task durations, allowing you to identify tasks that take disproportionately longer.
- **Event Timeline:** Within Spark UI, the event timeline showcases the start and end of various stages of an operation. A prolonged duration in any of these stages can clearly indicate a bottleneck.
- **SQL Performance Tab:** For SQL-based operations, Databricks provides an SQL Performance tab that offers visualizations of the query execution plan. You can determine which parts of your SQL query consume the most resources and time.

- **Metrics and Logging:** Leverage the logs to discern unusual behavior. Extended periods of garbage collection, for instance, can indicate memory issues. Databricks maintains structured logs that can be analyzed for such anomalies.
- **Data Skew Detection:** Check for uneven data distribution among partitions. If one partition has significantly more data than others, it can lead to some workers doing more work than others, causing delays.
- **Executor Metrics:** Dive deep into executor metrics to analyze the memory usage, disk spills, and task execution details. Overutilization of memory or excessive disk spills can be indicators of resource bottlenecks.
- **Custom `SparkListeners`:** For those comfortable with some coding, you can write custom `SparkListeners` to capture specific events or metrics, providing tailored insights into your application's performance.
- **External Monitoring Tools:** Tools like Grafana or Datadog can be integrated with Databricks. They provide a broader view of performance metrics, encompassing Spark-specific and infrastructure-related metrics.
- **Workload Review:** Sometimes, bottlenecks arise from inefficient code or operations. Periodically reviewing the workload, understanding the transformations being applied, and looking for redundancies can highlight areas of optimization.
- **Feedback Loops:** Regularly solicit feedback from end-users. They can often provide real-world insights into delays and performance issues that might not be immediately visible through metrics.

Identifying bottlenecks is the first and perhaps the most critical step in performance optimization. By leveraging a combination of built-in tools, external integrations, and periodic reviews, you can easily ensure that your Databricks environment runs smoothly, efficiently processing vast datasets and complex transformations.

Analyzing Query Execution Plans and Identifying Performance Hotspots

Query Execution Plans (QEP) offer a visual roadmap to how Spark executes a given query. Understanding and interpreting a QEP can uncover inefficiencies, anomalies, and performance hotspots. Here's how to analyze these plans and identify areas that might need attention:

- **Understanding Physical and Logical Plans:** Spark creates logical and physical plans for a query. While the logical plan represents the abstract intention of the query, the physical plan outlines how Spark will execute it on the cluster. Familiarize yourself with both to understand the translation from intent to action.

- **Spotting Wide vs. Narrow Transformations:** In the QEP, you'll notice wide and narrow dependencies. Wide transformations (like `groupByKey` or `reduceByKey`) can introduce shuffling and, thus, be expensive. Identifying and minimizing these can enhance performance.

- **Shuffle Read and Write Metrics:** Examine the Shuffle Read and Shuffle Write sizes in the QEP. High shuffle data can lead to network and disk IO overheads. If these metrics are high, consider revisiting your transformations to reduce data shuffling.

- **Node Details and Task Descriptions:** Each node in the QEP gives information about a specific operation, like a filter or join. Hovering over or diving into the details of these nodes can provide insights into the data processed and the time taken, helping identify performance hotspots.

- **Tungsten's `WholeStageCodeGen`:** Modern Spark versions use `WholeStageCodeGen` to compile entire stages into single JVM functions, improving efficiency. In the QEP, stages with a filled star symbol indicate they've been code-generated. Ensure that critical stages benefit from this optimization.

- **Join Optimizations:** If your QEP indicates a join operation, analyze its type (Broadcast, Merge, Hash, and more). Broadcast joins are usually faster when one data frame is small enough to be broadcast to all nodes. Spotting unintentional shuffle-based joins can lead to query refinement opportunities.

- **Inefficient Filters:** Filters executed later in the plan might cause more data to be processed earlier. Reordering operations to filter data as early as possible can improve efficiency.

- **Storage and Data Formats:** The QEP also provides insights into the data sources and formats. Leveraging columnar formats like Parquet or Delta can significantly enhance scan speeds.

- **User-Defined Function (UDF) Utilization:** While UDFs offer flexibility, they might not always be optimized for performance. If your QEP involves UDFs, consider their overhead and see if there's a native Spark function that can achieve the same result more efficiently.

- **Caching Strategy:** Based on the QEP, if you notice specific stages often recomputed or computationally expensive, consider caching the results for faster subsequent access.

By regularly analyzing Query Execution Plans and using them as a guide, one can unveil hidden inefficiencies and performance-sapping operations. Tailoring your queries based on insights from the QEP can lead to dramatically faster execution times and a more resource-efficient Databricks environment.

Strategies for Optimizing Complex Transformations and Joins

Complex transformations and joins are commonplace in data engineering, especially when dealing with large datasets from multiple sources. However, without careful management, these operations can become major performance bottlenecks. Here are strategies to optimize these intricate processes in Databricks:

- **Leverage Broadcast Joins:** Consider using broadcast joins when joining a large data frame with a smaller one. You can avoid the costly shuffling associated with standard joins by broadcasting the smaller data frame to all nodes. In Spark, this can be achieved using the **broadcast()** function.
- **Avoid Cartesian Joins:** A Cartesian join (or cross join) pairs every record of the first DataFrame with every record of the second one. It can exponentially increase the amount of data and should be used judiciously. Always ensure that you have proper filtering conditions when performing joins.
- **Repartition Before Joining:** If you know that a join will result in data shuffling, preemptively repartitioning your DataFrames based on the join key can reduce shuffle costs. The **repartition()** method can help distribute data evenly across partitions.
- **Minimize Wide Transformations:** Operations like **groupByKey** cause wide transformations, which can lead to data shuffling. Instead, consider using alternatives like **reduceByKey** that combine data at the partition level first, reducing the data that needs to be shuffled.
- **Leverage the Salting Technique for Skewed Joins:** If one key has a disproportionately large number of values, it can create a skew during joins. By adding a random "*salt*" value to each key and then performing the join, you can distribute the skewed key's values more evenly across partitions.

- **Optimize Data Serialization:** When shuffling data between nodes, the format of serialization matters. Using efficient serialization libraries like Kryo can speed up the data transfer process.
- **Use Appropriate Data Structures:** If transformations involve operations like searching or sorting, appropriate data structures (like a broadcasted hash map for lookups) can improve performance.
- **Limit the Number of Shuffle Partitions:** By default, Spark might create many shuffle partitions. Based on your data size and cluster configuration, consider adjusting the `spark.sql.shuffle.partitions` setting to a more optimal number.
- **Column Pruning:** Always work only with the necessary columns, especially during joins. Dropping unused columns early in the process can save memory and computational overhead.
- **Leverage Databricks' Z-Ordering and Data Skipping**: Particularly with Delta Lake, using features like Z-Ordering (which optimizes the data layout) and data skipping can drastically speed up certain join operations.
- **Test and Iterate:** Given the variability in data distributions and workflows, there's no one-size-fits-all. Regularly benchmark different strategies, analyze performance, and refine your approaches.

By being aware of the intricacies of complex transformations and joins and proactively employing optimization strategies, you can ensure that these operations, while intricate, do not impede performance in your Databricks workflows.

Conclusion

As we delved into *Chapter 8, Performance Tuning and Optimization*, the significance of achieving peak performance extends beyond quick results – it's about cost-efficiency, maximizing resource utility, and ensuring the overall reliability and stability of data operations.

We learned key performance optimization techniques in Databricks, such as caching, data skipping, and careful management of data shuffling and serialization, are essential tools in an engineer's toolkit.

As we journeyed deeper, proper cluster configuration, adaptive scaling, and isolation of workloads emerged as vital strategies. Balancing cost and performance involves ensuring that clusters are appropriately sized, and resources are adeptly managed. Lastly, our focus shifted to identifying and resolving performance bottlenecks – a critical optimization.

In the next chapter, we will learn how to deploy our jobs into production and make our solution scalable.

Key Terms

- **Performance Optimization:** Adjustments and improvements to maximize Databricks system efficiency.
- **Caching:** Storing frequently accessed data to speed up subsequent operations.
- **Data Skipping:** Skipping non-relevant data blocks based on metadata to speed up queries.
- **Data Shuffling:** Redistributing data across Databricks partitions.
- **Resource Management:** Allocating and efficiently using computational resources in Databricks clusters.
- **Cluster Configuration:** Setting up Databricks clusters for optimal performance and resource use.
- **Auto-Scaling:** Dynamically adjusting resource allocation based on real-time Databricks tasks.
- **Performance Profiling:** Analyzing Databricks operations' runtime to identify bottlenecks.
- **Query Execution Plan:** Sequence of operations in Databricks to execute a query, used to spot performance hotspots.
- **Z-Ordering:** An optimization in Delta Lake to collate related data information in the same set of files.

CHAPTER 9
Scalability and Deployment Considerations

"The true test of a system isn't how it behaves during normal operations, but how it handles growth and unpredictability."

— Werner Vogels, CTO of Amazon.com

Introduction

In today's data-driven world, data engineering solutions must be practical and adaptable to the ever-increasing volume, velocity, and variety of data. As organizations embark on their data journey, they inevitably encounter challenges in efficiently scaling their systems and deploying solutions that ensure flexibility and robustness. This chapter, titled *Scalability and Deployment Considerations*, dives deep into ensuring that your Databricks solutions are robust, scalable, and deployable across different cloud environments.

By the end of this chapter, you'll be equipped with the knowledge and insights needed to scale and deploy your Databricks solutions effectively, ensuring they remain resilient, adaptable, and performant in the face of evolving data needs. Let's embark on this enlightening journey together.

Structure

In this chapter, the following topics will be covered:
- Scaling Data Engineering Solutions in Databricks
- Cloud Deployment Options and Considerations
- Handling Data Growth and Future-Proofing Strategies

Scaling Data Engineering Solutions in Databricks

The concept of scalability is pivotal in the world of data engineering. Organizations are constantly inundated with increasing data loads as the data landscape evolves. Addressing this surge without compromising on processing speed or efficiency becomes paramount. Databricks, with its unified analytics platform, offers a robust framework to handle these challenges. This section delves into the intricacies of scaling data engineering solutions within Databricks. We will begin by understanding the foundational importance of scalability in data engineering, followed by exploring techniques to augment data pipelines and processing workflows. Additionally, we will shed light on the specific horizontal and vertical scaling options provided by Databricks, guiding you on how to harness them based on varied requirements. As we navigate this section, you'll gain valuable insights and tools to ensure your Databricks operations scale gracefully with your data growth.

Importance of Scalability in Data Engineering Solutions

Scalability, in data engineering, is not just a technical term but a fundamental requirement. It pertains to a system's ability to effectively grow and manage increased demands. As data continues to be the lifeblood of organizations, understanding the significance of scalability becomes crucial. Let's dive into the key reasons why scalability holds paramount importance in data engineering:

- **Growing Data Volumes**: Every day, organizations generate and receive vast amounts of data, be it from user interactions, business transactions, or IoT devices. A scalable solution ensures that as this data volume grows, the system can handle it without hiccups.

- **Variable Data Velocity**: Data doesn't always arrive at a constant rate. There can be spikes during certain events or times of the day. Scalable data engineering solutions can accommodate these fluctuations, processing data swiftly during high-velocity periods and scaling down during quieter intervals.
- **Ensuring Performance**: As data grows, a lack of scalability may lead to potential degradation in system performance. A scalable system maintains consistent performance, irrespective of the data load, ensuring timely insights and actions.
- **Cost-Effective Growth**: Scalability isn't just about managing more data; it's about doing so efficiently. Properly scaled solutions optimize resource usage, ensuring that organizations only use and pay for needed resources, leading to cost-effective growth.
- **Future-Proofing Solutions**: Data trends and technologies are ever-evolving. Scalable solutions provide a cushion against unforeseen future requirements, ensuring that the system can adapt without exhaustive overhauls as new data sources emerge or data structures change.
- **Meeting Service Level Agreements (SLAs)**: Many organizations have SLAs that dictate specific performance and uptime requirements. Scalability ensures that these SLAs are consistently met, even as data loads increase, safeguarding business continuity and trust.
- **Flexibility and Adaptability**: Scalable systems offer the flexibility to adapt to different data processing needs. Whether it's batch processing large datasets or real-time streaming analytics, scalable solutions can switch gears as needed.

In essence, scalability in data engineering bridges burgeoning data and the consistent, efficient processing. Ensuring scalability means ensuring that the valuable insights derived from data are timely, accurate, and actionable, irrespective of the data's volume or velocity.

Techniques for Scaling Data Pipelines and Processing Workflows

In the dynamic ecosystem of data engineering, merely recognizing scalability's importance is insufficient. It's vital also to understand and implement techniques that allow data pipelines and processing workflows to scale effectively. Here, we'll explore some of the paramount techniques leveraged to achieve this within the Databricks environment:

- **Distributed Processing:** One of the core strengths of Databricks is its ability to distribute data processing tasks across multiple nodes. By splitting large datasets into smaller chunks and processing them in parallel, Databricks harnesses the power of distributed computing to expedite tasks and handle massive data volumes.
- **Elasticity:** Databricks offers the ability to automatically add or remove resources based on the workload. This elasticity ensures that you're not over-provisioning resources during periods of low activity or under-provisioning during peak times, optimizing costs and performance.
- **Optimized Data Formats:** Leveraging data storage formats like Delta Lake or Parquet, which are columnar and support efficient compression, can significantly improve processing speed. These formats are designed to work seamlessly with Databricks, enhancing query performance.
- **Pipeline Parallelism:** Instead of executing tasks sequentially, Databricks supports pipeline parallelism where multiple tasks are run concurrently. This not only speeds up processing but also ensures better resource utilization.
- **Auto-scaling:** This feature in Databricks automatically adjusts the number of nodes in a cluster based on the workload. As data loads or processing requirements surge, the cluster scales out, and as they diminish, it scales in, ensuring optimal resource usage.
- **Caching:** Frequently accessed data can be cached in memory to avoid redundant read operations from disk. Databricks' in-memory caching capabilities, combined with the power of Spark, make iterative operations and frequent data access exponentially faster.
- **Workflow Optimization:** Beyond technical scaling, periodically reviewing and optimizing the workflow logic, removing redundancies, and employing best practices can have a substantial impact on scaling capabilities.

By implementing these techniques, data engineers can ensure that their pipelines and workflows within Databricks meet current data processing requirements and are poised to handle future growth seamlessly.

Horizontal and Vertical Scaling Options in Databricks

In the context of scalability, the terms horizontal and vertical often surface. These two approaches provide distinct paths to augmenting the capacity of systems, and understanding their nuances is crucial, especially within a platform as versatile as Databricks. Here, we'll delve into both these options as available in Databricks.

Horizontal Scaling (Scale-Out)

Horizontal scaling involves adding more nodes to the system, essentially growing the system outwards. It's akin to adding more lanes to a highway to handle increased traffic.

Databricks Application: Databricks clusters are inherently designed to support horizontal scaling. As data processing needs amplify, Databricks can dynamically add more worker nodes to a cluster.

Advantages of Horizontal Scaling:
- **Elasticity:** Easily scales with workload demands. You can start small and expand as your needs grow.
- **Cost-Efficiency:** Since nodes can be added or removed based on demand, you pay only for what you use.
- **Distributed Processing:** Allows for effective parallel processing, as tasks are distributed across multiple nodes.
- **Considerations:** It's essential to ensure that data is effectively partitioned and distributed across nodes to prevent data locality issues and ensure balanced workloads.

Vertical Scaling (Scale-Up)

Vertical scaling means increasing the resources of an existing node, similar to adding more memory or CPU. Think of it as upgrading a car's engine for better speed rather than adding more cars to the road.

Databricks Application: In Databricks, vertical scaling can be achieved by selecting larger Virtual Machine (VM) types with more memory and CPU for driver and worker nodes.

Advantages of Vertical Scaling:

- **Immediate Performance Boost**: Increasing resources can offer an instant performance uplift for specific tasks.
- **Simplicity:** Generally, scaling up is simpler as it involves adjusting the resources of existing nodes rather than adding new nodes.

Considerations:

- **Hardware Limits:** There's an upper limit to how much you can scale up based on available hardware specifications.
- **Potential Cost Surge:** Scaling up might lead to higher costs, especially if larger VM types are employed continuously, even during low workloads.

Strategic Scaling in Databricks

While horizontal and vertical scaling have their merits, a strategic combination often yields the best results in Databricks. Data engineers might opt for a blend of both methods depending on the nature of the data, the processing tasks, and the cost considerations. For instance, routine tasks might benefit from horizontal scaling, leveraging the distributed processing strength of Databricks. In contrast, certain resource-intensive tasks, like machine learning model training, might benefit more from a vertically scaled environment.

In essence, the choice between horizontal and vertical scaling in Databricks isn't binary but rather a matter of identifying the optimal configuration that aligns with the specific needs and constraints of a given data engineering scenario.

Cloud Deployment Options and Considerations

In today's dynamic data landscape, cloud platforms have risen to prominence, offering unparalleled flexibility, scalability, and performance benefits. With their vast capabilities, cloud deployments have become an indispensable facet of modern data engineering solutions. As Databricks inherently integrates with the cloud, understanding the nuances of its deployment options is pivotal for any professional aspiring to leverage its full potential.

This section will illuminate the various cloud deployment avenues available for Databricks. We'll embark on a journey that takes us through the various cloud providers, emphasizing their strengths, compatibilities, and the different services they offer in tandem with Databricks.

Firstly, we'll provide a broad overview of the cloud deployment options available, ensuring you have a clear roadmap of the landscape. Subsequent discussions will delve into a comparative analysis, aiding in the evaluation of different cloud providers and services. This comparative exploration is designed to equip you with the knowledge to make informed choices tailored to your organization's unique requirements.

We'll also spend dedicated time focusing on Databricks' integration with Amazon Web Services (AWS) - a popular cloud provider choice. Here, you'll learn the specifics, from deployment intricacies to optimizing costs and performance in the AWS ecosystem.

The objective is clear: by the end of this section, you should possess a robust understanding of how Databricks fits into the cloud matrix, ensuring that when it comes to deploying Databricks solutions, you're making choices that are both informed and strategically aligned with your broader data engineering goals. Let's delve in.

Overview of Cloud Deployment Options for Databricks

Today's cloud ecosystem is vast and diverse, with various providers offering various services tailored to specific needs. When considering Databricks deployment, selecting the right cloud platform becomes pivotal. This subsection will discuss the primary cloud options for deploying Databricks, emphasizing their unique features and benefits.

- **Amazon Web Services (AWS)**:
    - **Integration**: Databricks integrates seamlessly with AWS, leveraging its myriad of data storage, computation, and analytics services.
    - **Features**: With AWS, users can tap into services like Amazon S3 for storage, EC2 for computing, and Redshift for data warehousing. Additionally, AWS offers a host of security features, ensuring data privacy and compliance.
    - **Benefits**: AWS's global reach with its numerous data centers ensures low latency and high availability. Its pay-as-you-go pricing model also makes it cost-effective for varying scales of deployment.

- **Microsoft Azure**:
  - **Integration**: Databricks also has a robust partnership with Azure, giving birth to Azure Databricks, an Apache Spark-based analytics platform optimized for Azure's infrastructure.
  - **Features**: Integration points include Azure Blob Storage, Azure Data Lake Storage, and a deep link with Azure Active Directory for security.
  - **Benefits**: Azure's enterprise-grade capabilities, combined with its focus on security and compliance, make it a favored choice for businesses invested in Microsoft's ecosystem.
- **Google Cloud Platform (GCP)**:
  - **Integration**: Though historically Databricks has been more tightly integrated with AWS and Azure, there's growing support for deploying Databricks on GCP, capitalizing on its advanced AI and machine learning capabilities.
  - **Features**: Integration with GCP primarily centers on services like Google Cloud Storage and BigQuery.
  - **Benefits**: GCP stands out for its machine learning and AI capabilities, making it an intriguing option for those who wish to leverage Databricks for advanced analytics and machine learning tasks.
- **Private Cloud and On-Premises**:
  - **Integration**: While Databricks shines in public cloud environments, there are deployment options for private clouds and on-premises infrastructure for organizations with specific compliance or data residency requirements.
  - **Features**: This deployment method often requires additional configurations and integrations to link Databricks with on-site storage and computation resources.
  - **Benefits**: Provides more significant control over data, addressing data sovereignty and compliance concerns.

Selecting the right cloud deployment option is not just about the platform's technical features but also about aligning with organizational priorities, existing infrastructure investments, and future scalability considerations. Whether you're leaning towards AWS's vast service ecosystem, Azure's enterprise compatibility, GCP's AI prowess, or the controlled environment of a private cloud, the key lies in understanding the unique requirements of your data engineering projects and the broader organizational objectives.

Evaluating Different Cloud Providers and Services

In today's data-driven landscape, organizations have a plethora of choices when selecting a cloud provider for deploying their Databricks workloads. The decision becomes crucial as it can impact scalability, costs, performance, and the range of services available. In this section, we'll break down the criteria you should consider when evaluating different cloud providers and their services:

- **Compatibility with Databricks**:
  - **Description**: Ensure the cloud provider has strong support and integration with Databricks. Some cloud platforms offer native integrations, making setup and management simpler.
  - **Consideration**: Azure Databricks is a collaborative venture between Microsoft and Databricks, providing a seamless experience on the Azure platform.
- **Service Diversity**:
  - **Description**: Examine the range of services the cloud provider offers. This includes data storage, computation, analytics, and advanced AI/ML capabilities.
  - **Consideration**: AWS, for example, has a vast ecosystem of services, from S3 for storage to Lambda for serverless computing, offering flexibility in how you design your data solutions.
- **Cost Structure**:
  - **Description**: Understand the pricing model of the cloud provider. Some might offer pay-as-you-go, while others may have reserved instance pricing or even sustained-use discounts.
  - **Consideration**: GCP's sustained-use discounts can make it a cost-effective choice if you have continuous and consistent workloads.
- **Security and Compliance**:
  - **Description**: Evaluate the security features, protocols, and compliance certifications the cloud provider offers.
  - **Consideration**: Azure, being deeply entrenched in the enterprise sector, provides extensive security and compliance tools, making it a go-to for organizations with stringent regulatory needs.

- **Global Reach and Data Centers**:
  - **Description**: The geographical distribution of data centers can influence latency, availability, and compliance with regional data laws.
  - **Consideration**: AWS's vast global network of data centers ensures that you can deploy solutions closer to the end-users, ensuring faster response times.
- **Integration with Existing Infrastructure**:
  - **Description**: If your organization already uses certain cloud services, continuing with the same provider or ensuring the new provider integrates well with the existing infrastructure might be beneficial.
  - **Consideration**: Azure might offer smoother integrations if you're already using Microsoft's suite of products.
- **Support and Community**:
  - **Description**: Check the kind of support the cloud provider offers. A strong community can also be a boon when troubleshooting or seeking best practices.
  - **Consideration**: AWS and Azure boast robust support plans and have a vast community of users, ensuring you're never truly on your own when facing challenges.
- **Innovation and Future-Proofing**:
  - **Description**: Cloud providers constantly innovate, offering new services and features. Opt for providers at the forefront of technology, ensuring your solutions remain contemporary.
  - **Consideration**: GCP, with its strong emphasis on AI and ML, might be the choice for organizations looking to delve deep into advanced analytics.

Evaluating cloud providers comprehensively ensures that your Databricks deployments are robust, scalable, and aligned with your current needs and future growth aspirations.

Exploring Databricks with AWS

Amazon Web Services (AWS) stands as one of the giants in the cloud services realm. Its diverse ecosystem, combined with its agility and scalability, makes it a prime choice for many enterprises. When integrating Databricks with AWS, there are many benefits and considerations. Here's a deep dive into how the two seamlessly work together:

- **Seamless Integration with Amazon S3**:
  - **Description**: Databricks integrates natively with Amazon Simple Storage Service (S3), AWS's object storage service. This allows for efficient data storage and retrieval without complex configurations.
  - **Application**: Data engineers can store massive datasets in S3 buckets and directly read and process them within Databricks. This integration leverages the advantages of S3, such as data durability, availability, and scalability.
- **EC2-based Cluster Deployment**:
  - **Description**: Databricks on AWS utilizes Amazon EC2 (Elastic Compute Cloud) for deploying clusters. This ensures flexibility in selecting the right instance type based on workload requirements.
  - **Benefit**: Whether it's memory-intensive tasks or compute-heavy operations, EC2's diverse instance types cater to varied needs, allowing for cost-effective and performance-optimized cluster deployments.
- **Integration with AWS Data Lakes**:
  - **Description**: AWS offers robust data lake capabilities, primarily through Amazon S3 and Amazon Redshift. Databricks can directly connect to these data sources, enhancing analytics capabilities.
  - **Use Case**: An organization can build a comprehensive data lake on AWS and then employ Databricks for advanced analytics, AI, and ML tasks, making the most of both platforms.
- **Security with AWS Identity and Access Management (IAM)**:
  - **Description**: Databricks leverages AWS IAM roles for fine-grained access control, ensuring that only authorized personnel can access specific resources and datasets.
  - **Advantage**: This tight integration ensures data security and governance, making it easier to comply with various regulatory requirements.
- **Enhanced Monitoring with Amazon CloudWatch**:
  - **Description**: By integrating with Amazon CloudWatch, Databricks allows users to monitor their workloads closely, capturing metrics, setting alarms, and gaining insights into application and infrastructure health.

- o **Outcome**: Proactive monitoring ensures timely identification of any potential issues, reducing downtime and ensuring smoother operations.
- **Serverless Capabilities with AWS Lambda**:
  - o **Description**: Databricks can invoke AWS Lambda functions, allowing users to run code without provisioning or managing servers.
  - o **Scenario**: Imagine a use case where after certain data processing in Databricks, a Lambda function is triggered to send notifications or initiate another microservice. Such automations enhance operational efficiency.
- **Connectivity with AWS Networking Services**:
  - o **Description**: Integration with AWS Virtual Private Cloud (VPC) and Direct Connect ensures secure and optimized connectivity between Databricks and other AWS resources or on-premises data centers.
  - o **Benefit**: This connectivity ensures data transfer speed, security, and consistency, especially when dealing with large datasets or real-time analytics.
- **Cost Management with AWS Cost Explorer**:
  - o **Description**: AWS Cost Explorer can track Databricks-related expenses, clearly showing resource utilization and helping optimize cost.
  - o **Advantage**: Keeping a tab on costs ensures budget adherence and highlights areas for potential savings.

Together, AWS and Databricks create a formidable combination, enabling organizations to harness the power of big data, advanced analytics, and cloud scalability. Leveraging the strengths of both platforms ensures that data engineering solutions are not just efficient but also future-ready.

Handling Data Growth and Future-Proofing Strategies

As the digital universe expands, data volume, variety, and velocity grow unprecedentedly. Handling this massive influx of data, especially in platforms like Databricks, is no longer a luxury but a necessity. This section focuses on understanding the challenges and strategies associated with managing ever-growing data sets and preparing our data engineering solutions for the future.

Data growth is about handling increased volumes and ensuring data quality, relevance, and timeliness. As the data landscape evolves, the technologies and strategies that once seemed adequate might soon become obsolete. Hence, future-proofing becomes equally crucial. It's about having a vision and preparing your data infrastructure to accommodate future needs and unforeseen challenges.

We will delve into the following:

- Strategies that can help manage and accommodate the rapid data growth within Databricks, ensuring that the system doesn't get overwhelmed and continues to perform optimally.
- Techniques that will guarantee the longevity and relevance of your data engineering solutions. This involves monitoring emerging technologies and trends and ensuring that the systems we build today don't become archaic tomorrow.
- A closer look at the evolving landscape of data engineering, identifying technologies and practices on the horizon that promise to reshape how we think about and work with data.

By the end of this section, you'll be equipped with knowledge and strategies not only to handle the data deluge but also to ensure the longevity, scalability, and efficiency of your data solutions.

Strategies for Managing and Accommodating Data Growth in Databricks

Managing burgeoning data effectively is a pivotal concern for organizations, especially in today's data-driven landscape. With tools like Databricks, handling vast volumes of data has become more streamlined, yet it's essential to employ strategic methods to ensure that data is not only stored but also utilized efficiently. Here's a deep dive into some key strategies that aid in managing and accommodating data growth within the Databricks ecosystem:

- **Partitioning**: Breaking data into smaller, logical chunks based on certain attributes can significantly speed up query performance. For instance, partitioning data by date can allow systems to swiftly locate records from a specific period without scanning the entire dataset.
- **Delta Lake**: Using Databricks' Delta Lake can efficiently manage massive datasets. Delta Lake offers ACID transactions, scalable metadata

handling, and unified streaming and batch data processing. It enhances data reliability and ensures consistent data access.

- **Optimized Storage**: Employing optimized storage solutions, like Parquet, can compress data efficiently without compromising data quality. This not only saves storage space but also speeds up data retrieval processes.
- **Data Pruning**: Regularly evaluating the data to remove obsolete or redundant information helps optimize storage costs and ensures that the data being analyzed is relevant.
- **Data Lifecycle Management**: Establishing policies that define how long data should be retained, when it should be archived, or when it can be deleted. Tools like Databricks provide features that enable automated data lifecycle management, ensuring that older data doesn't clog the system.
- **Monitoring and Alerts**: Setting up monitoring tools within Databricks to monitor data growth trends can help anticipate storage needs and ensure the system is always ready to handle incoming data. Additionally, setting alerts for unusual spikes in data ingestion can also hint at potential issues or anomalies.

By implementing these strategies, organizations can ensure that their Databricks environment remains scalable and performs optimally despite the ever-increasing volumes of data. It's about proactive management, ensuring that data growth doesn't hamper performance or lead to increased costs.

Techniques for Future-Proofing Data Engineering Solutions

In the rapidly evolving world of data engineering, ensuring that your solutions stand the test of time is crucial. Future-proofing doesn't just mean adapting to handle more data but also ensuring that your solutions remain agile, adaptable, and efficient in the face of emerging technologies and evolving business needs. Here are some pivotal techniques to make your data engineering solutions future-ready within the Databricks environment:

- **Modular Architecture**: Design your data pipelines and workflows modularly. This ensures that individual components can be upgraded or replaced without overhauling the entire system. It promotes adaptability and reduces the impact of changes.

- **Continuous Learning and Training**: Data engineering is always in flux. Regular training sessions for the team on new tools, technologies, and best practices can ensure that your organization is always at the forefront of innovation.
- **Embrace Automation**: Automated testing, data validation, and deployment can streamline operations, ensure consistency, and reduce human errors. Databricks supports various automation tools that can be harnessed for smoother operations.
- **Version Control**: Use version control for your data engineering scripts and workflows. This helps in tracking changes and allows for easy rollback in case of issues. It's a safety net that ensures stability.
- **Hybrid Solutions**: While cloud solutions are the rage, it's wise to design systems that can operate both on-premises and in the cloud. This hybrid approach offers flexibility and ensures that your solutions can adapt to changing infrastructure needs.
- **Regular Audits**: Periodically audit your data engineering processes. This helps in identifying inefficiencies, redundancies, or areas that need upgrades. An audit can also highlight potential future challenges, giving you a head-start in addressing them.
- **Feedback Loops**: Incorporate feedback mechanisms into your systems. Whether it's feedback from end-users, stakeholders, or the system itself (in the form of logs and alerts), this continuous feedback helps in iterative improvement.
- **Scalable Infrastructure**: Invest in infrastructure that can scale horizontally (adding more machines) and vertically (adding more power to existing machines). Databricks offers seamless scalability, ensuring that your infrastructure can keep pace as your data needs grow.
- **Stay Updated with Emerging Technologies**: Keep an eye on the horizon. New data storage solutions, processing frameworks, or data formats can offer significant advantages. Being an early adopter can set you ahead of the curve.

By implementing these techniques, you ensure that your data engineering solutions in Databricks aren't just robust for today but poised to tackle tomorrow's challenges. The key is to remain agile, receptive to change, and proactive in your strategies.

Evaluating Emerging Technologies and Trends in Data Engineering

As data continues to burgeon and play a central role in decision-making processes across industries, the field of data engineering is under constant evolution. The continual emergence of new technologies and trends often presents both opportunities and challenges. It's vital for data engineers, especially those working within Databricks, to stay abreast of these developments to harness potential advantages and stay competitive. Here are some essential aspects to consider when evaluating emerging technologies and trends:

- **Understanding the Problem it Solves**: Before jumping onto any new trend or technology, it's crucial to understand the specific problems it addresses. Does it cater to an existing pain point in your current workflows? If not, it might not be worth the effort of integrating.

- **Integration Capabilities**: Determine how easily this new technology can be integrated into your existing Databricks environment. Seamless integration can save time and reduce potential disruptions, while a complicated integration might lead to more challenges down the road.

- **Cost Implications**: While some emerging technologies may promise revolutionary changes, they might come with hefty price tags. It's essential to balance the cost of adoption with the potential long-term benefits it might provide.

- **Community and Support**: Technologies backed by an active community and robust support tend to be more reliable. An active community can be a rich source of documentation, best practices, and troubleshooting help.

- **Flexibility and Scalability**: Consider how flexible the technology is to changes and how it scales. Given the dynamic nature of data engineering, adopting rigid systems can be counterproductive in the long run.

- **Performance Metrics**: Before adoption, analyze the performance metrics associated with the technology. How does it stack up against current speed, reliability, and efficiency solutions?

- **Security Considerations**: In the world of data, security cannot be an afterthought. Ensure that any emerging technology adheres to industry-standard security protocols and doesn't introduce new vulnerabilities into your system.

- **Feedback from Early Adopters**: Before fully integrating a new technology, gathering feedback from early adopters is wise. Their experiences can provide insights into potential challenges and best practices for implementation.
- **Future Roadmap**: Investigate the future development roadmap of the technology. This can hint at its longevity and how it might evolve, ensuring you're investing in a technology with a future.
- **Training and Skillset Requirements**: New technologies might require new skills. Consider the training needs and whether your team possesses the necessary expertise or if there's a learning curve involved.

By systematically evaluating emerging technologies and trends in data engineering, you can make informed decisions about what to incorporate into your Databricks environment. Staying updated ensures that your data engineering solutions remain cutting-edge, efficient, and poised to handle the ever-evolving landscape of data challenges.

Conclusion

We began by delving into the fundamental importance of scalability in data engineering solutions. Various techniques were discussed, highlighting the balance between horizontal and vertical scaling options, and emphasizing that the optimal path often requires a mix of both. Furthermore, we delved into the comparison and evaluation of different cloud providers and services, highlighting the value of selecting the most appropriate cloud environment tailored to specific needs.

In the next chapter, we will learn about the data security and Governance part of the project and what Databricks offers in that section.

Key Terms
- **Horizontal Scaling:** A scaling method where new instances or nodes are added to a system to manage increased load.
- **Vertical Scaling:** Adding more power (CPU, RAM, storage) to an existing node or system.
- **Cloud Deployment:** Launching and managing applications, services, and solutions on cloud platforms.
- **Data Growth:** The increase in the volume, velocity, and variety of data over time.

- **Future-Proofing:** The process of anticipating developments and ensuring solutions can handle future requirements.
- **Emerging Technologies:** New technologies that are currently being developed or will be developed within the next five to ten years and which will substantially alter the business and social environment.
- **Deployment Considerations:** Factors and elements that one must take into account when deploying a solution, especially in a cloud environment.
- **Data Engineering Trends:** The latest methods, techniques, and best practices in the field of data engineering.
- **Cloud Provider Evaluation:** The process of assessing and comparing various cloud service providers to determine the best fit for specific needs.

Chapter 10
Data Security and Governance

"Trust, but verify."

— Ronald Reagan

Introduction

This chapter delves into the nuances of Data Security and Governance, presenting a comprehensive guide to establishing airtight security measures and maintaining the integrity of data assets within the Databricks environment.

As data ecosystems evolve and become increasingly complex, the importance of a unified system for metadata management and data discovery also grows. In the first section, we introduce the Unity Catalog in Databricks – a central repository that facilitates data discovery, governance, and metadata management. The benefits it brings to an organization's data governance strategy cannot be overstated.

The second section delves into the intricate world of data privacy and compliance, discussing the significance of adhering to data protection regulations and highlighting the measures that Databricks offers to ensure compliance. In an era where breaches and non-compliance can have catastrophic repercussions, both financially and reputationally, understanding these practices is crucial.

Section three equips readers with the knowledge to design stringent access policies and elucidates techniques to encrypt data both at rest and during transit, ensuring no unauthorized entity can misuse sensitive data.

Lastly, the chapter rounds off by exploring best practices in data governance. By establishing solid governance frameworks, policies, and practices, organizations can ensure that their data remains a valuable asset rather than a potential liability.

Structure

In this chapter, the following topics will be covered:
- Unity Catalog
- Ensuring Data Privacy and Compliance in Databricks
- Implementing Access Controls and Data Encryption
- Data Governance Best Practices

Unity Catalog

In today's intricate data landscapes, understanding where data originates from, how it transforms, and where it resides is a challenge that many organizations grapple with. This complexity necessitates a unified system that streamlines data discovery and management. Enter the Unity Catalog in Databricks. Designed as a central hub for all your data-related needs, the Unity Catalog offers an organized repository for metadata management, data discovery, and governance.

This section takes a closer look at the Unity Catalog's core functionalities and their significance in the broader context of data engineering within Databricks. We will start by familiarizing ourselves with its foundational concepts and then move on to understanding how it fosters efficient data governance and simplifies metadata management. Through the Unity Catalog, organizations can gain a clearer view of their data ecosystem, ensuring that data assets are not only secure but also easily accessible and understandable for relevant stakeholders.

Understanding the Unity Catalog in Databricks

Data is an invaluable asset in today's digital world, but without a proper understanding and management system, it can quickly become overwhelming and challenging to harness its full potential. The Unity Catalog in Databricks aims to alleviate these challenges by providing a centralized metadata repository for all your data assets. This crucial tool makes it easier to navigate vast datasets, ensuring that users can quickly find and use the data they need.

- **Centralized Metadata Repository**: One of the primary functions of the Unity Catalog is to serve as a single point of reference for all metadata associated with your data assets. This centralized approach means that users don't need to hunt through disparate sources or systems to get the metadata information they require.
- **Integrated with Databricks Ecosystem**: Unity Catalog is not a standalone tool; it's deeply integrated with the Databricks ecosystem. This ensures seamless interoperability with other Databricks services and tools, making it more straightforward for users to derive insights without shifting between platforms.
- **Enhanced Data Discovery**: With the vast amounts of data that organizations deal with, finding a suitable dataset can be like searching for a needle in a haystack. The Unity Catalog simplifies this process, allowing users to easily search for and locate datasets based on metadata attributes.
- **Standardized Data Views**: Consistency is key in data management. Unity Catalog provides standardized views of datasets, ensuring that irrespective of where the data comes from, users get a consistent and unified perspective, making analysis and reporting more straightforward.

By providing a more precise understanding and organization of datasets, the Unity Catalog ensures that businesses can leverage their data assets more effectively, translating to faster insights and more informed decision-making processes.

Overview of Metadata Management and Data Discovery in Unity Catalog

Metadata, essentially the data about data, forms the backbone of efficient data management. Properly harnessed, metadata can simplify data-related tasks, leading to enhanced efficiency and precision. In Databricks, Unity Catalog is the torchbearer for these operations, championing streamlined data discovery and effective metadata management.

- **Comprehensive Metadata Capture**: Unity Catalog comprehensively captures a variety of metadata types from diverse sources. This includes structural metadata (like table schemas), descriptive metadata (annotations or descriptions), and operational metadata (data lineage or usage statistics).

Example: Consider a financial dataset containing daily transaction records. The structural metadata would outline the schema, such as transaction ID, date, amount, and vendor. Descriptive metadata might include notes about the source of the data, perhaps a specific bank or financial institution. Operational metadata, on the other hand, could indicate how often the data is accessed and by which department.

- **Efficient Data Discovery**: Unity Catalog's integrated search capabilities allow users to identify the datasets they need swiftly. With specific metadata attributes or keywords, locating the required data is simplified.

  Example: A data analyst looking for sales data from the last quarter can input relevant keywords or use metadata tags such as Q2 Sales to retrieve the dataset from Unity Catalog swiftly.

- **Metadata Versioning**: Data evolves, and so does metadata. Unity Catalog's metadata versioning tracks these changes, allowing users to understand data evolution and ensuring that they base their analyses on the most recent and relevant information.

  Example: If a dataset originally contained ten fields and later was updated to incorporate two additional areas, the metadata versioning would show this change, thus keeping data users informed about the dataset's current structure.

- **Data Lineage Visualization**: Unity Catalog offers a feature to visually represent data's journey, showcasing its origin and subsequent transformations.

  Example: A dataset might begin as raw logs from a website, undergo initial cleaning to remove anomalies, and then be enriched with customer data before being utilized for analysis. The data lineage visualization would display this entire process, ensuring clarity about the data's journey.

- **Collaborative Metadata Enhancement**: Unity Catalog allows for a communal approach to metadata. Users can supplement system-generated metadata with user-defined tags, comments, and annotations.

  Example: A user might add a tag indicating that a particular dataset has been validated for accuracy or perhaps leave a comment noting a specific quirk about the data that other users should be aware of.

- **Integration with Data Quality Tools**: Unity Catalog ensures that metadata genuinely mirrors the actual health and quality of datasets. By integrating with data quality tools, Unity Catalog provides insights that help build trust among data consumers.

Example: Suppose a dataset contains customer feedback. Integration with a data quality tool could highlight sentiment scores within the metadata, allowing users to quickly gauge the general sentiment of the feedback without diving deep into the data.

In essence, Unity Catalog's functionalities ensure that users have a complete and clear understanding of their data landscape. By emphasizing these capabilities, Databricks makes sure that organizations are best positioned to glean insights from their data with clarity and confidence.

Leveraging Unity Catalog for Efficient Data Governance and Metadata Management

The Unity Catalog in Databricks is not just a passive repository of metadata. Instead, it's a dynamic tool that can drive the data governance strategy of an organization. By efficiently managing metadata, the Unity Catalog can be pivotal in ensuring data quality, security, accessibility, and usability. Here's how organizations can leverage the Unity Catalog for maximum efficacy:

- **Unifying Metadata Across Multiple Data Sources**: Unity Catalog brings together metadata from various sources, ensuring that it's organized and accessible from a singular platform. This consolidation helps in providing a unified view of data assets, making data discovery straightforward.

  Example: An organization using cloud storage, on-premises databases, and third-party data sources can have all its metadata cataloged coherently within Unity Catalog, enabling users to locate and understand data from disparate sources quickly.

- **Facilitating Automated Data Classification**: By understanding the metadata, Unity Catalog can assist in automated data classification, thereby aiding in the identification of sensitive or critical data that may require special handling or protection.

  Example: Metadata indicating fields named "credit card number" or "SSN" can trigger Unity Catalog to classify datasets containing such fields as sensitive, necessitating enhanced security measures.

- **Enhancing Data Stewardship**: Unity Catalog, through its detailed metadata capture and visualization capabilities, enables data stewards to maintain the health and accuracy of datasets more effectively.

- **Example:** By visualizing data lineage, data stewards can quickly identify the origin of any anomalies in the data, ensuring data integrity throughout its lifecycle.
- **Empowering Collaboration and Knowledge Sharing**: User-generated annotations, tags, and comments in Unity Catalog promote collaborative metadata enhancement, ensuring that tribal knowledge about datasets gets captured and shared.

  Example: An analyst finding a novel use-case for a dataset can annotate this within Unity Catalog, guiding future users towards potential applications of the data.
- **Driving Compliance and Auditing**: With the granular metadata and versioning capabilities, Unity Catalog becomes an ally in ensuring regulatory compliance, facilitating comprehensive audits by maintaining a detailed record of data transformations and usage.

  Example: For industries under strict regulations, like finance or healthcare, Unity Catalog can trace every change made to a dataset, providing an audit trail that proves compliance with industry standards.
- **Optimizing Data Usage with Usage Statistics**: By capturing operational metadata, Unity Catalog can provide insights into dataset popularity and usage patterns, guiding decisions on data storage, caching, or archival.

  Example: Datasets accessed frequently could be moved to faster storage solutions or cached, while rarely accessed data might be archived, optimizing costs and performance.

In the context of modern data engineering, Unity Catalog does more than just store metadata; it serves as the bedrock of efficient data governance. Leveraging its features ensures not only streamlined data operations but also the fostering of a culture of data-driven decision-making within organizations. Through Unity Catalog, Databricks equips users with the tools they need to navigate the vast oceans of data confidently.

Ensuring Data Privacy and Compliance in Databricks

Data has been rightfully termed as the new oil in today's digital age. But as organizations navigate this ocean of data, the tides of privacy and compliance challenges rise against them. In this section, we'll guide you through the importance of data privacy and compliance, especially in data engineering environments such as Databricks. We'll also delve deep into the techniques Databricks offers to ensure that data stays private, compliant, and secure.

The importance of data privacy cannot be understated. It forms the foundation of trust between organizations and their clients or customers. With data breaches becoming commonplace and with stringent regulations in place, ensuring data privacy is both a moral and legal obligation. And when we consider Databricks, which offers powerful tools for processing massive data volumes, the question arises: How can we process this data responsibly without violating any privacy norms?

Furthermore, different regions and sectors come with their set of regulations, whether it's the General Data Protection Regulation (GDPR) of the European Union or the California Consumer Privacy Act (CCPA) in the U.S. Navigating these regulations requires a blend of technical and regulatory understanding.

In the upcoming subsections, we'll explore how Databricks provides avenues to ensure data privacy and helps organizations stay compliant. From understanding the gravity of data privacy in data engineering to implementing techniques for data protection – like anonymization and data masking – and ensuring that all operations align with global data protection laws, we've got a comprehensive journey ahead.

So, fasten your seatbelts as we embark on this journey to understand and implement best practices to ensure data privacy and compliance in Databricks. Whether you're a data engineer, a compliance officer, or a curious reader, this section has something vital to offer to everyone.

Importance of Data Privacy and Compliance

In our increasingly data-driven world, the significance of data privacy and compliance extends beyond merely checking regulatory boxes; it's about fostering trust and ensuring ethical data handling. Let's understand this in the context of data engineering, particularly within platforms like Databricks.

- **Foundation of Trust**: At its core, data privacy builds a foundation of trust between organizations and their stakeholders. When customers provide personal information to a company, they place trust in the organization's ability to protect and handle that data responsibly. In data engineering, where vast volumes of data get processed, maintaining this trust is paramount.

    Example: Consider a retail company using Databricks to analyze customer shopping behavior. If customers discover that their data has been mishandled, trust erodes, leading to potential losses in customer loyalty and revenue.

- **Regulatory Obligations**: With data breaches becoming more frequent, various regulations, like GDPR and CCPA, have come into play. These regulations are stringent about how data should be stored, processed, and transferred. Non-compliance can result in hefty fines and reputational damage.

    Example: A European-based finance company, while processing transactional data in Databricks, must adhere to GDPR guidelines, ensuring data is anonymized and the right to erasure is upheld.

- **Ethical Data Use**: Beyond regulations, there's an ethical aspect to data handling. Ensuring privacy means making sure that the data won't be used in harmful ways or without the explicit consent of its owner.

    Example: A healthcare institute processing patient records in Databricks must ensure that the data won't be used for unauthorized research or sold to third parties without patient consent.

- **Business Continuity**: Companies that ignore data privacy might face disruptions in their operations. Data breaches can lead to direct financial losses, legal consequences, and the cost of damage control, which could involve public relations campaigns and compensations.

    Example: A tech giant using Databricks for user analytics must constantly monitor and upgrade its data security protocols to prevent potential data breaches that can cost millions in reparations.

- **Enhanced Data Quality**: When organizations prioritize data privacy, they often establish rigorous data handling and validation processes. These can inadvertently improve the overall data quality by ensuring only relevant and approved data is stored and processed.

    Example: An e-commerce platform integrating data pipelines in Databricks might set up automated data validation checks, ensuring that only accurate and relevant customer data flows into their analytics systems.

In essence, while data privacy and compliance might appear as mere regulations, they provide a structure that promotes trust, ethical operations, and high data quality in data engineering. Platforms like Databricks play a crucial role by offering tools and practices to ensure these standards are upheld.

Implementing Privacy Measures and Techniques in Databricks

When managing and processing vast datasets in platforms like Databricks, implementing efficient privacy measures becomes indispensable. Protecting sensitive information and ensuring data is used appropriately requires the fusion of technology and strategic planning. Here's an in-depth exploration of how to achieve this within Databricks:

- **Data Masking**: This technique involves masking specific data within a database so that the application users do not see the entire data, only a part of it. It's beneficial for safeguarding sensitive data elements like Social Security numbers or bank account details.

    Example: If an analyst within a financial institution uses Databricks to view transactional records, data masking can display only the last four digits of a credit card number, ensuring the total number remains confidential.

- **Tokenization**: It replaces sensitive data with unique identification symbols (tokens) that retain all the essential data elements without compromising its security. These tokens can then be mapped back to the original data via a secure lookup.

    Example: In a customer database, every email ID can be tokenized into a unique sequence of characters. Analysts using Databricks can still carry out their operations using these tokens, and the original email IDs remain secure.

- **Data Anonymization**: This approach involves removing personally identifiable information where identification of data can't occur. It ensures that even if a data breach occurs, the exposed data won't harm individuals.

    Example: A healthcare organization processing patient records in Databricks might replace names with random codes or eliminate demographic information that's not necessary for the analysis.

- **Differential Privacy**: A technique that adds noise to the data being queried, ensuring that the outputs do not compromise the privacy of the inputs. This is especially useful for datasets that have sensitive information across large populations.

Example: When a research institute uses Databricks to analyze a vast dataset of patient illnesses, differential privacy ensures that results don't inadvertently reveal information about individual patients.

- **Audit Trails**: They keep a record of data access and modifications. By maintaining a transparent and tamper-proof log of who accessed data and what changes were made, organizations can better monitor and ensure data privacy.

   Example: If an energy company is analyzing consumer usage data in Databricks, an audit trail can record which analysts accessed specific datasets and when, ensuring transparency and accountability.

- **Retention Policies**: Establishing clear data retention policies can minimize privacy risks. By determining how long data should be stored and setting automated data deletion procedures, organizations can ensure they're not unnecessarily holding onto data that could be breached.

   Example: A retail company processing customer transaction histories in Databricks might set a retention policy that automatically deletes transaction data older than seven years, in line with specific financial regulations.

To sum up, Databricks provides the tools and functionalities to implement these measures, but organizations must review and adjust their privacy strategies regularly. As data environments grow and evolve, so too do the challenges and solutions associated with data privacy.

Ensuring Compliance with Data Protection Regulations

In today's digital age, data protection has become more than just an IT concern. It's a regulatory, ethical, and business imperative. With global data breaches increasing in frequency and impact, various jurisdictions have introduced stringent regulations to protect personal data. For organizations using Databricks, ensuring compliance with these regulations, such as the General Data Protection Regulation (GDPR) in Europe and the California Consumer Privacy Act (CCPA) in the U.S., is essential.

- **Understanding the Regulations**:
  - **GDPR**: Implemented in 2018, GDPR imposes stringent rules on businesses and organizations in the European Union (and those outside the EU that handle EU residents' data). Key provisions include

Data Security and Governance 217

      the right to data access, the right to be forgotten, and the need for explicit consent for data processing.

    o **CCPA**: Enacted in California, it grants consumers the right to know about data collection and sales, deny the sale of their data, and benefit from equal service and price, even if they exercise their privacy rights.

- **Data Mapping and Classification**:
  - Knowing where data resides is the first step in compliance. By utilizing Databricks' powerful data analytics capabilities, organizations can create a map of where personal data is stored and processed.
  - **Example**: A global company using Databricks can classify datasets based on the nature of data, such as personal, sensitive, or public. This classification helps in applying the correct protection measures.
- **Consent Management**:
  - Both GDPR and CCPA emphasize explicit consent. It's essential to maintain a record of when and how permission was obtained and provide mechanisms for withdrawal.
  - **Example**: An e-commerce platform using Databricks for customer analytics can integrate consent management tools to capture user consent for specific types of data processing, ensuring clarity and compliance.
- **Right to Access and Data Portability**:
  - Individuals have the right to access their data and transfer it. Databricks can facilitate this by providing efficient data extraction and format transformation techniques.
  - **Example**: Upon a customer's request, a health platform can use Databricks to extract the user's health records in a standardized format suitable for transfer.
- **Data Minimization and Deletion**:
  - Only the necessary data for a specified purpose should be processed. Databricks can help in ensuring that redundant or unnecessary data is identified and removed.
  - **Example**: A financial institution can automate data pruning processes in Databricks to delete old transaction records that are no longer needed.

- **Incident Response**:
  - In case of a data breach or non-compliance, having a well-defined incident response mechanism is paramount. Databricks can assist in rapid data forensics to understand the scope and impact of a breach.
  - **Example**: In case of suspicious activity, an organization can use Databricks to analyze logs and identify potentially compromised data sets swiftly.

Ensuring compliance is an ongoing process. It requires collaboration between legal, IT, and business units. With tools like Databricks, combined with a clear understanding of regulations like GDPR and CCPA, organizations can ensure they are on the right side of the law, fostering trust and reliability with their customers.

Techniques for Anonymization, Pseudonymization, and Data Masking

In an era where data breaches and privacy concerns are prevalent, businesses must ensure that the personal information they hold is protected, not only to comply with laws but to maintain the trust of their stakeholders. Anonymization, pseudonymization, and data masking are three crucial techniques that enable organizations to use data responsibly while minimizing the risks associated with data exposure. In the Databricks environment, these methods can be integrated seamlessly to bolster data protection measures.

- **Anonymization**:
  - **Definition**: Anonymization refers to the process of irreversibly altering data so that a data subject cannot be readily identified. Once data is anonymized, it's no longer subject to data protection regulations because it can't be tied back to an individual.
  - **Example in Databricks**: Suppose a healthcare analytics firm is using Databricks for research. To protect patient identities, they could utilize algorithms to replace names and other identifying attributes with random characters, ensuring individual patients cannot be singled out in their datasets.
- **Pseudonymization**:
  - **Definition**: Unlike anonymization, pseudonymization is a reversible process. It involves replacing private identifiers with fake identifiers or pseudonyms. This allows data to be matched with its source,

but only through a controlled mechanism, ensuring added layers of security.
- o **Example in Databricks**: An e-commerce site wishes to analyze user purchase behavior without exposing individual identities. By replacing user IDs with pseudonyms, analysts in Databricks can still link multiple transactions to a single pseudonymous user, preserving the structure of data while enhancing privacy.

- **Data Masking**:
  - o **Definition**: Data masking is about hiding specific data within a database, making it inaccessible to unauthorized users. It ensures that sensitive data remains confidential and is only available to those with the correct permissions.
  - o **Example in Databricks**: A financial institution utilizing Databricks for its analytics operations might mask specific figures, like account balances or transaction amounts. When an unauthorized user accesses the dataset, they might see asterisks or Xs instead of the actual numbers.

- **Implementing Techniques in Databricks**:
  - o **Automated Workflows**: One can set up automated workflows in Databricks to anonymize or pseudonymize data as it enters the system. This ensures consistent application of privacy techniques and reduces manual intervention.
  - o **Data Quality Assurance**: After implementing these techniques, data quality checks can be performed in Databricks to ensure that the anonymization or masking doesn't inadvertently compromise the data's usability.
  - o **Monitoring and Auditing**: Utilize Databricks' logging and monitoring capabilities to ensure these techniques are consistently applied and to keep an audit trail for compliance purposes.

Incorporating anonymization, pseudonymization, and data masking within Databricks not only amplifies the security of data but also ensures that organizations can unlock the value of their data without compromising on privacy. As businesses move towards a more data-driven approach, adopting these techniques will become increasingly vital in the landscape of data protection and compliance.

Implementing Access Controls and Data Encryption

As our digital era accelerates, data is increasingly recognized as a significant asset but also a potential liability if not properly managed. With this recognition comes the imperative for stringent security measures. Within the domain of data security, two cornerstones have emerged as vital for any data-driven organization: access controls and encryption.

Access controls are pivotal in ensuring that only authorized individuals can interact with data, allowing them to perform only those operations for which they have permissions. This encompasses not just whether a user can access data but what they can do with it – can they view it, modify it, delete it, or share it? By finetuning these controls, organizations can create a robust shield against unauthorized data manipulation and breaches.

Equally important is data encryption, which focuses on encoding data so that only those with a specific key can decode it. Encryption operates at various stages, from data at rest (stored data) to data in transit (while being transferred). When combined with strong access controls, encryption ensures that even if a malicious actor accesses the data, they can't interpret it without the decryption key.

This section delves into the intricacies of implementing these pivotal security measures within Databricks. We'll explore the nuances of access controls, how to formulate policies ensuring optimum data protection, and the state-of-the-art techniques for encrypting data both at rest and in transit. Additionally, we'll cover key management and the best practices for storing and handling decryption keys securely. Let's embark on this journey to fortify our data infrastructure, ensuring it remains impregnable to threats while fostering a culture of trust and compliance.

Overview of Access Controls and Authorization in Databricks

In today's digital age, where data breaches are increasingly common and costly, ensuring robust access controls becomes paramount for any organization, especially within platforms like Databricks, which often house a plethora of sensitive and valuable data, defining who can access what and how is of utmost importance.

Access controls essentially determine and manage user permissions, defining what actions users are authorized to perform on specific data sets or resources. These controls range from simple read-only permissions to more complex configurations, such as allowing a user to modify, but not delete, specific datasets.

In Databricks, access control is intricately woven into its architecture:

- **Workspace Access Control**: Databricks employs a workspace-based structure, and with workspace access control, you can determine which users or groups can access a particular workspace and what they can do within it. For instance, one might grant a user permission to execute notebooks but prevent them from creating new clusters.
- **Dataset Access Control**: With sensitive data often being the norm rather than the exception, it's essential to specify which users can access which datasets. Databricks allows fine-tuned permissions at the dataset level, ensuring that only authorized users can access specific data.
- **Cluster Access Control**: Given the distributed nature of data processing tasks in Databricks, managing who can initiate, modify, or terminate a cluster is crucial. Cluster access controls are especially useful in ensuring efficient resource utilization and preventing unauthorized or accidental tampering.
- **API Access Control**: With automation and integration tasks commonly performed using APIs, managing API permissions is equally essential. This ensures that only authorized scripts or tools can interact with your Databricks environment, preventing potential vulnerabilities.

For example, consider a retail company using Databricks. They may have sales data that a data analyst needs for forecasting but should not have access to personal customer information. With Dataset Access Control, they can grant the analyst permission to view sales trends while keeping personal data restricted.

In conclusion, by understanding and properly configuring the diverse access controls in Databricks, organizations can create a more secure, efficient, and compliant data environment. This not only protects against potential threats but also fosters a culture of trust and responsible data usage among team members.

Designing and Implementing Access Policies for Data Protection

Designing and implementing effective access policies is a cornerstone of data protection. By setting boundaries and rules around data access, organizations can prevent unauthorized data exposure, maintain regulatory compliance, and build trust with their stakeholders. Databricks, as a leading data platform, offers various mechanisms for crafting and enforcing these policies. Let's delve deeper into the strategies and best practices to employ:

- **Role-Based Access Control (RBAC):**
    - **What it is:** RBAC allows administrators to assign permissions based on roles within the organization. Instead of individual user permissions, users are assigned to parts, and permissions are granted to these roles.
    - **Example:** A 'Data Scientist' role might have permission to run queries and create notebooks but not manage clusters. Conversely, a 'Cluster Administrator' would have rights to create and manage clusters but limited access to sensitive datasets.
    - **Best Practice:** Regularly review and update roles as the organization and its data needs evolve. Ensure that role definitions are clear and well-documented.
- **Principle of Least Privilege (PoLP):**
    - **What it is:** Grant users the minimal level of access required to perform their jobs effectively.
    - **Example:** If a data analyst only needs to read data for generating reports, they shouldn't be granted permission to modify or delete datasets.
    - **Best Practice:** Start with no access and incrementally add permissions as needed rather than granting broad access and then removing it.
- **Time-Based Access Controls:**
    - **What it is:** Grant access for specific periods or during particular time windows.
    - **Example:** Temporary project teams might be granted access to specific datasets only for the duration of the project.
    - **Best Practice:** Set reminders or automated systems to review and revoke time-based permissions once they are no longer necessary.

- **Auditing and Monitoring:**
  - **What it is:** Regularly monitor and audit access logs to ensure compliance with established policies and detect any unauthorized or suspicious activities.
  - **Example:** If there are repeated failed login attempts outside of regular business hours, it might indicate a security threat.
  - **Best Practice:** Implement real-time alerting systems to notify administrators of potential breaches or policy violations.
- **Layered Security Approach:**
  - **What it is:** Implement multiple layers of security controls, ensuring that if one layer is bypassed, others still protect the data.
  - **Example:** Even if a user has permission to access a dataset, they might need to go through multi-factor authentication or a VPN to access the Databricks platform.
  - **Best Practice:** Regularly evaluate and update security layers to counter evolving threats.
- **Data Classification and Labeling:**
  - **What it is:** Categorize data based on its sensitivity and importance, then craft access policies accordingly.
  - **Example:** Susceptible data like personally identifiable information (PII) can be labeled as 'confidential', with stricter access controls than less sensitive data.
  - **Best Practice:** Conduct regular data audits to ensure accurate classification and adjust policies as needed.

By understanding and deploying these strategies within the Databricks ecosystem, organizations can build a robust and adaptive data protection environment. It's not only about safeguarding data but also about facilitating its effective and compliant use by the right stakeholders.

Techniques for Encrypting Data at Rest and in Transit in Databricks

Ensuring data security is paramount, especially in today's digital age. Protecting data both at rest (when stored) and in transit (when being transferred) is a foundational aspect of this security. Databricks offers comprehensive tools and techniques to encrypt data, ensuring that sensitive information remains inaccessible to unauthorized users and potential threats. Here's a deeper dive into these techniques and how to best implement them within the Databricks platform:

- **Encryption at Rest:**
  - **What it is:** Encryption at rest refers to the security measure where data is encrypted when it's stored. This means unauthorized entities cannot access or decipher the stored data even if they physically get hold of it.
  - **How Databricks supports it:** Databricks automatically encrypts data stored in its managed storage using industry-standard algorithms. It leverages cloud provider capabilities, like Amazon's S3 server-side encryption, to ensure data remains secure.
  - **Example:** If an intruder tries to bypass system security and access the physical storage, the data they encounter would be unreadable and meaningless without the appropriate decryption keys.
- **Encryption in Transit:**
  - **What it is:** Encryption in transit means that data is encrypted while moving from one location to another, such as from a user's device to a server or between data centers.
  - **How Databricks supports it:** Databricks ensures that data in transit is protected using Transport Layer Security (TLS) encryption. This includes data moving between Databricks workspaces, notebooks, databases, and between the platform and other external resources.
  - **Example:** When a user queries data from a Databricks notebook, the data returned from the storage layer to the notebook is encrypted, ensuring it can't be intercepted and read during transfer.
- **Key Management:**
  - **What it is:** Key management pertains to the administration and handling of cryptographic keys. Proper management is crucial to ensure that encryption remains both secure and accessible to authorized users.
  - **How Databricks supports it:** Databricks allows organizations to manage their encryption keys through integration with cloud providers' critical management services, such as AWS KMS. This ensures secure key storage, periodic rotation, and fine-grained access control.

- o **Example:** An organization can set up a policy to automatically rotate encryption keys every 90 days, reducing the chance of key compromise.
- **Customer-Managed Keys (CMK):**
  - o **What it is:** Some organizations prefer to have more control over their encryption keys. With CMK, they can create and manage their encryption keys, granting them greater control over data security.
  - o **How Databricks supports it:** Databricks allows users to leverage their customer-managed keys for added security. This means organizations have the flexibility to manage the lifecycle, rotation, and access policies of their keys.
  - o **Example:** A healthcare company, due to stringent regulatory requirements, decides to manage its encryption keys. By doing so, they ensure that only specific personnel can access and manage these keys, further tightening data security.

Implementing encryption – both at rest and in transit – is a critical step in safeguarding data. Databricks, recognizing the importance of data protection, offers integrated tools and best practices to ensure that data remains confidential and protected, regardless of where it resides or how it's accessed.

Implementing Key Management and Secure Credential Storage Practices

Managing cryptographic keys and securely storing credentials are fundamental to maintaining a robust security posture. In the context of Databricks, this pertains to collecting the keys used for encryption and ensuring that credentials, such as API keys or database passwords, are stored safely. Let's explore how Databricks supports these security requirements:

- **Unified Key Management:**
  - o **What it is:** Unified key management consolidates the management of all cryptographic keys under a singular system, making it easier to administer and track them.
  - o **How Databricks supports it:** Databricks integrates with popular cloud-based critical management services such as AWS KMS, Azure Key Vault, or GCP's Cloud KMS. These services provide centralized control over cryptographic keys.

- **Secret Scopes:**
  - **What it is:** A secret scope is a collection of secrets, which can be anything from API keys to database connection strings.
  - **How Databricks supports it:** Databricks provides a Secrets API that allows users to create, read, and manage secret scopes. With isolated areas, you can securely store credentials and access them in your notebooks without exposing them.
- **Databricks-backed Secret Scopes:**
  - **What it is:** These are secret scopes stored in Databricks, with the platform managing their encryption and access.
  - **How Databricks supports it:** Users can create Databricks-backed secret scopes directly through the workspace UI, allowing them to store secrets encrypted at rest.
- **Credential Passthrough:**
  - **What it is:** Credential passthrough allows users to execute commands with their credentials rather than service credentials.
  - **How Databricks supports it:** With Azure Active Directory credential passthrough, users' credentials are used to authenticate to Azure Data Lake Storage, ensuring individual accountability and preventing misuse of service credentials.
- **Code Example for Using Secrets in Databricks:** To securely use secrets in a Databricks notebook, you'd typically use the Databricks utility library (**duties**). Here's a simple example of accessing a database password stored in a secret scope:

```
# Access a secret from a Databricks-backed secret scope
password = dbutils.secrets.get(scope="my-secret-scope", key="database-password")

# Use the secret in a connection string (without exposing the actual password)
db_connection = f"jdbc:mysql://my-database-host:3306/my-database-name?user=my-username&password={password}"
```

Figure 10.1: How to store secrets in Databricks

This code snippet fetches a password from a secret scope named "my-secret-scope" and uses it to form a JDBC connection string. By leveraging the Secrets

API, the password is never exposed in the notebook, ensuring that sensitive credentials remain confidential.

Effective key management and secure credential storage are foundational to data security. By using Databricks' built-in features and adhering to best practices, organizations can significantly reduce risks associated with data breaches or unauthorized access.

Data Governance Best Practices

In the evolving digital landscape, data has become one of the most valuable assets for organizations. As the volume, variety, and velocity of data grow, so does the necessity for effective management and oversight. Data governance emerges as a strategic priority, ensuring that data is trustworthy, consistent, and used responsibly. Within the Databricks ecosystem, the administration goes beyond mere data storage and touches upon its entire lifecycle – from acquisition to retirement.

This section sheds light on the significance of data governance in upholding data quality and integrity within Databricks. It offers insights into establishing comprehensive governance frameworks and policies tailored to the platform's unique capabilities. Furthermore, we will delve into the nuances of data lineage, metadata management, and data cataloging – core components that enable transparency and traceability in data operations. Wrapping up this segment, we'll discuss best practices for documenting data, stewarding it through its lifecycle, and maintaining its relevance and value over time. As we navigate through this section, you'll gain a holistic understanding of how Databricks can be an ally in your data governance journey, ensuring that your data remains a trusted and valuable asset.

Importance of Data Governance

The promise of data-driven decision-making rests upon the foundation of high-quality and reliable data. Data governance, at its core, ensures that this foundation remains robust, offering frameworks and protocols that guarantee data quality, integrity, and usability. Let's understand the pivotal role data governance plays, especially within the context of Databricks.

- **Trustworthiness of Data:** For any data-driven organization, ensuring that the data being utilized is reliable is paramount. Data governance protocols make sure that data entering the Databricks environment is vetted, validated, and cleansed, making it a trustworthy source for analytical processes.

Example: Consider an e-commerce platform that relies on user data to make product recommendations. Through data governance, it can ensure that erroneous or misleading data, such as bot-generated activities, doesn't skew its recommendation engine.

- **Consistency Across Datasets:** As businesses scale, data sources often proliferate. Without governance, inconsistencies across these sources can lead to disjointed analytics and misleading insights. Implementing command guarantees that data, irrespective of its origin, adheres to a defined standard, ensuring consistency.

  Example: A multinational corporation uses Databricks to analyze sales data from various regions. Data governance ensures that all regional data aligns with a single format, enabling seamless global analytics.

- **Auditing and Compliance:** With rising concerns about data privacy and increasing regulations such as GDPR and CCPA, governance becomes a tool to ensure compliance. It helps maintain audit trails, ensuring that data is acquired, stored, and used in line with stipulated guidelines.

  Example: A healthcare provider using Databricks for patient data analytics can trace back every data point to its source, ensuring it was acquired with proper consent and used ethically, adhering to regulations like HIPAA.

- **Data Lifecycle Management:** From its acquisition to its eventual retirement, data undergoes numerous stages. Governance provides the necessary oversight during each of these stages, making sure that data remains relevant, updated, and valuable throughout its lifecycle.

  Example: A streaming service utilizing Databricks to analyze viewership trends can, through governance, ensure that older, less relevant data is archived or retired, maintaining the efficiency of its analytics engine.

- **Stakeholder Collaboration:** Effective governance in Databricks fosters collaboration. With clear protocols, data producers, consumers, and stewards can work in tandem, ensuring that data is not just well-managed but also well-utilized.

  Example: In a manufacturing unit, while engineers ensure that sensors generate accurate data, analysts leverage this data for insights, and governance ensures that both parties can work seamlessly, deriving maximum value from the data.

In sum, data governance isn't just a set of rules or protocols – it's the linchpin that ensures data's reliability and value within the Databricks ecosystem. When implemented effectively, it transforms data from a mere resource to a strategic asset.

Techniques for Data Lineage, Metadata Management, and Data Cataloging

Data lineage, metadata management, and data cataloging are pivotal components of a comprehensive data governance strategy. They provide clarity, traceability, and organization to the vast volumes of data that flow through an enterprise. Databricks, with its advanced functionalities, offers a suite of tools and techniques to streamline these aspects. Let's explore them in detail:

- **Data Lineage for Traceability:**
    - **Purpose:** Data lineage offers a visual representation of the data's journey through the system – from its source to its end-use. This traceability helps in identifying bottlenecks, ensuring data quality, and maintaining compliance.
    - **Databricks Application:** Databricks integrates with tools like Apache Atlas and other lineage-capturing software. When utilized, it provides a clear lineage map showing how data moves, gets transformed, and is consumed.
    - **Example:** In a retail company, tracking a specific pricing data point from its origin (supplier) through transformations (discounts, taxes) to its final representation on the website can be mapped using data lineage in Databricks.
- **Metadata Management for Data Context:**
    - **Purpose:** Metadata (data about data) offers context, aiding in understanding data's source, nature, transformation, and relevancy.
    - **Databricks Application:** Databricks' Delta Lake supports a variety of metadata operations, allowing for the easy addition, retrieval, and management of metadata.
    - **Example:** An insurance company, while analyzing claim data, can use metadata to understand when the data was last updated, by whom, and what transformations it underwent.

- **Data Cataloging for Organization:**
  - **Purpose:** Data cataloging involves creating a centralized repository where datasets are indexed, categorized, and made discoverable. It aids users in finding the correct data efficiently.
  - **Databricks Application:** Databricks Unity Catalog serves as a centralized data catalog that organizes and indexes data assets across the platform. It also provides functionalities like search, categorization, and documentation.
  - **Example:** In a research institution, scientists can navigate the Databricks catalog to find datasets on specific experiments, complete with descriptions, source information, and related documentation.
- **Implementing Data Annotations and Tags:**
  - **Purpose:** Annotations and tags add additional layers of information to data, making it easier to search, categorize, and manage.
  - **Databricks Application:** Within the Databricks environment, users can add custom tags and annotations to datasets. This enriched metadata aids in better cataloging and discoverability.
  - **Example:** A finance firm, when cataloging transactional data, can use tags like Q1, Domestic, Forex, and more, allowing analysts to filter and find relevant datasets quickly.
- **Maintaining Version History:**
  - **Purpose:** Keeping track of data versions ensures that users always have access to both current and historical data states.
  - **Databricks Application:** Delta Lake in Databricks maintains a versioned history of datasets, allowing users to roll back to previous states or track changes over time.
  - **Example:** In an e-commerce company, product inventory data can have multiple versions as it's updated daily. Databricks can help trace these versions to understand inventory flow over time.

Proper implementation of these techniques within Databricks ensures a streamlined approach to data governance. It not only aids in compliance and quality assurance but also fosters a data-driven culture where information is accessible, traceable, and understandable.

Best Practices for Data Documentation, Stewardship, and Data Lifecycle Management

Achieving an optimum level of data governance, particularly in sophisticated platforms like Databricks, demands rigorous practices in data documentation, stewardship, and lifecycle management. These practices not only bolster data integrity and trustworthiness but also facilitate smoother data operations and collaborations. Here's a deep dive into each:

- **Data Documentation for Clarity and Reusability:**
  - **Purpose:** Data documentation aims to describe data in detail, capturing its essence, transformations, dependencies, and more.
  - **Best Practices in Databricks:**
    - **Centralized Repository:** Maintain a central location within Databricks where all documentation is stored and easily accessible.
    - **Detailed Descriptions:** Every dataset, transformation, or workflow should have a detailed description covering its purpose, structure, and any other relevant details.
    - **Example:** For a marketing analytics dataset, documentation should explain the data sources (for example, website analytics, CRM, social media), the transformations applied, and the metrics derived.
- **Data Stewardship for Accountability and Quality:**
  - **Purpose:** Stewardship involves assigning responsibility for datasets to specific individuals or teams, ensuring data quality, security, and compliance.
  - **Best Practices in Databricks:**
    - **Designate Data Stewards:** Appoint specific individuals or teams for different data domains or departments.
    - **Regular Audits:** Encourage data stewards to conduct regular data quality and compliance audits.
    - **Example:** In a financial organization, a designated steward for transactional data ensures its accuracy, timeliness, and adherence to regulatory standards.
- **Data Lifecycle Management for Organized Data Operations:**
  - **Purpose:** Managing data throughout its lifecycle, from creation to deletion, ensures optimal storage, usage, and compliance.

- **Best Practices in Databricks:**
    - **Define Lifecycle Stages:** Clearly delineate stages like data creation, transformation, storage, archiving, and deletion.
    - **Implement Retention Policies:** Determine how long data should be stored in its active state before being archived or deleted.
    - **Automate Lifecycle Transitions:** Use Databricks to automate data transitions from one stage to another, like moving old data to cold storage.
    - **Example:** In an e-commerce setup, customer clickstream data might be actively used for analysis for a few months, after which it's archived. After a few years, if it's no longer deemed valid, it could be scheduled for deletion.
- **Consistent Terminology and Naming Conventions:**
  - **Purpose:** Consistency in naming ensures that data elements are easily recognizable and reduces confusion.
  - **Best Practices in Databricks:**
    - **Standardize Names:** Establish a set of naming conventions for datasets, tables, and columns and ensure they are uniformly applied.
    - **Regularly Review:** Periodically review the datasets to ensure that naming standards are being maintained.
    - **Example:** If a healthcare institution uses the term `Patient_ID` in one dataset, it should avoid having `P_ID` or `PatID` in others.

Incorporating these best practices within the Databricks environment ensures that the organization's data is well-documented, managed, and overseen. A diligent approach to data governance not only enhances operational efficiency but also fosters a culture of accountability and data-centric decision-making.

Conclusion

In this chapter, we started with the Unity Catalog, an essential tool for metadata management, offering enterprises a unified way of cataloging and discovering data assets. By using such a catalog effectively, organizations can foster a cohesive environment where data assets are clearly understood, effectively utilized, and easily accessible.

As we delved into the intricacies of data privacy and compliance, we recognized the profound importance of adhering to global data protection regulations like GDPR and CCPA. Databricks provides a myriad of features that help businesses implement privacy measures, from anonymization to data masking, ensuring that sensitive data remains protected while still being functional.

As we navigated through this segment, it became evident that constructing well-defined access policies, coupled with robust encryption practices, forms the backbone of data protection.

Lastly, the essence of data governance was highlighted. It's not just about securing data but ensuring its quality, lineage, and appropriate usage.

To conclude, as data continues to be an invaluable asset, the imperatives of securing and governing it grow equally. Databricks offers a potent combination of tools and best practices to help organizations stay ahead in this endeavor.

Key Terms

- **Unity Catalog:** A feature in Databricks that offers a unified system for metadata management, helping users in efficient data governance and metadata management.
- **Metadata Management:** The administration and oversight of data associated with data assets to ensure information can be integrated, accessed, shared, linked, analyzed, and maintained to the best effect.
- **Data Privacy:** The practice of ensuring that sensitive information remains confidential and accessible only to those with the proper permissions.
- **Compliance (for example, GDPR, CCPA):** Adhering to rules and regulations set by specific data protection acts and standards. General Data Protection Regulation (GDPR) is a regulation in EU law on data protection and privacy. At the same time, California Consumer Privacy Act (CCPA) gives consumers more control over the personal information that businesses collect about them.
- **Anonymization:** A data protection technique that removes personally identifiable information where identification of data cannot occur.
- **Pseudonymization:** The practice of replacing private identifiers with fake names or pseudonyms, making data less identifiable but still useful for data analysis and processing.
- **Data Masking:** The method of disguising original data with modified content but structurally similar to the original data.

- **Access Control:** Procedures that are designed to restrict access to data based on a user's role or responsibilities within an organization.
- **Encryption (Data at rest and in transit):** Converting data into a code to prevent unauthorized access. Data at rest refers to data that is not actively moving through the network, and data in transit refers to data that is being transferred over a network.
- **Data Governance Framework:** An integrated set of processes, roles, policies, standards, and metrics that organizations use to ensure that their primary data assets are formally, proactively, and efficiently managed throughout the enterprise.

Last Words

Recap of the Journey

As we close this time, let's take a moment to traverse the journey we've undertaken. We began with the foundational understanding of data engineering, demystifying its role in our data-centric world. Databricks emerged as the unified platform, enabling us to harness the full potential of data, transforming raw bytes into actionable insights. Through the chapters, we dived deep into the specifics - from the intricacies of Delta tables and efficient ETL processes to the paramount importance of data quality, validation, and governance. The nuances of scalability, deployment, and stringent security requirements provided a comprehensive view of the multifaceted world of data engineering with Databricks.

Continuous Learning and Upgradation

In the rapidly evolving domain of data engineering, resting on one's laurels isn't an option. The tools, techniques, and best practices of today might undergo transformations tomorrow. Continuous learning becomes the backbone of any successful data engineering endeavor. It's not just about keeping up with Databricks' updates or the next big thing in data processing. It's about cultivating a mindset of curiosity, questioning the status quo, and constantly seeking improvements. Books, courses, seminars, and peer discussions are invaluable, but what truly sets one apart is the drive to always be a learner. In the words of Alvin Toffler, "The illiterate of the 21st century will not be those who cannot read and write, but those who cannot learn, unlearn, and relearn."

Encouragement for Practical Application

Knowledge, when not applied, is like a dormant volcano – full of potential but bereft of any impact. This book has equipped you with tools and methodologies, but their true power will only be unveiled when you implement them in real-world scenarios. Whether you're just starting out or are a seasoned professional, challenge yourself. Design a new data pipeline, optimize an existing process, or perhaps restructure your data storage – the possibilities are endless. Mistakes, undoubtedly, will be made, but they are the stepping stones leading towards mastery. Remember, theoretical knowledge gains depth and dimension only when juxtaposed with practical application.

Final Motivational Note

At this juncture, as you stand with a compendium of knowledge and insights, remember that the journey of data engineering, much like any other discipline, is filled with challenges, roadblocks, and constant evolution. But within these challenges lie opportunities, opportunities to innovate, to lead, and to transform. The realm of data is vast and uncharted, waiting for pioneers like you to shape its future.

Data is often likened to the new oil. But unlike oil, the reservoirs of data are inexhaustible. Every day, zettabytes of data are generated, and hidden within are patterns, trends, and knowledge waiting to be discovered. You, as a data engineer, are the modern-day alchemist, with the power to transform this raw data into gold – insights that can change businesses, societies, and potentially the world.

Go forth with vigor and enthusiasm. Let the challenges inspire you, let the successes humble you, and always remember – in the world of data, you're only limited by your imagination. The future beckons, and you're more than equipped to shape it. Embrace the journey, for it promises to be a rewarding one.

Index

A

Access controls
  Databricks,
      authorization 220, 221
  data, Encrypting 223, 225
  data privacy policies 222, 223
  secure credential
      practices 225, 226
ACID transactions
  about 27, 28
Adaptive Query Execution
      (AQE) 170
ALTER TABLE 43
Amazon Web Services (AWS)
  benefits 195
  Databricks, exploring 198-200
  features 195
  integration 195

Apache Spark 12
Avro
  advantages 65
  characteristics 65
  working 65

B

business use case
  sales, forecasting 117

C

cloud databricks
  reference link 18
cloud deployment
  about 195
  considerations 194, 195
  Data growth, handling 201
  emerging technologies,
      evaluating 204, 205

future-proofing, strategies 201
services and providers,
    evaluating 197, 198
cloud deployment,
    accommodating 201, 202
cloud deployment data,
    solutions 202, 203
cloud deployment, options
  Amazon Web Services (AWS) 195
  Google Cloud Platform
      (GCP) 196
  Microsoft Azure 196
  Private Cloud and
      On-Premises 196
cloud storage extracting,
    techniques
  cloud-specific,
      connecting 62
  Delta Lake 62
  direct access 62
Cluster Optimization
  about 176
  Auto-scaling,
      strategies 180, 181
Cluster Optimization, operation
  adjust, monitoring 178
  dynamic, allocating 178
  executor size, setting 178
  limit partitions 178
  oversubscription, avoiding 178
  right instance, choosing 177
  spot instances, leverage 177
  storage, configuring 178
  workload, understanding 177
Cluster Optimization, techniques
  Auto-scalling 179
  cost tools, managing 179
  data, cleaning 179
  idle clusters, terminating 179
  job schedule, optimizing 179
  spot/preemptible instances 179
  storage, optimizing 179

strategically, caching 179
workload prioritization,
    implementing 179
workloads consolidate 179
Common Data Extraction
    Techniques
  batch processing 84
  Change Data Capture
      (CDC) 84
  incremental, loading 84
  streaming 84
Common Data Transformation
    Techniques
  clean, processing 86
  data enrichment 86
  data, mapping 86
  grouping 87
  selection, filtering 86
CSV (Comma-Separated Values)
  compactness, simplicity 68
  processing 68
  schema lack 68

D

Data Anomalies
  business, impacting 115
  business cases, using 116
  causes 115
  contextual, identifying 116
  data, importance 115
  detecting 115
  handling 114
  Outliers, comparing 114
Data Anomalies, analysis
  capping, flooring 117
  contextual analysis 117
  data imputation 116
  discretization, binning 117
  removal 117
  robust statistical methods 117
  transformation 116
  transformation functions 117

Index 239

Databricks
  about 10
  analytics platform 10
  data ingestion 50
  Data validation 110, 111
  Delta tables 26, 27
  key features 11, 12
  setting up 18-21
Databricks Architecture 12
Databricks Architecture, components
  Clusters 14
  data storage 14
  Notebooks 14
  Workspace 14
Databricks Architecture, types
  Customer Account 14
  Databricks Cloud Account 13
  interactions 14
Databricks, components
  centralized workspace 10
  down silos, breaking 11
  flexibility 11
  integration simplify 10
  interactive analysis 10
  reproducibility 11
Databricks data transformation, techniques
  aggregations 80
  broadcast 80
  column, pruning 81
  DataFrame API 80
  dynamic, partitioning 81
  file, coalescing 81
  persistence, caching 80
  Spark SQL 80
  User-Defined Functions (UDFs) 80
  window functions 80
Databricks implementing, roles
  dashboards, monitoring 103
  data, profiling 102

  data quality, checking 102
  lineage, tracking 103
  notifications 103
  quality reports 103
Databricks notebooks
  about 16
  practices 21-23
Databricks notebooks, roles
  code execution 16
  documentation 17
  data visualization 17
  external tools, integrating 17
  reproducibility 17
Databricks Workspace
  about 15
  setting up 18
Databricks Workspace, functionalities
  clusters 15
  collaboration 16
  integration 16
  jobs 15
  libraries 15
  Notebooks 15
Data compaction
  about 141
  aggregate, summarizing 142
  benefits 141
  compression 142
  Databricks, optimizing 141
  data, partitioning 143
  deduplication, cleaning 142
  lifecycle, managing 142
  metadata, indexing 142
  pruning 142
  retention policies 142
Data engineering
  about 3
  core concepts 7, 8
  data analytics, enabling 4
  data-driven, supporting 5, 7

modern organizations 3
  scope 7
  summary 8
Data engineering, concepts
  data governance 9
  data integration 8
  data modeling 8
  data pipelines 8
  data transformation 8
Data engineering optimization, reasons
  cost efficiency 168
  data insights, ensuring 168
  future-proofing 169
  processing speed, enhancing 168
  resource, utilizing 168
  user, satisfying 169
Data engineering, roles
  data governance 5
  data preparation 4
  data wrangling 4
  pipeline development 5
  scalability 5
Data extraction
  about 57
  API data, extracting 69
  AWS S3 Connector 63, 64
  cloud storage, using 62
  JDBC connector, working 59-61
  practices 61, 62
  semi and unstructure, handling 68
  sources, implementing 57
  techniques, implementing 64
  Web scraping, extracting 70, 71
Data extraction, methods
  API integration 58
  cloud storage, extracting 58
  file-based, extracting 58
  Relational database 58
  Web scraping 58

Data governance
  best practices 227
  data annotations, implementing 230
  data, cataloging 230
  data lineage traceability 229
  importance 227-229
  lifecycle management practices 231, 232
  Metadata, managing 229
  version, maintaining 230
data ingestion
  about 50
  appropriate method 52
  implementing 55
  importance 51
  key considerations 53
  rules 56
  key reasons 51, 52
data ingestion considerations, factors
  data privacy 54
  data sources, formating 54
  error handling, monitoring 55
  metadata, managing 55
  transformation, integrating 54
  volume, velocity 54
data ingestion, method
  batch processing 52
  data characteristics 53
  frequency, updating 53
  hybrid approach 53
  latency requirements 53
  streaming 52
  system capabilities 53
data integration 9
Data lakes
  about 133
  use cases 133
  warehouse 133, 134

Data modeling
  about 123
  best practices 129-131
Data modeling, fundamentals
  cost efficiency 124
  data integration 124
  data quality, consistency 124
  flexibility 124
  query performance 124
  scalability 124
  structure organization 124
Data modeling key, types
  conceptual data 125
  dimensional data 125
  hierarchical data 126
  logical data 125
  NoSQL data 126
  object-oriented data 126
  physical data 125
  relational data 126
data partitioning
  about 138
  benefits 139
  considerations 141
  effectiveness consideration 139
  key concepts 138
  optimization, strategies 138
  tailored benefits 140
data partitioning, techniques
  combination 140
  custom criteria 140
  hash-based 140
  location-based 140
  range-based 140
  time-based 139
Data pipelines
  about 9
  advantages 150
  automated data,
      implementing 149
  components 149
  Databricks jobs,
      scheduling 154-156

Data pipelines, principles
  documentation 150
  error, handling 150
  modularity 150
  monitoring 150
Data pipelines, scenarios
  E-commerce, optimizing 150
  financial, analysis 150
  Healthcare analytics 150
Data Privacy and Compliance
  Anonymization 218
  Databricks, ensuring 212, 213
  Databricks, implementing 219
  Data masking 219
  data protecting regulations,
      ensuring 216-218
  importance 213
  privacy measures,
      implementing 215, 216
  Pseudonymization 218
Data Privacy and Compliance,
    context
  business continuity 214
  data quality, enhancing 214
  ethical data, using 214
  obligations, regulatory 214
  trust foundation 213
Data processing
  Databricks, leveraging 92-94
  performance, optimizing 90
  strategies 91, 92
  transformation, operations 94, 95
Data quality
  Databricks, implementing 102, 103
  integrity, ensuring 98
  practical example 103, 104
Data quality, issues
  cross-validation 101
  data, cleansing 101
  data enrichment 101
  data, profiling 101
  feedback loop 102
  outlier detection 101

rule-based, validating 102
statistical analysis 101
timeliness, validating 102
Data quality, key points
decision-making, informing 99
experience, enhancing 99
operational efficiency 99
regulatory compliance 99
trustworthy insights 99
Data quality validation, rules
automated checks 100
business rules 99, 100
critical fields, indentifying 100
data anomalies, handling 100
techniques, selecting 100
Data shuffling
about 174
broadcast, using 174
minimizing 174
data storage options
about 132
hybrid approaches 133
utilizing 131
Data transformation
about 9, 76
Apache Spark, using 87, 88
building 76
business analysis 86
Databricks, using 80
data, extracting 84
efficient pipelines,
    designing 78
importance 77
relational database,
    extracting 85, 86
significance 77, 78
target system, loading 88
Data transformation, challenges
data consistency 85
data security 85
data validation 85

Data transformation, data flow
access methods 84
data formats 84
source considerations 84
Data transformation, importance
aggregation 86
data, cleansing 86
data, structuring 86
enrichment 86
Data transformation scalability,
    types
clear objectives 78
data formats, optimizing 78
data movement 79
data, partitioning 79
incremental, processing 79
in-memory, processing 79
parallelize, partition 78
performance, monitoring 79
quality checks, implementing 79
right tools, choosing 78
Data validation
about 105
case study 111, 112
data consistency 108, 109
key takeaways 114
methodologies 106, 107
rules, constraints 107, 108
Data validation constraints, rules
data type, implementing 107
enforce format 107
ensure integrity 108
establish clear rules 107
nulls with care, allowing 108
range validations 107
Data validation, goals
cross-field consistency 108
Data completeness 108
data matching 109
data profiling, accuracy 109
domain-specific 109

Index   243

integrity verification 109
statistical measures 109
time-series, validating 109
user-defined rules 109
Data validation
    methodologies, key
  business logic 106
  pattern, matching 106
  referential integrity 106
  Rule-based 106
  statistical analysis 106
Data warehouse
  about 134
  scenarios 134
decision-making, roles
  data governance, compliance 6
  data integration 5
  quality assurance 6
  scalability 6
  transformation and aggregation 6
  visualization and accessibility 6
Delta Lake
  about 32
  machine learning 36
  architecture 34
  existing 36
  file organization 36
  history 32, 33
  integrations 36
  transaction log 37
Delta Lake, core
  aggregation 35
  ingestion tables 35
  refined tables 35
Delta Lake, data inputs
  batch, processing 35
  streaming 35
Delta Lake file organization,
    key aspects
  Delta Table 37
  file compaction 37
  file versions 37

Delta Lake schema evolution
  about 39
  handling 40
Delta Lake transaction log,
    key aspects
  ACID transactional 38
  data consistency 39
  data versioning 38
  Write-Ahead Log (WAL) 37, 38
Delta tables
  about 26, 27
  capability 30, 31
  data reliability, consistency 27
  data, versioning 30
  time travel 31
  use case 31
Delta tables, key aspects
  ACID transactions 27, 28
  consistency checks 28
  data versioning 28
  schema evolution 28
  write optimization 28
Delta tables optimization, features
  column pruning 29
  data, skipping 29
  indexing mechanisms 29
  predicate pushdown 29
Delta tables time travel, working
  data comparison 31
  historical data, querying 31
  point-in-time, recovery 31
Delta tables versioning, advantages
  data, auditing 30
  historical analysis 30
  reproducibillty 30
Dependencies
  about 152
  Databricks workflows,
      managing 153
  Databricks workflows,
      techniques 153, 154
  data engineering 151

Data pipelines, scheduling 151
  task, workflows 152
Dependencies, forms
  data dependency 152
  task dependency 152
  time dependency 152
Dependencies, matters
  efficiency 152
  error, preventing 152
  resource, managing 152

E

e-commerce
  practical use, analysis 172, 173
Effective data modeling
  about 123
  analytical, working 127
  designing 122, 123
Effective data modeling, principles
  business, understanding 127
  data integrity enforcement 127
  data relevance 127
  documentation 127
  naming conventions 127
  normalization 127
  over-engineering, avoiding 127
  scalability 128
ETL pipelines, components
  extract 82
  load 82
  transformation 82
ETL process 81
ETL process, components
  data extraction 83
  data, loading 83
  data sources 83
  data transformation 83
  quality assurance 83
  workflow, managing 83

F

FinTrust
  about 111, 112
  issues 112

G

Google Cloud Platform (GCP)
  benefits 196
  features 196
  integration 196

H

Horizontal scaling
  about 193
  advantages 193
hybrid approaches 129

I

indexing mechanisms 29
indexing mechanisms, key
  Bloom filters 29
  Z-Ordering 29

J

Java Database Connectivity (JDBC) 59
JavaScript Object Notation (JSON)
  data volume 67
  processing 67
  schema flexibility 67
  semi-structured nature 67

L

Loading data
  case study 90
  data, transforming 89
  key consideration 89
  techniques 89

M

Microsoft Azure
  benefits 196
  features 196
  integration 196

O

Optimized Row Columnar (ORC)
  advantages 65
  characteristics 65
  working 65

P

Parquet
  advantages 65
  characteristics 64
  working 65
Performance optimization 168
Performance optimization, fundamental
  Adaptive Query Execution (AQE) 170
  cluster, configuring 170
  data, partitioning 169
  data serialization 170
  data, shuffling 169
  data skipping, caching 169
Performance profiling
  about 182
  complex transformations, optimizing 185, 186
  Query Execution Plans (QEP) 183
  tools 182, 183

Private Cloud and On-Premises
  benefits 196
  features 196
  integration 196

Q

Query execution
  Databricks auto, caching 171
  Data skipping, benefits 171
  Data skipping, caching 171
  data, utilizing 170
  Delta Cache, understanding 170
  practical tips 171
Query Execution Plans (QEP)
  about 183
  anomalies 184, 185

R

repartition() 185
Resource Management 175, 176
Resource Management, resources
  distributive nature 176
  dynamic resource, allocating 176
  execute memory, cores 176
  feedback loop, monitoring 177
  resource overheads 177
  resource pools 177

S

Scaling data engineering
  concept 190
  data pipelines 191
  horizontal and vertical, scaling 193
  importance 190
  workflows, techniques 192
Scaling data engineering, reasons
  adaptability 191
  cost-effective growth 191
  data variable, velocity 191
  data volumes, growing 190
  future-proofing 191

performance, ensuring 191
Service Level Agreements
        (SLAs) 191
Schema evolution
  about 40
  handling 43, 44
  leveraging 42
  practices 45
Schema evolution, challenges
  backward compatibility 41
  data consistency 41
  data, migrating 41
  validation, cleansing 41
  workflows, processing 41
Schema evolution, techniques
  enforcement 42
  evolution compatibility 42
  metadata, managing 42
  storage unified 42
  time travel capability 42
Schema-on-Read, key aspects
  data, exploring 129
  flexibility 128
  late, binding 128
  storage efficiency 128
Schema-on-Read (SoR) 128
Schema-on-Write, key aspects
  data integrity 129
  data, validating 129
  predefined structure 129
  query performance 129
Schema-on-Write (SoW) 129
Serialization
  optimizing 174
  shuffle partitions 175
  Shuffling issues, monitoring 175
Service Level Agreements
        (SLAs) 191
SparkListeners 183
storage format
  appropriate 134
  data types 135-137

Strategic, scalling
  Databricks 194
Structured data formats,
        working 64-66
Structured data storage 132
Structured data storage, options
  data lakes 132
  data warehouses 132

T

task dependencies
  complex handling 156
task dependencies practices,
        execution
  dependency, mapping 156
  documentation 157
  error, handling 156
  monitoring 157
  parameterization 157
  scalability, planning 157
  testing, validation 157
  version control 157
  workflow modularity 156

U

Unity Catalog
  about 208
  Databricks, handling 208, 209
  data governance,
        leveraging 211, 212
Unity Catalog Metadata,
        managing
  collaborative 210
  comprehensive capture 209, 210
  efficient data 210
  lineage visualization 210
  quality tools 210, 211
  versioning 210
Unstructured data storage 132
Unstructured data storage, options
  data lakes 133
  object storage 132

V

Vertical scaling
 about 193
 advantages 194

W

WholeStageCodeGen 184
Workflow automation
 about 147
 analysis, handling 148, 149
 Databricks jobs 148
 Notebooks 148
Workflow automation, benefits
 big jobs, handling 148
 efficiency boost 148
 fewer mistakes 148
 on time, every time 148
 resources, saving 148
Workflow automation with Databricks
 implementing 147
Workflow Execution
 Databricks, optimizing 163
 debugging tools 163, 164
 error detection 159, 161
 error handling 158
 Retries techniques 161, 162
Workflow Execution, strategies
 custom scripts 159
 Metrics, logging 158
 notifications, alerting 159
 resource, monitoring 159
 troubleshooting 159
 visualization 159
Write-Ahead Log (WAL) 37, 38

X

XML (eXtensible Markup Language)
 hierarchical structure 67
 processing 67
 schema, using 67

Made in the USA
Coppell, TX
18 October 2024